The Fashion Handbook

The Fashion Handbook is the indispensable guide to the fashion industry. It explores the varied and diverse aspects of the business, bringing together critical concepts with practical information about the industry's structure and core skills, as well as offering advice on real working practices and providing information about careers and training.

The Fashion Handbook traces the development of the fashion industry and looks at how fashion can be understood from social, cultural and commercial perspectives. Each chapter contributes to the knowledge of a particular academic or vocational area either through building on existing research or through the dissemination of new research undertaken into specialist vocational disciplines.

The Fashion Handbook uses case studies, interviews and profiles and includes chapters written by recognised academics and fashion industry experts. Specialist topics include fashion culture, luxury brands, fashion journalism, fashion buying, design and manufacturing, retailing, PR and styling.

The Fashion Handbook includes:

- A unique and broad overview of the fashion industry
- Chapters on specialist topics
- Contributions from recognised experts in both academia and the fashion industry
- Expert advice on careers in fashion retailing.

Tim Jackson is a Principal Lecturer at The London College of Fashion specialising in fashion marketing and luxury. He has produced a number of publications relating to these topics including *Mastering Fashion Buying and Merchandising Management*. Following a career in the fashion industry, he regularly commentates on fashion business issues across various broadcast media.

David Shaw currently works as both a freelance buying and marketing consultant and as an academic at The London College of Fashion, having worked for 20 years in the fashion industry for companies such as Top Shop, Dorothy Perkins, Principles, Burtons, Debenhams, Dolcis and Bertie. He is the co-author of *Mastering Fashion Buying and Merchandising Management*.

Media Practice

Edited by James Curran, Goldsmiths College, University of London

The *Media Practice* handbooks are comprehensive resource books for students of media and journalism, and for anyone planning a career as a media professional. Each handbook combines a clear introduction to understanding how the media work with practical information about the structure, processes and skills involved in working in today's media industries, providing not only a guide on 'how to do it' but also a critical reflection on contemporary media practice.

The Fashion Handbook

Tim Jackson and David Shaw

Routledge
Taylor & Francis Group

LONDON AND NEW YORK

First published 2006
by Routledge
2 Park Square, Milton Park, Abingdon, Oxon OX14 4RN

Simultaneously published in the USA and Canada
by Routledge
270 Madison Ave, New York, NY10016

Reprinted 2009

Routledge is an imprint of the Taylor & Francis Group,
an informa business

© 2006 Tim Jackson and David Shaw

Typeset in Times and Helvetica by
Florence Production Ltd, Stoodleigh, Devon
Printed and bound in Great Britain by
CPI Antony Rowe, Chippenham, Wiltshire

British Library Cataloguing in Publication Data
A catalogue record for this book is available from the British Library

Library of Congress Cataloging in Publication Data
A catalog record for this book has been requested

ISBN10: 0–415–25579–1 (hbk)
ISBN10: 0–415–25580–5 (pbk)
ISBN10: 0–203–32117–0 (eBook)

ISBN13: 9–78–0–415–25579–0 (hbk)
ISBN13: 9–78–0–415–25580–6 (pbk)
ISBN13: 9–78–0–203–32117–1 (eBook)

Contents

Figures

....

Tables

....

Boxes

....

Notes on contributors

Dr Tony Hines is Research Coordinator for the Marketing Group at Manchester Metropolitan University's Business School, with research interests in retail strategies. He is a leading marketing educator, having taught, examined and researched in Sri Lanka, South Africa, south Korea, Europe and the USA. He is the author of *Supply Chain Strategies: Customer Focused, Customer Driven* (Elsevier 2004) and co-editor of *Fashion Marketing: Contemporary Issues* (Elsevier 2001).

Pamela Church Gibson is Reader in Historical and Cultural Studies at the London College of Fashion. She has published widely on fashion, film, fandom, history and heritage. Her co-edited collections of essays include *Fashion Cultures: Theories, Explorations and Analysis* with Stella Bruzzi (Routledge 2001). She is currently writing on the relationship between consumption, cities and cinema.

Tim Jackson is a Principal Lecturer specialising in fashion marketing at the London College of Fashion and member of the editorial panel of the *Journal of Fashion Marketing and Management*. He is the Research Coordinator for the School of Fashion Promotion and Management and chairs the inter-college Fashion Management Research Group. Having worked both in retail management and in buying and merchandising for a number of fashion retailers, including Dash, Jaeger and Burton Menswear, he and David Shaw wrote the first UK textbook on fashion buying and merchandising management; other publications include papers and book chapters on luxury branding and fashion trend prediction. Tim comments on fashion and luxury business issues in the media, supervises Ph.D students researching luxury and fashion trends, and works as an external examiner for fashion marketing courses at a variety of universities.

Carmen Haid is UK Head of Communications for Celine, a post to which she was appointed in 2002. Prior to this Carmen was the UK PR Manager at Yves Saint Laurent for four years. Carmen's career has also included a period at the UK *Vogue* and has published a paper in the *Journal of New Product Development and Innovation Management* on the Gucci Group co-authored by Tim Jackson. In addition to her full-time employment, Carmen has been acting as a marketing consultant for the bi-annual lifestyle and photographic magazine *EXIT* since 2000.

David Shaw is a Senior Lecturer and Course Director in Fashion Retailing and Marketing at the London College of Fashion. His background as a buying and merchandising Executive and Director of high-street retailer brands including Top Shop, Dorothy Perkins and Burton Menswear has directly informed his explanation and analysis of contemporary buying and merchandising issues. While still consulting for the industry David also acts as a retailing consultant for the charity shop sector and is a non-executive director of Minds Matter Ltd. He is co-author of *Mastering Fashion Buying and Merchandising Management* (Palgrave 2001). He has lectured at many universities in the UK and Australia on business subjects, including marketing and retailing, at undergraduate, postgraduate and professional levels.

Bill Webb is a Senior Lecturer and Course Director at the London College of Fashion. He is an Exhibitioner of Trinity Hall College, Cambridge, and has a Masters degree in Economics. He has held marketing management positions with Jaeger, Johnson and Johnson and Storehouse, and has carried out retail strategy and concept development assignments with specialist agencies in thirty countries. He has published numerous articles on retail management issues in academic and professional journals, and has presented over forty conference papers, most recently in Beijing and Frankfurt. Bill is a Freeman of the City of London and a member of the Marketing Society and EAERCD.

Brenda Polan is a freelance journalist who specialises in fashion and design. She has worked for most of the UK's national newspapers and important magazines. An art historian by education, she was a sub-editor on the *Guardian* when the Women's Page editor decided she looked smart enough to fill the vacant post of fashion editor. Six years later she herself became editor of the women's page, initiating a broader, more reflective, coverage of style and design, and also wrote about architecture for the paper. Since leaving the *Guardian* in the early 1990s she has worked, either on the staff or as a freelance, for many papers and magazines, including the *Daily Mail* and the *Mail on Sunday, The Financial Times, The Times*, the *Daily Telegraph*, the *Independent on Sunday, Tatler, Harpers & Queen* and *Good Housekeeping*. Additionally, she was launch editor of Harvey Nichols's magazine. She has been a member of the Design Council and a lecturer, consultant and external examiner on MA and BA courses in fashion and journalism. She currently teaches journalism on BA (Hons) courses at the London College of Fashion and the Surrey Institute.

Matthew Jeatt has worked as Director of Promostyl UK, the world's leading fashion forecasting and trend research consultancy, for over ten years. In that time he has been responsible for the development of Promostyl's special contract work in the UK and elsewhere. Matthew is a regular keynote speaker at Promostyl's 'Influences' and 'Colour, Print, Shape' seasonal presentations at Première Vision in Paris and at the Victoria & Albert Museum in London; he also presents these and other specialist works around the world. Prior to becoming involved in the fashion business, Matthew worked for many years in the music industry where his awareness of and keen interest in youth trends began. This early career saw him work with a wide variety of performers, including Gladys Knight, Meat Loaf, Genesis and Duran Duran. Recently he has featured in press and magazine articles across various publications, including the *Financial Times, Harpers Bazaar, Zest* and *Homes & Gardens*. Other media involvement includes commentary on fashion and future trends for a variety of programmes on both the BBC and ITV. Matthew has consulted across a variety of different product areas for global businesses, which include the BBC, Boots, Selfridges, Ellesse, Kohler, Sara Lee, Nokia, Panasonic, Swarovski, and Unilever. He has also made presentations and lectured on style and design trends at the London College of Fashion and Central St Martin's College of Art and Design, among other colleges. He believes strongly in the 'fun of fashion' and the ever increasing value of 'self-expression', both personal and corporate.

Acknowledgements

....

We wish to thank all those who have contributed to the chapters of this book and the others, named below, for their varied support and assistance in the production of the book.

Mrs K. Miel	(Mum and researcher!)
Gary Aspden	Adidas
Carl and Rachel Bromley	Sienna Couture
Ian Cartwright	Base London
Emma Fripp	Arcadia Group
Brenda Hegarty	*International Herald Tribune*
Stephen Henly	i2
Sian Hession	Long Tall Sally
Nick Hollingworth	Austin Reed
Fritz Humer	Wolford
Bob Jolley	JDA
Ginny Jones	Shore to Shore
Robin Laing	Retail Human Resources
June Lawlor	House of Fraser
Anne Leeming	Late of City University Business School
Errin Mackness	Halpern Public Relations
Jodie Pritchard	Mercedes Australian Fashion Week
Ann Priest	London College of Fashion
David Riddiford	Lane Crawford
Sally Smitherman	Retail Human Resources
Alison Thorne	George
Roger Tredre	Worth Global Style Network
Elaine Tulloch	Jasper Conran
David Walker-Smith	Selfridges
Dilys Williams	London College of Fashion
Charles Harrision Wallace	London College of Fashion (retired)
Ken Watson	Fashion Industry

We thank in particular Karen Jackson for all her patient support over the many weekends devoted to writing.

Abbreviations

....

ADS	Approved Destination Status
ATC	Agreement on Textiles and Clothing
B&M	buying and merchandising
BFC	British Fashion Council
Bhs	British Home Stores
CAD, CAM	computer-aided design/manufacture
CBI	Caribbean Basin Initiative
DC	Distribution Centre
DOS	directly operated store
DTI	Department of Trade and Industry
FMCG	fast moving consumer goods
GATT	General Agreement on Tariffs and Trade
GDP	gross domestic product
GIS	geographic information systems
GM	gross buying margin
H&M	Hennes and Mauritz
HNWI	high net-worth individual
IHT	*International Herald Tribune*
IT	Information Technology
KPI	key performance indicator
M&A	merger and acquisition
M&S	Marks & Spencer
MBWA	management by walking about
MD	mark down
MFA	Multi-Fibre Arrangement
MRTW	men's ready-to-wear
MU	mark up
NAFTA	North American Free Trade Area
NAMAD	net achieved margin after discount
NIC	newly industrialising country
ONS	Office of National Statistics
OPT	outward processing trade
PLC	product life cycle

POS	point of sale
PPR	Pinault Printemps Redoute
PV	Première Vision
QR	quick response
ROCE/ROI	return on capital expenditure/investment
RFID	radio-frequency identification
RHR	Retail Human Resources
RIS	Retail Information System
ROII	return on increased investment
RSP	retail selling price
RTW	ready-to-wear
SKU	stock-keeping unit
TQM	total quality management
U-HNWI	ultra-high net-worth individual
V&A	Victoria and Albert Museum
WGSN	Worth Global Style Network
WRTW	women's ready-to-wear

Introduction

....

For many people, fashion is something they read about and buy in stores. In this sense fashion is about change and about replacing the old with something new. The liberal use of the word 'fashion' to reference everything from the latest fad in clothing accessories to a medium-term shift in people's taste for minimalist interior design indicates a wide difference in how change is understood and in the timescales involved. A fad may come and go within a season whereas a trend may survive a number of years. Equally ambiguous is the notion of innovators being 'fashionable' when in fact most fashion is defined by mass acceptance, a point where innovators have moved on to something else. So fashion is linked to change but not in any defined or prescribed way, especially as today's 'fashion' is an eclectic mix of almost everything and is expressed by individuals who have less concern for seasonal looks or fashion rules than in the past.

However, changes in fashions can provide insights to social motivations and beliefs, as fashion clothing provides us with an archive of the past and a vehicle through which to document, examine and explain social, economic and cultural changes. It is a lens through which we can observe changes in people's attitudes and values as dress and adornment represent conspicuous means of expressing identity. Consumerism and the consumption of fashion have become a replacement for religion for many, as individuals shop to feel better and researchers analyse and debate the implications of this new behaviour. Fashion can also be a stimulus for engaging debate about the meaning and purpose of designers' work as haute couture has evolved into a workshop for ideas that are communicated through a global fashion press.

Fashion is all these things and a multi-billion-dollar global business that covers a diverse range of commercial activities, ranging from the unglamorous world of mass garment production to celebrity-patronised fashion shows and the associated reportage in the fashion press.

This book aims to provide readers with insights to a range of subjects that are significant to the study and practice of fashion. Each chapter adds to the knowledge of a particular academic or vocational area either through building on existing research or disseminating new research undertaken into specialist vocational disciplines. This is achieved through the contributions of both academics, who are recognised experts within their fields, and fashion industry experts who provide unique insights, knowledge and understanding of subjects that are not widely documented in the public domain. The latter include coverage of fashion styling and PR, fashion journalism, buying and merchandising, and luxury.

Chapter 1 provides the reader with an overview of the clothing and textile industries, revealing the enormous changes in sources of global garment production. Chapter 2 develops a more commonly documented aspect of fashion, examining how the subject may be understood from social and cultural perspectives. Chapter 3 explores historical aspects of fashion design and provides insights to the significant trade fairs and shows which inform the process of designing fashion clothing. Chapter 4 provides a detailed analysis of global luxury brands, documenting and discussing data and views from within the industry that are rarely accessible within the public domain. Chapter 5 delivers a fundamental understanding of the processes involved in garment manufacture, as clothing represents the building blocks of most fashion collections. Chapter 6 reviews the significance of fashion retailing to the modern fashion industry and charts significant events and changes within the field. Chapter 7 is concerned with buying and merchandising, one of the important vocational areas of fashion that is narrowly represented in academic or trade literature, and reveals the nature and workings of modern buying and merchandising functions. Chapter 8 explains how the vocational subject of fashion journalism impacts on the wider industry. Chapter 9 offers a rare insight into the often misrepresented roles of fashion PR and styling through a very experienced industry contributor. Chapter 10 examines careers in fashion retailing with significant input from the Arcadia Group and Retail Human Resources, both of which provide expert and balanced perspectives on a major area of employment within the fashion industry. The final chapter looks towards the future through the eyes of one of the world's leading fashion trend research consultants, Matthew Jeatt – director of Promostyl. In Matthew's view,

> Fashion has changed dramatically in recent years and will continue to do so. Today's consumer is very well informed and sometimes difficult to please. We can now see the incredible impact of both the 'vigilante consumer' and the 'brand evangelist' as a direct consequence of today's 'wired world' in which an individual can utilise technology and network as never before. Fashion and technology both have to come to terms with the aspirations and needs (both physical and emotional) of today's consumer. They both have to adapt to the human body and soul instead of expecting humans to adapt to them as they have in the past.

These broad topics are collected together in an attempt to provide some coherence to what is a fascinating but very disparate and fragmented subject, which can be open to wide interpretation.

1 The nature of the clothing and textiles industries: structure, context and processes

Tony Hines

T his chapter is structured to give the reader insights to the nature and structure of the clothing and textile industries. Nature and structure will be considered, first, in historical context, to provide patterns of development through time from a UK perspective; second, the UK sectors are considered in their contemporary context nationally and, finally, in an international context – from a European perspective and then in a global context. Global supply chains serve as a lens through which to view the interconnectedness of firms and national economies. Finally, future industry challenges and opportunities are considered in a national and international context.

The nature of the clothing and textiles industries

It is perhaps apposite to consider the nature of the clothing and textiles industries by demonstrating their interconnectedness and the similarities and differences that occur between them. Viewing a supply chain from its origin through to final consumption is a useful framework for this discussion. Figure 1.1 illustrates the main stages linking the chain. Primary producers are located either in agriculture for natural fibres (e.g. wool and cotton) or in the chemical industry for man-made fibres (e.g. nylon and acrylics). Essentially, outputs of these two primary producing sectors (agriculture and chemicals) form the basis of inputs to the textile industry. It is at this stage of the journey that conversions begin with natural or chemical-based products entering the textile supply chain to become textile-manufactured outputs (e.g. fabrics). These fabrics then become raw-material inputs to the clothing manufacturing industry by which they are converted into items of clothing – apparel. Moving on from this stage clothing outputs are passed from converters (manufacturers) to wholesale and retail distribution firms acting as intermediaries between suppliers and customers. Customers may be the ultimate consumers of products or they may simply be further intermediaries, for example, a mother purchasing clothing for members of her family or a retail store purchasing from a wholesaler. Consumption takes place at the end of the chain. This linear forward model of a textile clothing supply chain is presented merely for clarity about the processes involved. It is important to recognise that the drivers of this chain are often retailers who interpret customer demand patterns and trigger demand for clothing manufacturers, textile mills and primary producers.

Increasingly management of the supply network has been controlled by large national and international retail organisations or through large suppliers of branded clothing.

Time is an important dimension within the textile clothing supply chain. It is useful to think of the major stages in the chain as cycles, each cycle taking a specific time to run its course. For example, it takes half a year to grow crops or produce wool; it takes anywhere between 12 and 24 weeks to secure textile fabric in the specified quantities, qualities and colours from a textile mill; it takes anywhere between 2 weeks and 16 weeks to secure finished goods inventories from clothing manufacturers; and, if you add to all these inefficiencies idle time in warehousing and shipping logistics, sourcing trips, design concepts, fabric testing, sampling and selection, then more time is consumed in these processes too.

Similarities and differences between textiles and clothing

It is important to understand economic differences between the textile and clothing industries. The textile industry is capital-intensive, requiring significant investment to develop even the smallest textile mill. A small-scale polyester plant in a relatively low-cost location may require a US$10–15 million investment. The economics of textile production are based on efficiency. Having made the investment in the asset the

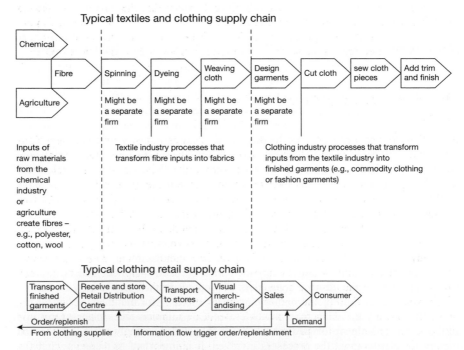

Figure 1.1 Main stages in textiles–clothing supply chain

Source: Hines (2005).

organisation wants to generate an appropriate level of return on the capital expended/ invested (ROCE/ROI). The consequence is that it is important to fill plant capacity and keep it running round the clock to ensure maximum output from a given resource input. Hence, productivity is an important performance indicator for the textile industry. Higher levels of productivity reduce unit costs. In competitive markets lowering unit costs is essential. Large retail organisations, their agents or supplier networks often book mill production capacity months in advance of production to ensure that they will receive fabrics on time for their clothing manufacturers to produce garments for their stores at the right time. In contrast clothing manufacture is a labour-intensive industry, requiring little capital investment by comparison with textile firms. Often a space with sewing machines, cutting tables and storage facilities is the minimum requirement. It is in this sense more of a footloose industry, meaning that light manufacturing equipment and facilities can easily be moved between locations across the globe. It is not so easy to move a textile plant, having made the investment. It is a heavy industry. Clothing manufacture has become an industry that needs to focus its attention on being responsive to customer needs (usually those of a retailer, buying office or agent). Not only must the clothing manufacturer be responsive but also it must strive for efficiency if it has higher labour costs than its competitors.

A brief history of textiles and clothing in the UK

There are a number of salutary lessons to be drawn from the accounts that follow since in many ways we are still making history, except that the context has shifted from Britain to other parts of the globe. The stories of conservative businessmen, accusations of capitalist exploitation, worker resistance to technical innovations that reduce their wage-earning capacity and migration from countryside to towns may sound familiar to people who populate the first industrial industry across the world.

Eighteenth-century Britain – the birth of the textile industry

In 1700 the most important part of the British textiles industry was woollen cloth manufacture. It was the largest English export, with three areas in particular responsible for the majority of manufacture: East Anglia, the West Country and the West Riding of Yorkshire. Merchant clothiers dominated the industry: usually men of great wealth and substance. Raw material (wool) was cleaned and dyed; then combed to separate long and short strands or carded to turn it into a workable roll. It was then spun into yarn and woven into cloth which was fulled, washed, stretched, bleached and dressed. The factory system of the Industrial Revolution had not yet developed and many of these jobs were performed by part-time workers in the 'domestic system' (men, women and children), endeavouring to increase their main income drawn from the land. In the specialised areas workers were employed full-time and were craftsmen of the wool trade. Fulling and dressing required the use of mills powered by water or horses, and dye and bleaching processes needed equipment that was too large for cottages. However, the key processes of spinning and weaving were conducted in the homes of workers. The word 'spinster' originally applied to the women who carried out these processes (men usually did the weaving). Spinning-wheels and hand-looms could easily be set up in the cottages. Merchants controlled the whole process, buying raw materials from farmers, moving it through the various processes, before selling on the finished cloth. These merchants were the capitalists who paid for materials and various wage costs before drawing their profits from the sale of finished cloth. This general pattern of development was similar in the silk trade and other textiles, and the industry was dominated by a few wealthy men. So important was the wool trade to the British economy that these men had their own lobbyists at Parliament and acts had been passed to regulate the price, quality, weights and methods of drying and dyeing. During Charles II's reign every person who died on English soil had to be buried in a woollen shroud. In William III's time the developing Irish wool trade was stifled by excessive export duties. In the early 1700s the woollen merchants did their best to kill off the developing cotton trade by forbidding the import of printed fabrics from Asia. Nevertheless, the prohibition of foreign trade simply acted as a catalyst, stimulating the English cotton industry which would come to rival woollens and challenge for supremacy.

Wealthy wool merchants who had little incentive to change a system that served them well stifled technical progress. However, the newly establishing cotton and silk industries were more open to change. Cotton had to fight for supremacy with wool, and the silk trade was forced by strong French competition to become more efficient. The increasing use of water power in silk production was epitomised by the factory set up by Thomas Lombe on an island in the River Derwent, Derbyshire, between 1718 and 1722. It contained silk-throwing machines based on Italian designs and smuggled into England. Despite being a success for Lombe, resulting in his knighthood, silk remained a minor industry in the UK, and was conducted mainly in the Peak District. The greatest-impact early development was Kay's flying shuttle in the 1730s when he worked for a clothier in Colchester, Essex. Kay, a native of Bury, Lancashire, was an ingenious mechanic, having already developed a carding process more efficient than anything previous, and had now developed a gadget for saving the weaver time and labour at the loom: the flying shuttle. The shuttle worked by being struck to and fro by hammers which the weaver controlled by strings, and it made it possible to produce wider widths of cloth since the weaving width was no longer limited by the length of the weaver's arms, as in the previous process. It was very unpopular with weavers, who saw the invention as depriving them of their livelihood. Kay was forced to leave Colchester by the strength of feeling, moved to Leeds, where manufacturers adopted his shuttle without paying him for his patent, and then back to his native Bury, where once again he was forced to leave after riots in which his house was sacked. He died penniless in France.

The cotton industry firmly established itself in South Lancashire during the first half of the eighteenth century. The location was no accident: a major port in Liverpool; rapid streams for water power; a damp climate with little change in temperature and a humid atmosphere suited to cotton thread. There was growing demand for cotton cloth (muslin and calicoes) both at home and overseas. Output grew as demand grew, and cotton was better suited than wool to the machine age because it was finer and easier to handle by machine processes. Spinners had always struggled to meet the demands of weavers because they were unable to supply sufficient yarn in time. The flying shuttle had exacerbated this problem by halving the time that weavers needed to produce cloth. The urgent industry need was to find a way of increasing the output of spinners. Around 1765 James Hargreaves, a Blackburn weaver, invented the spinning jenny, a machine that could spin 6 threads at once, although later it was developed to spin 80 threads at once. In its original form it was designed for use at home by hand. It came into widespread use in Lancashire and 10 years after Hargreaves's death in 1778 there were 20,000 or more spinning jennies used in England. A second important development occurred in 1769 when Richard Arkwright, originally from Preston, invented the water frame, a device similar to an earlier invention by Lewis Paul which had been less successful than Arkright's. It was much bigger than the spinning jenny, using rollers to stretch threads, and the yarn produced was much stronger than that of the spinning jenny, but it did require power to drive it. So began the factory age, as large mills began to be established. Arkwright was more businessman than inventor, and some doubt that he was truly the originator of the water frame, alleging that he cribbed his ideas from a number of previous inventors. Nevertheless, he did indeed apply the invention vigorously in his growing empire of mills stretching from Cromford, Derbyshire on the banks of the Derwent (opened 1771) through to Lancashire and (in conjunction with David Dale) on to the New Lanark mills on the banks of the Clyde, Scotland.

In 1779 a further spinning invention by a Bolton weaver, Samuel Crompton, produced a machine that was a mix of the spinning jenny and the water frame which was given the name 'The Mule'. It combined rolling with a moving carriage to produce fine strong yarn. Unfortunately for Crompton he did not patent his invention, unlike Arkwright, and made little money from it. He died a poor and broken man in 1827 after inventing a carding machine, which he then destroyed, fearing others would profit from this too. Originally William Kelly, manager at the New Lanark Mill, harnessed the Mule to water power in 1790 and its use spread rapidly as British manufacturers began to produce high-quality yarn to rival those of Indian craftsmen (fine muslins). This branch of the cotton industry established itself on the banks of the Clyde and in Bolton. Steam power was first applied to spinning machinery in 1785 and spread during the 1790s. Mills were no longer restricted to locating by rivers for water power and so began to migrate to towns and cities. In the early part of the century weavers had often been unemployed while waiting for yarn to be spun; but now, at the turn of the new century, there were not enough weavers to satisfy the demand for cloth. As a consequence wages were driven upwards. Bolton weavers, who earned 3s 6d a yard for fine muslins, adopted airs and graces and often wore £5 notes in their hatbands to display their new-found wealth. However, this golden age did not last, as unskilled men rushed to satisfy the growing demand for weavers, attracted by high rates of pay and partly by the dislocation of the industry as the Napoleonic wars with France developed.

A further major development occurred in 1784 when Edmund Cartwright, a clergyman and professor of poetry at Oxford University, developed a loom driven by power, after hearing a discussion in which Manchester weavers claimed that it was impossible. Cartwright built a factory with 400 steam-powered looms which attracted fierce opposition from hand-loom weavers and they burned it down in 1792, though the power loom came into widespread use in both cotton and wool manufacture throughout the nineteenth century. These technical developments marked the start of the Industrial Revolution in Britain.

The British textiles and clothing industry in the nineteenth and twentieth centuries

Cheaper clothing came at a price. Social consequences from these economic developments were many, and the trends established in the textile industry in eighteenth and nineteenth centuries in Britain have been repeated the world over, as well as having established the foundations and pattern for life as we know it today in the UK. As steam became the prominent source of power, Leeds, Bradford, Huddersfield and other Yorkshire towns became great centres of the woollen industry, just as Lancashire with Manchester at the centre had become the great centre for 'King Cotton' (The Cottonopolis). Within a few years the populations of these towns grew tenfold. Slums, overcrowding, disease, squalor and misery for many were the tangible results of this economic progress. Town planning did not exist; there were few public health regulations, and lighting, drainage and clean water supplies were a hit-and-miss affair. It was during this period that row upon row of poorly built, two-up, two-down houses were established for the growing bands of workers attracted to the large industrial centres like Manchester. People toiled fourteen hours a day, and child labour was prevalent and without regulation. Simple economics dictated that women and children were more widely employed, as they were generally cheaper as labour and less vocal in protest than men. Factory conditions were generally poor, with lighting, ventilation, health and safety being low on the list of priorities for owners. It was during this time that punctuality became a major issue for working times and deductions were made for lateness, illness and singing at work which was regarded as disruptive to production. Rigid discipline and conditions of work akin to those of a prison became the norm for the new factories. Workers began to form trade unions to fight for better working conditions in factories but this did not go unnoticed by the capitalist mill owners. It was significant that the Combination Acts prohibiting trade unions were passed by Parliament in 1799. The development of an improved communication and transport infrastructure, with the canal system at the latter part of the eighteenth century, continuing until the railway system developed in the 1830s and throughout the nineteenth century, facilitated industrial development.

It is estimated that textiles accounted for 7–8 per cent of output measured as gross national product (GNP) for the UK economy in 1812, rising to 11 per cent by 1836. In 1851 the UK textile and clothing industries combined accounted for 21 per cent of employment, representing 10 per cent of the total population (Deane and Cole 1969). Briscoe (1971) estimated that employment levels rose to nearly 2 million people by 1923 with 1.3 million in textiles and a further 651,000 in clothing manufacture. Competition from newly industrialising countries (NICs) and other developed economies had taken their toll throughout the twentieth century as employment levels and output began to fall from the 1930s onward. Britain's involvement in two world wars (1914–1918 and 1939–1945) also impacted on these industrial sectors. Output levels began to fall as a proportion of total manufacturing as other heavy industries developed, particularly iron and steel, ship-building and coal-mining. By 1969 the textile industry employed 580,900, with clothing employing 390,000, and the manufacturing industries combined represented close to 4 per cent of the total output for the UK economy (Jones 2002: 6).

Analysing the place of the textiles and clothing industries within their wider manufacturing context is important in establishing just how important has been their contribution to the UK economy. Mathias (1969) recognises that the peak year for all manufacturing in the UK economy was 1861, when it represented 41 per cent of the GDP; just after the turn of the century, in 1907, it had fallen to 37 per cent. Employment in the total manufacturing sector began to fall more rapidly in the 1960s as the service sector of the economy began to develop and competitive pressures from NICs increased. Moore (1999) noted that in the three years 1979–82 when the Thatcher Conservative Government took office one-fifth of all manufacturing jobs disappeared from the UK economy.

Britain's position in the world economy had been in decline since the 1950s, and statistical analysis shows that it performed worse than most other manufacturing economies during the period from 1950 to 1980. A number of explanations for the decline have been put forward by commentators, including: poor industrial relations, poor productivity in the manufacturing sector, inadequacies of the education sector to meet the challenges of a competitive economy, a failure of successive governments to implement effective industrial policies and class bias against manufacturing, which manifested itself within a banking system that was ill-equipped to support manufacturing firms adequately, particularly through growth phases. In essence it could be argued that the capitalist system was failing the manufacturing capitalists. Structural economic changes were inevitable as a consequence.

The contemporary context of the textiles and clothing industries

It is not simply in the UK that manufacturing decline has taken place: an analysis of the US economy would reveal that between 1950 and 2000 manufacturing employment fell from 40.5 per cent to 19.5 per cent of total employment. The textiles and clothing industries have undergone many changes. The early influencing factors – markets, location of production facilities based on factor costs and technological developments – remain. However, the balance of power in production shifted away from suppliers during the latter part of the twentieth century and towards the new large retail organisations with their significant purchasing power fueled by increasing consumer demand in Europe, US and Japan. These large retail groups have enormous buying power, enabling them to supply high volumes at increasingly low prices. One impediment to retail power and market forces was the establishment of the Multi-Fibre Arrangement (MFA) in 1974.

The MFA and protectionist measures
The textiles and clothing industries are no strangers to protectionism. From the early days of the Industrial Revolution in the UK, those whose wealth derived from a specific commodity have lobbied governments and politicians to protect their interests from the forces of competition. The 'mercantilist' system, as it was known in the UK, introduced a series of customs, duties and tariffs to protect particular economic activities from the forces of competition in the form of 'free trade' – recall the wool merchants demanding that cotton imports be subject to tariffs to protect their interest. Such lobbying has been replayed throughout the world as international trade and competition damaged a domestic industry's stronghold on markets. In the latter part of the twentieth century protectionism was revived in the guise of a derogation from the General Agreement on Tariffs and Trade (GATT), which in 1944 was set up to establish a fair system of world trade development. The MFA was set up in 1974 essentially as a quota-based system to control patterns of development. Initially established for a four-year period to run until 1978, it was not until the trade talks at the Uruguay Round concluded at the end of 1993 that decisions were finally taken to phase out the MFA by January 2005 under the new Agreement on Textiles and

Clothing (ATC). The MFA had been designed as a reintegration mechanism to establish desired patterns of development in textiles and clothing which, it was argued, would limit global shifts that could be damaging to developed, newly industrialised and developing countries. Essentially it was a re-emergence of mercantilism on a global scale.

Jones (2002: 206) records the impact of the MFA in its first two periods of implementation by comparing statistics on import penetration of the UK, noting that between 1973 and 1982 it rose from 11 to 35 per cent, and it has continued to rise despite the protectionism offered under the MFA. This demonstrates that in practice many parts of the textiles and clothing industries remained unrestricted, probably as a consequence of diversion tactics by large corporations. For example, if quota restrictions applied in one country of operation which had used its full quota, and was as a result unable to supply, it might simply move production to another country that still had unused quota to supply. While the MFA did succeed in controlling countries restricted under the agreement it is argued that there were so many alternative cheap sources that were unrestricted that it failed to halt the increasing import penetration both of the UK and of the US. For example, during the third phase of the MFA countries with preferential trade agreements with the European Union (Turkey, Morocco, Tunisia, Egypt, Malta and Cyprus) were able to substantially increase their exports to the EU (Khanna 1994: 22).

It became increasingly evident throughout the 1970s and early 1980s that market penetration was having an impact on the US textiles industry as large retail customers keen to get products to market faster began to import more Asian textiles, despite the restrictions under the MFA. Protectionism had been an important US governmental policy towards its own textile and clothing industries. In the 1960s the US had established preferential trading agreements through item 807 of the tariff schedule operated by US Customs and Excise, which encouraged garment manufacturers to undertake apparel assembly in lower-cost Caribbean and South American countries. The duty payable on the garment was then limited to the value-added component since leaving the US and being re-imported as a finished item. In effect duty was paid only on the labour cost element. The US established the Caribbean Basin Initiative (CBI) in February 1986 which allowed access to US markets, under specific conditions, for garments produced in the Caribbean (Steele 1988). Item 807.0010 of the US Customs and Excise schedule, more commonly referred to as 807a, was added to the existing 807 programme. The main difference between the two programmes was critical for the US textile industry. Whereas 807 allowed the use of fabric imported from anywhere in the world so long as it was cut in the US before being exported to the low-cost labour country, 807a demanded that only US-produced fabric be used within the scheme. This addition removed an earlier major objection from textile suppliers that had continually been levelled at the original 807 scheme. The major developing countries to benefit from the 807a programme have been the Dominican Republic and Mexico.

The more recent North American Free Trade Agreement (NAFTA), established between the US, Canada and Mexico for a twelve-year period from 1992, effectively replaced the 807a programme for Mexico. NAFTA's terms covered 360 million people, making NAFTA the largest trading bloc in the world. As far as textiles are concerned any production outsourced to Mexico would need to use fabric developed in US mills in the same way as the 807a schedule.

If protectionism doesn't work then faster response times might improve competitiveness

The US textiles industry controlled 80 per cent of its domestic market in 1981, and 6 years later it had lost 20 per cent to imports, mainly from Asia. Searching for competitive advantage, US industry leaders appealed to patriotism through an initiative called 'Crafted with Pride in the USA Council Inc'. The 500 members of the council paid US$100 million to advertise and promote the initiative to support US-made clothes, but failed to realise that even patriots have an eye for a bargain. In 1986 the council commissioned Kurt Salmon Associates to study US clothing (they use the term 'apparel') supply chains and discovered that time in the supply chain on average was fifteen months from textile loom to retail store. The industry-wide cost of this was US$25 billion per annum, roughly equivalent to a quarter of the industry's annual turnover at that time. This wastage had in effect been passed on to the consumer until trading became tough and imports penetrated the domestic markets to such an extent that the competition was threatening the very existence of many long-standing household textiles firms. Large US textiles firms and their retailers, like Milliken working with Wal-Mart, became interested in reducing process time through 'quick response' (QR). The study revealed that of the 66 weeks tied up in the supply chain only 11 weeks were needed to manufacture products and the other 55 weeks were consumed in storing or moving the products to different parts of the chain. In essence inventories in warehouses are simply goods in transit at zero miles an hour (Hines 2004).

Throughout the 1980s and 1990s QR gained further adoption as computing power increased, making it possible to process the large amounts of data to run QR programmes. Many supplier firms viewed QR as a way of increasing their own competitive position within the supply chain: they may not be the cheapest, but they can respond the fastest was the principle. Visibility of inventories within the supply chain through efficient information exchange created transparency to remove blockages, reduce time and replace inventories. It is well documented in the literature that Benetton, the Italian knitwear retailer, was able to respond quickly to consumer demand in store through its QR piece dyeing of garments in the colours that are in demand. The electronic point of sale (EPoS) data from the retail store transmits colour, size and style data back to the production centres, located in Italy where they react quickly to deliver, wherever in the world, the required product within seven days, often sooner (HBS 1984; Bull *et al*. 1993). QR promised much to domestic-supply firms but has not delivered all it promised (Hunter 1990; Fisher *et al*. 1994; Fiorito *et al*. 1995; KSA, 1997; Lowson *et al*. 1999). Ko and Kincade (1997) and others have measured the success of QR initiatives in the US apparel sector. There is no doubt that some firms improved their competitiveness as a consequence of adopting QR techniques. However, sustainability is the issue, because techniques can be imitated and many organisations in different parts of the world have established their own QR systems to improve their competitiveness in world markets.

Contemporary global markets

It is also important to draw comparisons between the textile and clothing industries in the UK within the international economy. Table 1.1 shows the employment record of developed countries in Europe and North America between 1995 and 2002.

Table 1.1 Employment in textiles and clothing, ATC countries (1,000s)

	1995	1996	1997	1998	1999	2000	2001	2002	2002 employment as % of 1995
Textiles									
Canada	54	55	51	60	59	54	51	54	100.00
United States[a]	688	660	653	642	614	595	539	489	71.08
France[b]	134	129	126	126	123	19	116	109	81.34
Germany	261	209	188	194	184	168	154	146	55.94
Italy	332	340	326	351	334	352	344	335	100.90
Portugal	99	87	83	101	101	100	106	104	105.05
Spain	108	91	94	99	99	101	101	99	91.67
United Kingdom[b]	188	185	184	178	162	149	135	120	63.83
Clothing									
Canada	92	80	92	98	97	85	94	80	86.96
United States[a]	814	743	700	639	556	497	427	358	43.98
France	137	128	121	115	106	95	87	81	59.12
Germany	122	133	128	120	114	117	118	105	86.07
Greece	66	65	60	52	50	50	51	45	68.18
Italy	274	243	235	229	209	206	206	198	72.26
Portugal	143	131	124	176	164	156	151	143	100.00
Spain	117	114	120	111	126	123	125	116	99.15
United Kingdom[b]	173	165	163	159	133	109	88	78	45.09

Notes
a Data based on establishment surveys.
b Data basedon official estimates.

Source: ILO (2004).

The final column is added to illustrate the changes during this eight-year period. It is significant that textiles employment, because of its capital intensity, has not shifted as much as that of clothing employment, which is more labour-intensive and foot-loose. Nonetheless, the USA, Germany and the UK have suffered substantial job losses.

The picture for clothing is much worse, with most countries apart from Portugal, with its low labour cost relative to most of the 15 EU countries and its close proximity to the EU market, suffering substantial job losses. Germany, with its strategy of out-ward processing trade (OPT), has also managed to stave off significant job losses, essentially by shipping partly constructed garments to lower labour cost countries for final make-up where processes are labour intensive. The USA and the UK have lost over half of their jobs in the clothing industry during this period.

Price deflation in clothing

Examining the period from 1988 through to the end of 2004 (Table 1.2) a clear pattern emerges between the whole UK economy (given by the all-prices index) and the clothing and footwear index. Up to 1995 there was a steady rise in the index for all prices while clothing and footwear showed increases between 1988 and 1991 and thereafter a steady decline. Whereas the index for all prices is now 11.2 per cent higher than in 1996, clothing and footwear prices are lower at 64.7 per cent of the prices in 1996. Effectively you would be able to purchase clothing and footwear that may have cost £1 in 1996 for 65 pence in 2004. These lower costs correlate with the shift in employment patterns and the lower volumes of supply sourced from UK manufacture.

Table 1.2 Data for the UK economy (all-prices index) and the clothing–footwear index 1988–2004

Year	All-prices index	Clothing–footwear index
1988	72.1	100.6
1989	75.8	105.0
1990	81.1	108.9
1991	87.2	110.7
1992	90.9	109.3
1993	93.2	107.5
1994	95.1	105.5
1995	97.6	103.3
1996	100.0	100.0
1997	101.8	97.5
1998	103.4	93.8
1999	104.8	88.8
2000	105.6	82.3
2001	106.9	76.2
2002	108.3	70.7
2003	109.8	68.0
2004	111.2	64.7

Source: CSO (2005).

Competition intensifies – at the micro level

A number of alternative and equally valid reasons can be given for the fall in prices that has occurred in the UK context. First and foremost, competitive pressures in the UK market have intensified since 1997 when Zara opened its first UK store in Regent Street, London. This retail subsidiary of Spain's Inditex Corporation has had a significant impact on the high-street retailers already in place. Zara was able to supply fashionable merchandise quickly from its supply base in northern Spain. It operated a vertically integrated business model that was finely tuned to customer demand, with the major twist of not being tied to replenishment ordering patterns. Zara simply offered in-demand styles, in season, faster than anyone else. This drove footfall through their stores and gained market share from major competitors who were locked into seasonal business models established in the 1960s in Britain. Simultaneously, competitive pressures were emerging in the shape of new competitors at home from the grocery supermarkets. George at ASDA has established itself as a fast-growing clothing brand run out of a major, if mainly northern-based, supermarket with its HQ in Leeds and its George brand offices in Leicester. This, however, was only the start. Tesco was developing its clothing brands, particularly Cherokee, to compete with high-street retailers such as Marks & Spencer (M&S), Next, Arcadia and Bhs, H&M and other international retailers had watched Zara's successful launch in the UK with interest and embarked on their own invasion. Volumes were rising but prices were falling as a consequence of this intensifying competition. Established retailers began to feel the pinch as their margins were eroded and their volumes hit by these new entrants to the market. The established retailers needed to respond but found it difficult to match the price points being set, particularly by supermarkets and by the new foreign invaders who seemed to be offering fast fashion at remarkably low prices by UK standards. There was only one thing for it: UK retailers needed to cut their costs and follow the examples being set by the new competition.

In the early 1990s M&S prided itself on being British and this meant having merchandise in store that was made in the UK. It was the largest UK retailer with £1 in every £7 spent on clothing going through its tills. UK-based manufacturers supplied almost 90 per cent of its products. So significant was the contribution of this single retailer that indeed it was often said in the 1990s that its purchase of UK manufactured clothing was equivalent to the UK trade balance deficit for clothing (i.e. UK clothing export minus imports). However, in 1997 M&S too began to feel the chill wind of a retail recession that seemed to impact on it more than it did on many of its competitors. The board decided to take drastic action and a key decision was taken to source more product from overseas where costs were lower than in the UK. In 2001 M&S strengthened its resolve to achieve a lower cost base and ended contracts with a number of long-standing clothing suppliers, notably William Baird with whom M&S had an acrimonious and very public dispute about the legality and morality of the decision. However, after the blood had been let M&S, in just a few years, managed to turn its supply equation into approaching 90 per cent from overseas sources and 10 per cent from UK sources. Many of its existing suppliers helped with the move to offshore supply. Initially, some of its main suppliers were encouraged to set up offshore production facilities in North Africa, particularly Morocco with its proximity to Europe (and the UK market) and its relatively low-cost labour base (Hines 2001).

The end of the MFA

The elimination of MFA quotas since January 2005 increases the nature of competitive pressure. The quota system provided protection to developed economies and to a number of developing countries that benefited from having quotas and, as a result, they were able to build their own manufacturing capacity. Figure 1.2 illustrates the relative market shares in textiles and clothing markets between 1992 and 2002. Under protection from the MFA the developing countries have managed to increase their relative market share from 49 per cent in 1992 to 64 per cent in 2002. The NICs of Asia (Hong Kong, Macau, Singapore, South Korea and Taiwan) have suffered. The Asian NIC share of the global textile and apparel market fell from 24 to 12 per cent between 1992 and 2002. China steadily increased its share of world markets from 21 to 25 per cent over the same period. You can draw your own conclusions about the causes.

The growing impact of China on world textiles and clothing markets

It is estimated that China has 40,000 textiles and garment manufacturing firms and 24,000 textiles mills. China has 15 million people employed in textiles and clothing manufacture and a forecast growth rate of 17 per cent per annum to increase its capacity further (WTO 2004 and World Bank reports). China's clothing imports into the UK stood at £1.7 billion in 2002 and they are expected to increase to £2.8 billion by 2005 when 20 per cent of clothing purchases by consumers in the UK will have been made in China. China produced 20 billion garments in 2002, enough for each person on the planet to have 4 garments from China in his or her wardrobe. China

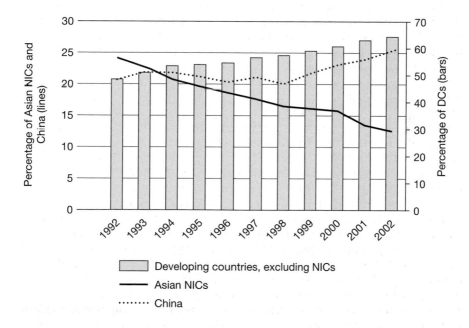

Figure 1.2 Textiles and clothing market share of NICs in Asia 1992–2002

Source: WTO (2004).

had a positive trade balance with the rest of the world which was US$54.6 billion, with US$50.4 being clothing and US$4.2 being textiles. Perhaps it is not so surprising that the country with the most people is so dominant in a labour-intensive industry such as clothing. Pure labour economics on the basis of supply and demand might lead us to conclude thus.

China's clothing exports to the US stood at just around US$9 billion in 1990, US$25 billion in 1995 and are forecast to rise to US$70 billion by the end of 2005. This acceleration in growth is fueled by the demise of the MFA quota system. Trade liberalisation will also have the effect of lowering the price of goods by 46 per cent in the US market and by 42 per cent across the EU, increasing further retail price cuts.

Leading exporters and importers – the macro picture

Table 1.3 shows that the top 15 exporting countries for clothing manufacture account for 78.6 per cent of the market at an estimated value of US$178.34 billion in 2003. Of these top 15 exporters the EU (15) has lost significant market share since 1980 but shows a slight recovery since 2000. China has seen major gains in market share from just 4 per cent in 1980 to 23 per cent in 2003. Other winners have been Turkey, Mexico, India, Bangladesh, Indonesia, Romania, Thailand, Vietnam, Morocco and

Table 1.3 Leading exporters of clothing (value in billions of US$ for 2003 and %s for share of markets 1980–2003)

Exporters	Value	Share in world exports			
	2003	1980	1990	2000	2003
European Union (15)	59.95	42.0	37.7	24.1	26.5
Extra-exports	19.04	10.4	10.5	7.4	8.4
China[a]	52.06	4.0	8.9	18.3	23.0
Hong Kong, China	23.15	–	–	–	–
domestic exports	8.20	11.5	8.6	5.0	3.6
re-exports	14.95	–	–	–	–
Turkey	9.94	0.3	3.1	3.3	4.4
Mexico[a]	7.34	0.0	0.5	4.4	3.2
India[b]	6.46	1.7	2.3	3.1	2.9
United States	5.54	3.1	2.4	4.4	2.5
Bangladesh[b]	4.36	0.0	0.6	2.1	1.9
Indonesia	4.11	0.2	1.5	2.4	1.8
Romania	4.07	–	0.3	1.2	1.8
Thailand[b]	3.62	0.7	2.6	1.9	1.6
Korea, Republic[a][b]	3.61	7.3	7.3	2.5	1.6
Vietnam[b]	3.56	–	–	0.9	1.6
Morocco[a][b]	2.83	0.3	0.7	1.2	1.3
Pakistan	2.71	0.3	0.9	1.1	1.2
Above 15	178.34	71.3	77.5	75.9	78.6

Notes
a includes shipments through processing zones
b includes secretariat estimates
c imports are valued Free on Board (FOB)
d 2002 instead of 2003.

Source: WTO (2004).

Table 1.4 Leading importers of clothing (value in billions of US$ for 2003 and %s for share of markets 1980–2003)

Importers	Value	Share of world imports			
	2003	1980	1990	2000	2003
European Union (15)	101.29	54.3	50.6	38.7	42.9
Extra-imports	60.39	23.0	25.2	22.9	25.6
United States	71.28	16.4	24.0	32.4	30.2
Japan	19.49	3.6	7.8	9.5	8.3
Hong Kong, China	15.95	–	–	–	–
retained imports	0.99	0.9	0.7	0.8	0.4
Canada[c]	4.50	1.7	2.1	1.8	1.9
Switzerland	3.93	3.4	3.1	1.6	1.7
Russian Federation[b]	3.71	–	–	1.3	1.6
Mexico[a,c]	3.03	0.3	0.5	1.7	1.3
Korea, Republic of[b]	2.50	0.0	0.1	0.6	1.1
Australia[c]	2.19	0.8	0.6	0.9	0.9
Singapore	1.94	0.3	0.8	0.9	0.8
retained imports	0.53	0.2	0.3	0.3	0.2
United Arab Emirates[b,d]	1.78	0.6	0.5	0.7	0.8
Norway	1.52	1.7	1.1	0.6	0.6
China[a]	1.42	0.1	0.0	0.6	0.6
Saudi Arabia	1.03	1.6	0.7	0.4	0.4
Above 15	220.60	85.8	92.8	92.6	93.5

Notes:
a includes shipments through processing zones
b includes secretariat estimates
c imports are valued FOB
d 2002 instead of 2003.

Source: WTO (2004).

Pakistan. Losers apart from the EU have been the Republic of Korea (i.e. South Korea) and the US. Hong Kong has become part of China during the period and the statistics are therefore of less relevance than they might have been had they have been independent of China.

Table 1.4 shows the top 15 importers of clothing manufactures between 1980 and 2003. Demand for imported clothing in the US has increased significantly over the period while EU (15) imports have actually fallen as a share of world markets in percentage terms.

Table 1.5 reveals regional flows of trade in clothes for 2003. Intra-Western European trade still accounts for the main share of trade and it is growing year on year. Latin America to North America trade appears to be stagnating while the trade flows from Asia to North America are growing. Similarly, Asian trade with Western Europe has grown significantly.

In contrast to clothing markets, textiles markets are dominated by intra-Asian trade worth US$41.8 billion in 2003 and intra-Western European trade worth US$41.1 billion (WTO, 2004). The statistical data supplied in the tables should provide the reader with some insight into world trade flows that currently exist in the contemporary textiles and clothing industries. It is intended that the commentary should also

Table 1.5 Major regional flows of exports of clothing in world trade (value in billions of US$ for 2003 and %s)

	Value	Annual % change		
	2003	1995–2000	2002	2003
Intra-Western Europe	55.5	0	9	18
Asia to North America	37.4	7	2	6
Intra-Asia	25.2	4	–5	11
Asia to Western Europe	23.7	4	3	15
Latin America to North America	18.9	22	–2	0
C/E, Europe/Baltic states/CIS to Western Europe	11.5	7	6	18

Source: WTO (2004).

help reveal trade patterns at the macro level and at the micro level where it impacts on individual companies operating in these global markets, and last but not least, on all of us as consumers or maybe as employees or employers.

Conclusions

The journey began in this chapter with an explanation of the nature and structure of the textiles and clothing industries set within a supply chain extending from its origins in agriculture or chemical processes to develop fibres for fabrics that could be transformed into products for consumption and distributed through retail networks. Key differences and similarities between the textiles industry and the clothing industry were established in terms of production process time, barriers to entry being relatively high for textiles investment and relatively low for clothing manufacture, textiles being capital-intensive and clothing being labour-intensive. Furthermore, the economics of textiles production are such that efficiency is a prime focus whereas in clothing responsiveness may be relatively more important than efficiency, although retail buyers would like both low-cost supply and responsiveness.

The antecedents for the contemporary patterns of production and market structures began with the Industrial Revolution in the UK and a number of key technological innovations enabled the early manufacturers to improve their efficiency and hence their competitive position. There was also a tendency to protectionism and conservatism in attitude towards new products and technological developments, not least from owners who saw their profits eroded and workers who saw their livelihoods threatened by machinery (capital) replacing labour in work processes. The textiles and clothing industries became integral to economic growth in the UK, and accounted for substantial employment and output measured by GDP throughout the eighteenth–twentieth centuries. These industries were responsible for the emergence of the factory system and industrialisation on a grand scale with incumbent economic gains and social costs. Development patterns established in the first Industrial Revolution were to be rehearsed and replayed time and again throughout the world as comparative advantage moved from region to region and nation to nation.

Despite the agreements designed to liberalise world trade following the Bretton Woods Agreement in 1944, when GATT was established, the textiles and clothing industries have by and large been subject to new mercantilist policies placing restrictions on trade and limits to industrial growth. The MFA was a major policy initiative designed to achieve these aims, but it has failed miserably to protect those it was designed for. Since January 2005 the MFA has been removed and ostensibly trade is freer. Nevertheless, protectionism remains in the form of tariffs agreed and applied through large trading blocs and at an individual national level. Nevertheless, global shifts in production continue and market growth occurs in unplanned ways. It is appropriate that at the micro level organisations continue to trade as they see fit within legal and ethical frameworks, allowing governments to continue their obsession with controlling economies at the macro-economic level.

The major challenge to UK-based businesses and those in the US is how to benefit from global shifts in production and consumption that alter the patterns of world trade. Competitive pressures have intensified during the last ten years and many once-famous household names in textiles and clothing have faded away or changed form. A cursory glance at the stock market pages of the *Financial Times* will indicate that textiles is not the important industrial sector it once was. Nevertheless, the UK, as is the case in Western Europe and North America, with its loss of manufacturing capacity has developed new skills and new important economic contributors such as retailing. Wal-Mart is not simply a US retailer but the largest retailer in the world, and it heads the Fortune list of the top 100 companies. With its acquisition of ASDA in the UK it has also acquired its own major clothing brand: 'George'. The company is responsible for major sourcing and production of its own clothes, manufactured in factories throughout the world, bought for lower cost than they could be manufactured in their home markets. Wal-Mart is not alone in doing so: all major clothing retailers now source and produce merchandise away from their domestic markets because of the advantage of achieving lower costs.

The entry of grocery retailers such as ASDA–Wal-Mart (UK), Tesco, Sainsbury and the discounters Matalan, Primark, TK Maxx, together with the intensifying competition between the high-street clothing retailers M&S, Bhs, Arcadia, Next and new entrants to the market such as Zara, Mango and H&M, will ensure that prices remain low across most clothing lines and will continue to eat into brand profits. Branded clothing retailers will be able to sustain their higher prices and higher levels of profitability only by offering something very different, be that the shopping experience, the fashionable clothes or the special service levels. Pockets of specialist UK clothing suppliers will remain in existence mainly because they will be able to offer QR through their proximity to the market. Some suppliers will also maintain and develop their design, sourcing and technical operations in the UK, close to their retail markets, while managing supply networks offshore to achieve lower production cost overall. Today China is viewed as the major sourcing opportunity; but if historical world trade patterns are observed it is merely a question of time before comparative advantage shifts to another centre of even lower cost. The critical success factor for any organisation operating within the complexities of the global textiles and clothing supply chain, be they a retailer, a manufacturer or a service provider, is simple: stay customer-focused. If at the micro level the organisation is completely focused on providing satisfaction for its immediate customer then it will innovate, improve and compete in whatever ways it can. If there is one thing that history and the evidence presented in this chapter teaches us, it is that success is difficult to sustain and that flexibility of thought is perhaps more important than anything else in order to create new opportunities – seeing solutions where others do not.

2 Analysing fashion

Pamela Church Gibson

Those of you who, for whatever reason, are starting to read through this handbook will already have a good idea of what you think 'fashion' is. You probably think, too, that the study of fashion – in a variety of ways – is a perfectly legitimate activity. You may go further and agree that, for a full understanding of the workings of any given society – including the globalised world in which we now live – the different ways in which people choose to adorn themselves must be studied carefully and, if you like, decoded. Only then can we fully understand the rules, the ideas, the behaviour and the attitudes of that society. And there has never been a society, however primitive, without bodily decoration of some kind.

It is still generally assumed that the function of dress is threefold – to provide protection if necessary, to serve the demands of modesty and, lastly, to adorn. Today, in different parts of the world, people in 'primitive' societies follow codes which date back to the formations of those societies. Those people may seem to us to be virtually naked, but the ways in which they modify and decorate their bodies tell those within their group of their identity and status, and inform outsiders about their values and customs. For example, a tribe which lives in the tropical rainforests of the Amazon River basin insert large disks of bone into their lower lips – and they must never be seen in public without these disks. Whereas in our society, modesty demands the covering of the genitals, there the rules are different.

In the West, again, we have always placed a premium on unblemished, unmarked, bodily skin – lately, young men on both sides of the Atlantic have even begun to wax their chests. In Central Africa, however, many tribes carefully, precisely, scar their bodies – both boys and girls are decorated in this way, as part of ceremonies around attaining adulthood that vary from tribe to tribe. Some go further, inserting beads underneath the scars and the skin. And in parts of the Pacific archipelago, male bodies are decorated with elaborate all-over tattooing or with carefully painted designs.

In Western society, we tend – wrongly – to assume that adornment and display are still the province of women. Elsewhere in the world, it is often the male of the species – as in the animal kingdom – who sports the more splendid plumage. After all, the actual origin of make-up and body-painting – and of the term 'war paint' – was the ritual decoration applied to themselves by the men of a tribe before they left the safety of their own encampment to confront enemies. Interestingly, the Wodaabe tribe of Africa still conducts an annual festival which reverses the conventional Western beauty pageant. The young men spend hours, even days, decorating their faces with yellow pigment and encircling their eyes with elaborate dark lines, before lining up for inspection as the marriageable young women make their choices of husbands.

In the study of Western history, the clothes, jewellery, accessories and hairstyles of a particular period can give us vital information, often relating to the decorative arts of the period in question. To give one example, in the last decade of the eighteenth century, after the French Revolution, the excessive female fashions of 1780s' Paris were replaced by the simplicity of the 'Empire line', where dresses fell straight to the ankle from below the bust. The waist and hips were no longer heavily empha-sised, since women had a part to play in the new post-revolutionary France which extended beyond the bearing of children – unfortunately, like the Empire line, this idea did not last.

Sadly, however, many historians have little or no interest in the vagaries of dress, while there might be plenty of academics in other fields of scholarship who would dispute my assertion that fashion is a vital area of study for us all, whatever our parent discipline. And those of us who think that fashion itself *is* an important area of academic study are still in a minority, often the subject of sarcastic remarks. Fashion is still seen by far too many as something quintessentially frivolous.

Yet the fashion industry today – in its diverse forms – occupies a vital place in the global economy, providing livelihoods for millions of people, while in the UK itself it is the fourth largest source of employment. And our ever-increasing interest in fashion, whether or not we are professionally involved, is obvious to anyone – particularly to journalists. Newspapers give fashion stories a far higher profile than they did, say, twenty years ago – clothes are no longer simply consigned to the fashion pages. Nowadays, a particularly innovative or eye-catching catwalk show will invariably make the front page of even the most serious broadsheet – a glimpse of breast, nipple or upper thigh is no longer necessary to make the front page – while takeover bids within the industry, designer sackings or other developments are usually reported in detail.

Fashion journalists, and their editors and publishers, too, have realised that we are increasingly fashion-literate. Magazine journalists have responded to the widening of female interest across a broader demographic spread than ever before – the raft of new titles that have appeared over the past ten years includes magazines targeted at pre-pubertal and post-menopausal markets. Most significant, however, are the developments within fashion journalism – and fashion imagery – since the revolu-tion in and around menswear in the 1980s, when the industry first discovered and then embraced the newly fashion-conscious younger man. Until the 1980s, most male models in the glossies were still besuited accessories for women. Elsewhere, they were invariably clean-cut chaps in knitwear consorting with a more 'ordinary' woman – the husband of OXO Katie in the TV campaign is a good example. Occasionally they might be glimpsed in their jockey briefs in advertisements for such products. However, in the 1980s mainstream fashion finally caught up with what had been happening on the streets and around popular music since the mid-1950s, gathering real momentum in the 1960s, that decade of upheaval and transformation.

The economic improvements of the 1950s gave young people more disposable income, while the 'baby boom' of the post-war years meant that in the 1960s, for the first time ever, those same young people constituted a majority of the population in England and the USA. The sharp-suited Mods of Carnaby Street, the long-haired hippies in their unisex kaftans, the glam-rock bands of the early 1970s, even the confrontational androgyny of punk – all these street styles were, in part, a way of men reclaiming fashion for themselves after more than a century of conformity.

In the 1980s, however, men moved to the very centre of the fashion stage. Male models were no longer anonymous tailors' dummies used as props, but subjects of fashion spreads in their own right. They were no longer pictured fully clad – now their newly honed torsos were used to sell every type of fashion-related product, from 'fragrances' to jeans. Nick Kamen, the model used in the famous Levi's campaign of the mid-1980s, not only increased the sales of the product he advertised by an unprecedented 200 per cent, he became a 'name' in his own right and moved into a career in the music industry.

Images of men stared down from billboards, glanced across from advertisements beside the escalator in the London Underground, and looked up from the pages not only of women's magazines but of the new publications that quickly appeared to satisfy this new consumer. First, journalists christened him 'New Man'. Supposedly a sensitive soul who helped with childcare and was in touch with his 'feminine side', he was offered the thoughtful glossy magazine *Arena* and a transformed version of an American import, *GQ*, to read. But in the 1990s, the most successful magazine in English journalism – across the board – was the newly launched *Loaded*, aimed at the more realistic figure of the 'New Lad'. Like 'old' lads before him, he watched football, liked girls, played with gadgets and went to the pub – but what made him 'new' was his desire for good clothes and the new male-grooming products. Now, ten years later, journalists have discovered a new archetype, the 'metrosexual'. This man shares all the stereotypical interests of gay men – fashion, interior décor and cooking – but is 'straight' in his sexuality. By the time *The Fashion Handbook* is printed, journalists will have come up with a new phrase to describe the 'metro-sexual' man – who continually changes and morphs.

It was in the 1960s, of course, that the female fashion model first became a recognised personality. Jean Shrimpton was the first, arguably, who emerged from anonymity, followed swiftly by Twiggy, who in 1966 became a national byword for extreme slenderness. The 'supermodels' of the late 1980s and early 1990s were familiar, named, highly desirable figures to many outside the industry, while model Kate Moss became so famous in the new century that her turbulent personal life made the front pages of the tabloids. She could be headlined simply as 'Kate', just as the late Princess Diana, another fashion icon, became 'Di'. Arguably, Diana's early popularity was not due just to her good looks and pleasant nature, but to her open interest in fashion and her capacity to set trends that others wanted to copy, from the heavy fringe and frilled blouses of 1980s 'Shy Di' to the gym-honed, Versace-wearing, woman of the 1990s.

Yet despite two decades of radical change and the re-emergence of the male consumer, there are still many who think that fashion is to be equated with the feminine – and talked about only by the feeble-minded. Before I discuss the ways in which fashion came to be studied and interpreted in the last hundred years, it's important, surely, to understand why it has been – and is – so demonised.

Since 'fashion' has traditionally been equated with 'the feminine', the misogyny that lurks within the Judaeo-Christian beliefs which inform the institutions of Western society might take some of the blame. Jezebel, that most scandalous of Old Testament villainesses, was cast down from the city walls and eaten by dogs for committing a series of offences that included the visible painting of her face. The cardinal sin of vanity is invariably represented in Western art by some representation of a feminine concern with appearance. In Bosch's painting of the late fifteenth century *The Seven Deadly Sins*, which now hangs on the walls of the Prado in Madrid, vanity is displayed through the figure of a solid bourgeois *hausfrau*, secretly trying on the latest fashionable headdress – it is the Devil himself who is holding up the mirror in which she admires herself. And it was seen as a short journey from vanity to sexual transgression in its many forms – in Renaissance painting, and thereafter, a courtesan was marked out by the loose hair that covered her shoulders, her display of jewellery and the mirror in her hand.

The links between fashion, femininity and sexual allure are behind the twentieth-century feminist attack on fashion. From Germaine Greer's broadside of 1969 *The Female Eunuch*, in which she reserves her most scathing prose for women foolish enough to follow fashion, to Naomi Woolf's *The Beauty Myth* in the 1980s – which reworks many of Greer's arguments – there's a misleading assumption that women who choose to take an interest in their clothes and their hair, and who wear make-up, do so only to attract men. Janet Radcliffe Richards took issue with this idea in *The Sceptical Feminist* (1980) but it took Elizabeth Wilson's seminal work on fashion, *Adorned in Dreams*: *Fashion and Modernity* (1985) to show women that they could dress fashionably without betraying the feminist cause and, more significantly, that fashion was a legitimate arena of academic study.

Readers are presumably aware that fashionable dress was, in the past, the province of the elite. 'Ordinary' people, quite simply, wore functional clothes, while until the twentieth century 'fashion', and the changes in style it brings, were reserved specifically for the upper echelons of society – which may have added to the suspicion surrounding it. Sir Thomas More, when he wrote *Utopia* in 1516, argued that ostentation in dress is wrong, since it is socially divisive. Not only does it show at a glance the status of the wearer, but also it gives those with money an added advantage, since they are always able to select clothes which suit them. In his imaginary, truly democratic, country of Utopia, all the inhabitants are obliged by law to wear similar simple garments – loose shifts in neutral colours and plain fabrics. This Utopian ideal was, of course, in sharp contrast to the actual laws of Thomas More's England and their dictates on dress. The Sumptuary Laws, which attempted to tax those who spent vast amounts on their wardrobes, more significantly restricted the wearing of fashionable garb to the higher social echelons, even creating forms of punishment for those who transgressed. These statutes were introduced in 1363 and enforced up until the 1560s, more than twenty years after More's execution. Interestingly, his ideas of the levelling power of simple dress were used in Maoist China, where all were required to dress in identical navy-blue peasant tunics and trousers, and did so for thirty-odd years.

In the century after More's death, the newly powerful Puritans, in England and elsewhere in Europe, adopted a new style of dress which was almost a uniform – plain black garments with white collars and cuffs, and, for women, simple white caps. This 'uniform' was intended to show that their minds were on higher things and that their spiritual beliefs were opposed to ostentation in any form, whether in church décor or in personal adornment. When, in 1642, civil war broke out in England, the Puritans were with Parliament against the overbearing, unpopular, wasteful king – and the Puritan leader Cromwell's 'Roundhead' army provided a stark visual rebuke to the Cavaliers, who supported the king, for male Cavalier dress involved elaborate lace collars and velvet doublets, their long hair curling around their faces.

The Cavaliers and their king may have been defeated – but the strict rule of the Puritans dismayed many. After eleven years of parliamentary rule, the restoration of the monarchy in 1660 brought with it the restoration of very elaborate, showy clothes for those men and women in the higher ranks of society. The period was noted for its 'fops', precursors of the 'dandies' – aristocratic, affected men with a keen interest in their appearance and a studiedly languid manner, who wielded their scented handkerchiefs, canes and gloves as deftly as any woman might her fan or parasol.

It is important to realise that men have been able to sport frills and furbelows, if that was the current fashion and if they came from the right sector of society. A century later, in the period before the Industrial Revolution made its radical impact on England's social map, men, like women, wore heavily powdered wigs. The more fashionable men powdered their faces, too, and decorated them with 'patches', black beauty spots cut from fabric, often positioned to cover smallpox scars. This potted costume history is necessary if the theories in fashion studies about the effects of the Industrial Revolution on male attire are to be fully understood.

What are these theories? There is still a general consensus in fashion studies that, after the industrialisation of Britain in the late 1700s and early 1800s, which meant, in effect, that the landed gentry ceded power to the new professional middle classes, extravagance in dress became confined to women alone. Serious, sober-minded professional men, the captains of the new industries, wished to show off their status, then as now, in what became the three-piece suit we know today. New, simple jackets, waistcoats and breeches swiftly evolved into an outfit that is still with us.

The German psychologist J. C. Flugel, writing in 1930, was the first to identify and discuss this phenomenon, naming it the 'Great Masculine Renunciation' – the term is still deployed, though his ideas may sometimes be contested. Flugel, a trained psychoanalyst, was a disciple of Sigmund Freud, and the first writer to study clothing from that particular perspective. This theory, one of his most influential, explained that these newly powerful professional men put aside fashion as frivolous, and instead displayed their wealth and power on the bodies of their wives, through the rich dresses, jewellery and sumptuous accessories which they encouraged them to wear and for which they paid. As the nineteenth century progressed, really competitive rich men could always encourage their wives to patronise the new couture houses of Paris, the first of which was, interestingly, opened by an Englishman, Charles Frederick Worth, in 1858. The idea of this 'renunciation' is still with us in fashion studies, though it's been contested by some in recent years. For instance, Anne Hollander suggests in her book *Sex and Suits* (1994) that these men, far from removing themselves from the admiring gaze of others, instead constructed a far more subtle way of self-display. The suit, she explains, accentuates the contours of the male body in a particularly flattering way, emphasising the shoulders, narrowing the waist, and lengthening the legs. Other fashion scholars have drawn attention to the fact that Flugel, although the first to investigate the psychology of dress, wanted clothes to be – quite literally – cast aside: like many Germans of his time, he was a passionate advocate of nudism – a strange irony for a man still linked firmly to the study of dress.

If you set out to study fashion in depth, you will encounter this notion of the 'renunciation', together with other persuasive ideas that Flugel introduced.

One of these was that dress is designed for sexual display or to gratify narcissism – or both. He was the first writer to make theoretical links between fashion and eroticism.

James Laver, costume historian and a central figure in fashion scholarship for thirty years – his publications date from 1937 to 1969 – picked up on this aspect of Flugel's work. He developed it and named it the 'Attraction Principle' or the 'Seduction Principle', arguing that this principle leads, in its turn, to what he christened the 'Shifting Erogenous Zone'. This notion explains the fashionable changes in the female silhouette as an indication of women's efforts to attract – and sustain – male sexual attention. The bust and the accompanying décolletage are vital at one moment, although the next few years could see the focus of interest shifting to the buttocks, and then – in the present century – the legs might become the object of interest. Fashion, he asserts, keeps changing the central object of the male gaze as part of women's perpetual competition with each other in the desire for male admiration, and as part of the ceaseless race to reproduce.

Laver worked in the costume department of the Victoria and Albert Museum (V&A) for thirty years, and a stroll through its collection will perhaps provoke the question: why does fashion today change so rapidly? Looking at fashions of the past, we can see how changes took place gradually, over a period of years – fashion moved at a different pace. The reasons for the acceleration of change in the modern era are complex, and form part of any study of fashion. Mass production, new methods of clothing manufacture, new fabrics are only a part of it – technological changes have their part to play, though they do not themselves inspire change, but only make it easier.

Thorstein Veblen's notion of 'conspicuous consumption', advanced in 1899 in his book *The Theory of the Leisure Class*, is surely more relevant than ever in 2006. Veblen's book was a study of the upper echelons of American society, including those who owed their vast wealth to the new industries rather than to inherited money and who could now, like the landed gentry, proudly proclaim that they need never work again. He studied and deciphered the ways in which they displayed their wealth, filling their studiedly tasteful homes with European antiques and decorating their wives in the most elegant, elaborate clothes, showing them off like all their other possessions. The way that women of fashion dressed at the time was a perfect illustration of Veblen's argument – with their trailing skirts and over-decorated garments, weighed down with fur stoles, massive hats and ostentatious jewellery, they showed off the wealth of the household and its male provider. Their only function was to be decorative, and they were expected merely to form a part of the lavish fixtures and fittings of a rich household.

Today, 'conspicuous consumption' is rampant as never before – but it's no longer confined to the higher social orders. Anyone with enough disposable income can participate, while women today who display their money through their designer clothes or expensive furniture conceivably have earned it themselves. It is in some ways, seemingly, more democratic. Footballers' wives can now be fashion leaders, while what has been nicknamed 'bling' – a particular way of wearing chunky gold jewellery and the odd diamond – is a style begun by black 'rap' stars, picked up on by their fans and filtered down to street level. Meanwhile, those very manicured lawns which so fascinated Veblen now show off the status of Middle England: what you need is cash rather than social cachet. Worryingly, in order to fund our conspicuous consumption, we have become a nation living on credit, and our obsession with designer labels has spawned a whole new industry around counterfeiting. Veblen would be fascinated – but, rightly, perturbed.

Georg Simmel, a Berlin-based philosopher whose work on fashion was published in 1904, was not, in fact, the originator of the 'trickle-down' theory used throughout the last century to explain the workings of the fashion system. Many, though, do associate him with this idea – though it forms only a small part of his study of the relationship between fashion and modernity. The theory – still of value, although there have been significant changes in the way fashions are created – is that fashions are created in, for and by the upper echelons of society. Couturiers create a style, which is displayed by 'fashion leaders'; it therefore becomes desirable to those lower down the social scale, where it is copied and popularised.

The 'fashion leaders' of Simmel's era were the high-profile ladies of elegant society, the odd 'Royal' such as Edward VIII's wife Princess Alexandra, and the most newsworthy actresses – some of whom were Edward VIII's mistresses. Today, fashion leaders still include actresses, although now they are more likely to be film stars rather than stage performers. In our celebrity-dominated culture we scrutinise the new crop of magazines to see who is wearing what – and among those whose pictures we study are singers, TV presenters, top fashion models and footballers. With the exception of the late Princess Diana, today's royals are more likely to be seeking tips than they are to be setting trends.

The other significant change since Simmel elaborated the trickle-down theory is the parallel existence – and arguably the dominance – of 'bubble-up' fashion, which, as the name implies, describes fashions created and popularised on the streets, and then filter upwards. Many sub-cultural styles, looks associated with a particular type of music or an individual youth icon, have, over the last fifty years, filtered upwards to become available on the high street. From James Dean's Levi's and white T-shirt, through Madonna's endless reinventions of her own image, to Britney Spears's bared midriff and visible thong knickers, the potency of 'bubble-up' is unquestionable. Perhaps the most interesting example is the extraordinary influence of the rap style of the 1980s. Not only did it put everyone in trainers, hooded tops and fleeces – still with us – but the ' bumbags' that were integral to 'rapper' style were actually copied on the catwalk: Karl Lagerfeld produced a quilted bumbag, embossed with the Chanel logo, which cost several hundred pounds.

The first systematic studies of fashion, as we have seen, coincided with the start of the twentieth century and the speedy proliferation of fashionable images through both still photography and the newly invented medium of film. And the first two decades of that century saw the most radical changes ever in women's appearance. As their social role altered and they won a measure of freedom, so their long locks and sweeping skirts were replaced by the short haircuts and skirts that characterised the 1920s. One of the freedoms for which they fought was the right to be educated – and when the first fashion design courses were set up in the 1930s women formed the majority of the first fashion students at both the Royal College of Art and St Martin's School of Art. Of course, women had been employed for hundreds of years as seamstresses, dressmakers and, later, milliners. Coco Chanel herself started life as a milliner – and was lucky or enterprising enough to have had a rich lover who recognised and encouraged her obvious talent for other forms of design. Chanel and her great rival Elsa Schiaparelli were working in an industry where, then as now, women formed the bulk of the workforce, while the couturiers who dictated what they and other women might wear were, of course, men. Some of the new fashion students in the 1930s hoped to redress the balance, although among today's top designers, men still outnumber women – another interesting irony within fashion's curious workings.

These early fashion students studied costume history, not cultural studies as on the present-day courses at what is now Central St Martins School of Art. Costume history is still a part of fashion study – but sadly there is sometimes a degree of hostility directed at the new discipline of cultural studies. A few costume historians dislike the work of cultural studies' lecturers, with their interest in theory and questions of class, gender and economics. A key text in the analysis of fashion, Roland Barthes's *The Fashion System*, published originally in 1967, attracted some indignation because he was one of the first 'structuralists', the French theorists who attempted to reveal the structures underlying social and cultural life. Some historians prefer analysis to keep away from 'high theory' which they see as wilfully problematical.

This shift is mirrored in other disciplines. In literature and in art history there's been a move away from the idea of a canon of 'great works', and from the concept of the 'great artist' working in isolation. Instead, the new theorists argue that any artistic production – a book, a painting or a dress – is the product of the cultural and social forces within which the particular artist is working. Some would argue that in fashion design the innovative Chanel was simply responding to the needs of women in the new, transformed world that followed the First World War. Women were enjoying a new freedom, many of them going out to work – indeed, they were forced to do so because the deaths of so many young men on the battlefield meant that, for many women, marriage was no longer a career option. Another, related, example – Christian Dior's 'New Look' of 1947 – was, once again, not the product of a 'genius' working in isolation. No, it was the creation, arguably, of a man who had taken the social and cultural temperature of the immediate post-war period and made a clever judgement. He had divined, correctly, that after the recent horrors, the austerity of rationing and the practical clothes demanded by war work – trousers, turbans, short shorts and wedge heels – what women would now want were romantic, non-practical, feminine clothes that harked back to an earlier era, before Hiroshima and the Holocaust. I myself would suggest, too, that the massive success of the film *Gone With The Wind* in 1939 – set in a war, yes, but in a country far away and in a past made safe by distance – may have been in his mind. Certainly Vivien Leigh, star of that film, wearing her ethereal green dress, surrounded by a circle of enchanted young men, was a potent cinematic image. Brides subsequently have often cited that dress, with its low neckline, tiny waist and vast, sweeping skirts, as exemplifying the look they wish for on their wedding day.

Similarly, Mary Quant and André Courrèges did not *invent* the miniskirt, as both have claimed – rather, their designs reflected women's new-found freedom in an age when, finally, they could control their biology – and when, through a strange demographic blip, the majority of them were under 25.

Fashion since the 1960s is a fascinating subject for study. Why have the majority of designers ceased to look forward, instead starting to look not only backwards but also sideways, across other cultures, for inspiration? They seem to be engaged in a non-stop perusal of history books, copies of the *National Geographic* magazine and photographs of sub-cultural styles, past and present, for inspiration. At the start of a new millennium, it does seem strange that we are stuck in a 'retro' groove from which there is no visible escape as yet. The cultural study of fashion would attempt to explain this and other sartorial questions. For instance, sub-cultural styles and 'street style' in general were once claimed by some theorists to be 'subversive'. But these days, high street retailers pick them up so quickly that they lose their subversive potency. Nevertheless, the 'homeboy' style that involved very low-slung trousers for young men – with their designer briefs visible above the waistbands of their jeans – was perhaps too threatening and was bypassed by white suburban boys. Instead, their girlfriends took it up enthusiastically, thus robbing it of its original meaning: for the belts were removed and the trousers lowered towards the crotch by the young black men who started the trend in the US on the grounds that it's invariably black men who get arrested, usually for no reason, and the first thing to be confiscated in prison cells are those very belts. Interestingly, though, the style for women became so popular that no young girl, whatever her girth, seemed able to ignore it.

If you study fashion seriously, that's the kind of conundrum that you might try to solve. You will also study consumption – not only the patterns in fashion marketing and retailing, but also the cultural theories which attempt to look at those patterns within a much wider historical and social context. Earlier ideas that we are all hapless dupes of consumerism are still there, but they've been joined by oppositional theories suggesting that through different forms of consumption we can express our own identity. You might ask: if we are living on credit, how can that be really an expression of 'identity'? Or you might put forward another argument: can fashion consumption ever be truly ethical? The 'fair trade' movements are powerless against the exploitation of millions, elsewhere in the world, working in sweatshops so that English supermarkets can now offer jeans for the ridiculous price of £3. Nike's problems when its underpaid workers were discovered may be well known – others have been luckier and have escaped detection. Then there's the question to which the name 'Nike' gives rise – how can we look 'different' and express our 'identity' when everything on offer seems exactly the same, when the same shops are to be found on every high street from Prague to Preston?

Hopefully, by now, you can see the point of analysing fashion at a deeper level – in an attempt to make some sense out of the seesawing of hemlines rather than merely describing these changes. Fashion is a part of our lives, a basic means of self-expression, however limited, that must receive the status within academic work that it merits. You might start by reading Christopher Breward's recent study *Fashion* (2003) and Elizabeth Rouse's invaluable primer *Understanding Fashion* (1987), both of which will provide excellent introductions. I hope that your own study – whatever form it takes – is not only of use to you in career terms but provides some in-depth insight to this most fascinating and undervalued of disciplines.

3 Fashion design

Tim Jackson

Introduction

The aim of this chapter is to provide the reader with an appreciation of the scope and diversity of fashion design. There is a mix of historical fact, explanation of industry activity and analysis of contemporary fashion design issues.

Today fashion is a ubiquitous feature of life, from the label on our clothes to the mobile phone in our bags. Fashion matters to people because it says something about who they are and how they want to be seen. Modern life is much faster and more fragmented than at any stage in the past and it is unsurprising therefore that people buy for many different occasions according to the diversity of their lifestyles. Add to this the fact that styles and brands come and go very quickly and it makes the task of designing fashion for a season a very involved and finely balanced activity.

New global media provide the perfect vehicles for communicating fast-moving, disposable fashion, which is conceived by designers, creative directors and stylists. Reportage and analysis by fashion journalists and 'taste-makers' helps to identify and communicate trends. However, the initial spark or seed of a fashion concept often comes from observing what is new and unusual in our everyday lives.

The boundaries between celebrity, fashion and popular culture are becoming increasingly blurred. More than ever before fashion mixes comfortably with entertainment culture, including sport, music and television. TV shows such as *Sex in the City* and *Desperate Housewives* both introduce the names of designers and brands to the mass market and offer role models, and new attitudes and lifestyles. Consumers have become more familiar with designer names as fashion is frequently the central focus of many media interests, ranging from awards ceremonies, such as the Academy Awards (Oscars) to features on celebrity lifestyles.

The name Christian Dior will be familiar to many people for a variety of reasons. Some will remember the name as that of a famous designer and style icon of the 1940s and 1950s; others may know it because they have bought one of its mass-market perfume products such as Dune or Fahrenheit. But fewer people would know that the designer name is a brand owned by LVMH, which produces both ready-to-wear (RTW) and couture collections. Still less would know that John Galliano is the chief designer and artistic director for Christian Dior.

Although the term 'fashion' can be applied to a wide range of products and services it is most commonly associated with clothing and accessories. This is due in part to the historical significance of textiles trade shows as an indicator of trends prior to a season and the wide use of clothing as a statement about people's social standing. Many of the definitions of 'fashion' reflect a time when clothing and accessories provided social meaning through dress. Barnard (2002: 48) refers to definitions including 'the action or process of making a shape', 'a particular shape or cut' and 'conventional usage in dress'.

Haute couture

Many would argue that modern fashion can be traced back to the end of the nineteenth century when dress was the primary vehicle for communicating style in society. There are almost as many definitions of *haute couture* as there are couture designs that have paraded down catwalks over the years. It is a 'world of glamour, of history, of tradition and signatures' (Milbank 1985: 24), and is regarded by some as a laboratory in which designers can rehearse ideas for new ready-to-wear collections. Haute couture has also been described as a 'fusion of fashion and costume, the consummate arts of dressmaking, tailoring and constituent crafts to apparel and accessories' (Martin and Koda 1995: 21). Steele (1997: 1) gives a literal translation of haute couture as 'high sewing' referring back to its roots in dress-making. Common to most explanations is a notion of extravagance and theatricality that is shaped by craftsmen and associated with a by-gone age. In general it refers to custom-made luxurious garments and accessories that are 'fitted' on clients. One might question how recognisable or relevant that is for most people today. However, for those who could afford 'fashion' at the end of the nineteenth and the start of the twentieth centuries it was the way to dress. There were no global brands, fashion retailer chains or discount stores knocking out cheap runway imitations then as there are now.

The term 'haute couture' has always been associated with French elegance and luxury. This is unsurprising given that couture began in Paris, that contemporary couture shows are still held there and that the majority of couture originates in France. French couture first appeared to the public at the World Fair in Paris in 1900. Located in the Pavilion of Elegance, selected houses, including Worth and Doucet, exhibited to an international audience (Seeling 2000: 15). This was one of the earliest trade fairs for fashion, signalling the internationalization of fashion between Europe and the USA. This increased integration contributed to the rise in importance of RTW, which was popular in America. RTW increased in significance throughout and after the Second World War as clothing became less flamboyant and frivolous and more practical.

The houses of Worth, Doucet, Pingat and Poiret

Worth

One of the early founders of haute couture was the English dressmaker Charles Frederick Worth, who opened his own fashion house in 1857 at '7 rue de la Paix in Paris' (Coleman 1989: 9; Leymarie 1987: 21). Just as designer names such as Gucci, Prada and Chanel inspire 'fashion lust' in many women today, so 'it was the internationally held feminine fantasy of the second half of the nineteenth century to be dressed in a Worth creation' (Coleman 1989: 7).

Although Rose Bertin, minister of fashion to Marie Antoinette, is credited with being the first celebrated fashion designer (Milbank 1985: 24), Worth 'was the first couturier whose career outlasted the passing of governments and spanned international boundaries' (Milbank 1985: 24). Aside from his undoubted skill in dressmaking many regard Worth to be significant in marking the modern fashion era because of the way he did business. Before the opening of his house, dressmakers would visit their clients' houses and act on their instructions, frequently using fabric and trimmings supplied by the client (Milbank 1985: 12). However, clients of Worth had to visit his house and select from his creations, which were displayed on 'sosies' (models with physiques similar to those of his clients), before having the garments fitted on them (Leymarie 1987). This centralising of the activity on a single location brought the business of couture inline with other businesses and led to a broadening of its appeal. Worth was also the first to create a 'signature' for his clothing – in real terms, with a label, and metaphorically, through distinctive design (Milbank 1985: 26). He became famous for abandoning the crinoline (a hooped structure of wire used under skirts) in favour of a flat-fronted skirt with a bustle around the back, creating 'the first new silhouette ever single handedly introduced by any individual' (Milbank 1985: 27). Many couturiers in Paris during the mid to late nineteenth century shared premises and sold both RTW and custom-made products.

Doucet
Although Worth is credited with opening the first couture house, that of Doucet was classified in 1915 as the oldest of all the *maisons de couture*, rising to prominence in women's fashion under Jacques Doucet at the latter end of the nineteenth century (Coleman 1989: 137). He was the third generation of the Doucet family, which had been involved with tailoring since 1816 and had developed a reputation for lingerie and shirts from 1830. Jacques Doucet came to prominence after the death of Edouard in 1898 and is credited with creating the tailored suit, or *tailleur*, and making coats with 'fur on the outside', acting as a fabric (Coleman 1989: 145). Tailoring is believed to have its origins in thirteenth-century France when the coat replaced the tunic as the commonly adopted over-garment. The houses of Worth and Doucet received royal patronage, which enabled them to access appropriate clientele, namely women of the highest levels of society.

Pingat
During the second half of the nineteenth century Emile Pingat came to prominence as a couturier in Paris, advertising himself in the same way as Worth as a supplier of 'nouveautés confectionées', outfitter of fancy articles (Coleman 1989: 179). He is considered to have been one of the great couturiers but, unlike Worth and Doucet, had no family to pass on the business to and so the name was lost.

Paul Poiret
Poiret is regarded as a great artistic influence in fashion history. Having trained with both Charles Worth and Jacques Doucet, he opened his first haute couture salon in 1903 at Rue Auber 5, Paris. Poiret attracted attention through his extravagantly presented boutique, innovative garments and his ability to market himself in a way that would be innovative even by today's standards. He hosted exotic fashion shows

and parties, founded a school for applied art and established a perfume factory (*ibid.*). In 1908 his interest in fashion illustration, which had led to him being introduced to Doucet some years earlier, resulted in his publication of a book of his designs entitled *Les robes de Paul Poiret*. This pioneering album of fashion designs, illustrated by Paul Iribe, was used to promote Poiret's couture collection of that year. This combination of artistic flair and innovative activity produced great success for Poiret. However, having closed his fashion house during the First World War he did not seem to be able to repeat the original success on its re-opening after the war and he went bankrupt in 1929.

English couture

England has a long history of bespoke fashion and tailoring. Perhaps the best-known name associated with that history is that of Savile Row. Originally a location for prominent military figures and doctors in the eighteenth century, the location acquired a reputation for tailoring after Beau Brummel patronised the Burlington estate area. Born in 1778, Brummel is best known for being a 'dandy' who was responsible for a vogue for bespoke tailoring in wool. Many believe that his patronage of the Savile Row tailors established the location and developed its reputation for quality tailoring. Modern-day couture in England has really been dominated by Norman Hartnell and Hardy Amies. The reputations of both grew out of their royal associations: Hartnell was official tailor to the Queen and late Queen Mother.

Hardy Amies, Lachasse and Norman Hartnell
Hardy Amies and Norman Hartnell were designers synonymous with English couture. Amies began his career with an old English couture house called Lachasse in the early 1930s and went on to open his own house in 1946. Norman Hartnell began his career before Amies, and dressed many stars including Noel Coward and Marlene Dietrich. Both Amies and Hartnell were appointed as couturiers to the queen. Although they worked independently of each other the two famous names are now brands that are owned by the company Hardy Amies Plc, which is a publicly quoted company.

Italian couture

Although Paris has always been regarded as the original city of fashion, with magazines feeding on the city throughout the 1920s and 1930s (Milbank 1985: 15), centres of fashion began to emerge outside Paris after 1945. Since travel was easier and communication more sophisticated the fashion industry became more international (Healy 1996: 17). Italian haute couture began with the first Italian fashion show, held in Florence in February 1951 (Healy 1996: 17), before an audience of powerful international buyers and journalists. Following its success regular shows later relocated to the manufacturing province of Milan, precipitating what has become a major influence on modern style of Italian fashion from Pucci, Missoni, Krizia and Armani (Healy 1996: 17; Forti – Buxbaum 1999: 73).

Couture is the seed from which modern-day fashion has grown and flourished. It created the first stars of fashion, namely designers who could be recognised, and provided a forum and an opportunity for change in ways of dress. Select houses such as Poiret and later Chanel led the way in introducing new product categories such as perfumes to complement their clothing.

Much mass-market and high street fashion is still influenced by the ideas displayed on the runways of contemporary couture and ready-to-wear shows. The 1990s resurgence of hipster styles in trousers and jeans is credited by some to an Alexander McQueen show in which the style was more exaggerated through displaying the 'builder's bum' look on models. However, Top Shop (a brand of the Arcadia group) is challenging the view that high street brands simply copy 'designer fashion' by showing its Unique collection at London Fashion Week from Spring Summer 2006 onwards.

Changes to couture

There has been a decline in the number of French couture houses over the twentieth century (Table 3.1) according to Fraid Chenoune (Buxbaum 1999: 65).

Table 3.1 Decline in French couture houses

Year	Number of couture houses
1946	106
1952	60
1958	36
1967	19

'Dress is an industry whose "raison d'être" is novelty', declared Paul Poiret, the French couturier famous at the turn of the Twentieth Century (Leymarie 1987: 21). This still holds true today as many designers and couture houses maintain their couture operation in part to promote the more commercial RTW and mass-market products such as perfumes. This notion is supported by Pierre Bergé, business partner and some would say commercial brain behind Yves Saint Laurent. He is reported to have said: 'No we don't make a profit from the couture, but it's not a problem. It's our

Spring–summer 2005 couture membership categories and members

Members	Correspondent members	Guest members
Adeline André	Gorigio Armani Privé	Marc Le Bihan
Chanel	Valentino	Maurizio Galante
Christian Dior	Versace	Laurent Mercier
Jean Paul Gaultier		On Aura Tout Vu
Givenchy		Ralph Rucci
Christian Lacroix		Elie Saab
Jean-Louis Scherrer		Stéphanie Saunier
Dominique Sirop		
Frank Sorbier		
Emanuel Ungaro		

Source: www.modeaparis.com

advertising budget.'(Coleridge 1988: 168). This view is echoed by Bernard Arnault, chairman of LVMH, who sees couture as a key to the success of the Christian Dior brand, allowing the designer John Galliano an opportunity to 'go to extremes and limits' in a way that is more about ideas than about products and stimulates a debate between the press and the house of Dior (Arnault 2004: at a conference speech).

Today there are approximately a dozen established designers showing regularly at the biannual couture shows in Paris. There are three categories of membership in which a designer is allowed to show.

Displayed below is a list of those who showed at the autumn–winter couture shows in July 2003.

Couture designers at the autumn–winter couture shows, July 2003

Day 1	Day 2	Day 3	Day 4
Torrente	Chanel	Frank Sorbier	Ralph Rucci
Nicolas le Cauchois	Dominique Sirop	Emanuel Ungaro	Fred Sathal
Christian Dior	Christian Lacroix	Eymeric Francoise	Elie Saab
Anne Valérie Hash	Ji Haye	Hanae Mori	Grimaldi Giardina
Adeline André	Givenchy	Scherrer	
Versace		Valentino	

Source: www.modeaparis.com

The display below lists those who showed at the spring–summer couture shows in January 2005.

Couture designers, spring–summer, January 2005

Day 1	Day 2	Day 3
Giorgio Armani Privé	Chanel	Franck Sorbier
Stéphanie Saunier	Marc Le Bihan	Jean Paul Gaultier
Christian Dior	Christian Lacroix	Dominique Sirop
Maurizio Galante	Laurent Mercier	Jean-Louis Scherrer
Adeline André		On Aura Tout Vu
Valentino		Elie Saab

Source: www.modeaparis.com

In 2003, of the 21 designers scheduled 13 were either guest members or correspondent members, leaving 8 of La Chambre Syndicale's official couture designers showing. In 2005 16 designers showed, of whom 8 were either guest members or correspondent members, also leaving at 8 the number of full members who showed. This raises the question of how important La Chambre is to the survival of couture, if nearly two-thirds of those showing are not full members of the organisation. With the departure of Yves Saint Laurent from couture in 2002, there are relatively few of the original classical designers left. Giorgio Armani, Karl Lagerfeld at Chanel, Emanuel Ungaro and Valentino represent the remaining legends.

With the proliferation of global sportswear and casual-wear brands as modern-day cultural references (Adidas, Nike, Gap, Diesel), the future for expensive and finely sculpted dresses looks increasingly bleak. The taste and style preferences of the modern womenswear consumer are more disposable than the reverent aspiration of those of 30–40 years ago as characterised in the film *Mrs 'Arris Goes To Paris*, in which Angela Lansbury played a cockney housekeeper who had saved all her life to realise her aspiration of owning a genuine couture gown as worn by her mistress.

Fashion couture seems to embody a number of paradoxes. It is concerned with uniquely beautiful creations but is dependent on the sales of mass-market diffusion products for its survival. The houses, which produce what appear to be irrelevant dresses to the average person, are also household names. As couture labels receive unprecedented press coverage through sustained media interest in celebrities who wear the dresses and gowns, so the number of couture houses is falling.

Today's world of mass-market fast fashion, which is available in the latest runway style, is a relatively modern phenomenon. Even in the 1970s and 1980s, both decades of distinctive fashion, there was less choice in clothing and accessories available to consumers compared with today. Contemporary brands such as Tommy Hilfiger, Oasis, Zara, George (ASDA) and more recently 'per una' were either not significant or established in the UK prior to the 1990s. Equally, the subject of fashion was less prevalent in the mass media than it is today. In fact, the twentieth century has seen a gradual evolution of the interest, acceptance and availability of fashion to the vast majority of the UK population. As Coco Chanel said, 'Fashion does not exist unless it goes down into the streets. The fashion that remains in the salons has no more significance than a costume ball' (Roux 1981: 237).

Ready-to-wear

Prêt-à-porter, literally 'ready-to-wear', emerged as a strong alternative to couture in the 1960s. In 1960 a group of eleven couturiers from Paris effectively held the first prêt-à-porter show two weeks before the couture collections (Healy 1996: 15). The ranges were stocked in boutiques, a common enough concept today but one that was quite new at the time. A major difference between the couture and RTW fashions was the availability of the latter in standard sizes, which could be bought instantly from a boutique. By contrast, couture requires the buyer to spend time having the garment fitted.

By 1963 the genie was out of the bottle and French magazines were promoting the new RTW collections, which were held after the couture shows (Healy 1996: 17). Today, international designer fashion is still shown at both couture and RTW shows. The relationship between couture and RTW collections has changed little over the years, with the former used primarily as a theatrical marketing tool for design houses and the RTW businesses used to make money with mainlines and brand extensions, including accessories and perfumes.

Each year there are two seasonal couture weeks and two groups of seasonal RTW shows. Couture is shown in Paris and the principal RTW shows are held in New York, London, Milan, Paris. The RTW shows are collectively termed fashion weeks in whichever country they are hosted: London Fashion Week, Paris Fashion Week, and so on. These are discussed on p. 53.

The Fédération Française de la Couture, du Prêt-à-Porter des Couturiers et des Créateurs de Mode

The Federation was established in 1973. It is the executive organ of each Chambre Syndicale and is run by the Federation's president, Didier Grumbach. It derives from the Chambre Syndicale de la Haute Couture and is composed of:

• The Chambre Syndicale de la Haute Couture, created in 1868. This includes the haute couture houses and firms that are not registered under the label of 'Haute Couture' but which have a made-to-measure dressmaking activity in the Paris area. The organisation stipulates the requirements to qualify as a couture house to ensure tradition and quality. Président: Mr Didier Grumbach and Président d'honneur: Mr Jacques Mouclier

• The Chambre Syndicale du Prêt-à-Porter des Couturiers et des Créateurs de Mode, created in 1973. This is made up of couture houses and fashion designers of women's RTW. Président: Mr Ralph Toledano, who is also chairman and chief executive of the (Richemont Group) fashion brand Chloé.

• La Chambre Syndicale de la Mode Masculine, also created in 1973. This is made up of couture houses and fashion designers of men's ready-to-wear. Président: Monsieur Simon Burstein and Président d'honneur: Monsieur Pierre Cardin.

The Federation's main activities are organising and running the various runway shows in Paris, promoting French fashion and culture, and acting on behalf of its members in a variety of capacities, including copyright protection. Arguably, the most significant is organising the shows. After preliminary consultations with the various fashion houses participating in the shows, the press department sets the fashion show programme, making sure that there is no overlap. This ensures that the fashion press and buyers will be able to cover the various collections. The schedules are sent to journalists, agents, French and foreign buyers, and trading consultants. Every season, before the collections start, an application form and a regulation note are sent to the French and foreign newspaper and magazine editors who are officially recognised by the Chambre Syndicale de la Couture. Editors return the engagement form containing information concerning the publication (origin, periodicity, circulation figures, etc.). They also have to enclose a list of the journalists and, if necessary, the photographers, who will cover the shows. This list is given to the fashion designers so that they can send invitation cards to the journalists, ensuring that they will be well received in the fashion houses.

The Federation also organises group events outside France as its major purpose is to help maintain and develop the fashion industry on the international markets. The member houses of the Federation earn about 70 per cent of their turnover in exports.

Some historical landmarks in fashion design

- Nineteenth century: Worth abandons skirt crinoline for new silhouette of flat front and bustle on rear.
- 1923: Madeleine Vionnet created the bias cut.
- 1926: Gabrielle 'Coco' Chanel introduced the 'little black dress'.
- 1947: Christian Dior's first collection, Corolle line, described by US journalists as the 'New Look' – slim waisted with a high bust.
- 1950s: US youth culture – denim jeans, white t-shirt and leather jackets; James Dean and Marlon Brando.
- 1960s: The arrival of the 'mini' skirt/dress.
- 1970s: Anti-fashion: Vivienne Westwood and the punk revolution.

Leading designers

Although many contemporary fashion designers have been described as 'great' and as possessing genius, it is more commonly the case that 'greatness' is attributed posthumously. With the exception of Yves Saint Laurent, who has recently retired from the world of fashion, the following summary refers to designers of the past. It is impossible in a book of this sort to do justice to the many leading designers who have influenced fashion over the years, but the following have been selected as having a unusually strong impact in their life time and after their death.

Christian Dior

After the drab functionality of uniforms and sombre dress of the war period (1940–45), women sought something new that was fun and a distraction from the hardships of rationing. Immediately after the war, couturiers returned to what they had been designing in the 1930s. A new mood of change and austerity meant that the collections were treated critically as being extravagant and irrelevant.

It was in this context that Christian Dior showed his first collection in 1947. The impact of his collection was so considerable that it was dubbed the 'New Look'. Dior named his first collection the 'Corolle line', a reference to the ring of petals on a flower. It was a very feminine collection featuring soft shoulders, nipped waists and long, wide skirts. Christian Dior captured the imagination by creating a look that had been popular for evening occasions and converting it to daytime wear. His other great innovation was to introduce frequent changes to his collections every six months creating novelty and stimulating a sense of anticipation and excitement among his audience.

Throughout the 1950s he continued to create new looks. The H-line focused on the torso to create a youthful impression; the famous A-line delivered a triangular look with narrow shoulders and wide skirts; and the Y-line inverted the A-line look. Christian Dior died in 1957 having spent only around ten years designing, but his influence on fashion was significant and his name is still a major haute couture house with individuals such as Yves Saint Laurent and John Galliano having designed for it. In 1997 John Galliano became artistic director of the house, which is now owned by LVMH.

Gabrielle 'Coco' Chanel

In the early part of the twentieth century women's dress was very much governed by etiquette. A combination of the changing role of women, largely as a result of the world wars, and visionary designers such as Chanel significantly altered the status quo. In 1915 *Harper's Bazaar* wrote: 'The woman who hasn't at least one Chanel is hopelessly out of the running in fashion' (quoted in De La Haye and Tobin 1994: 20).Throughout the 1920s and 1930s she created stylish, comfortable and practical fashion, introducing new ways of dressing, including the sporty look in jerseys and tweeds for women wanting to reflect a particular lifestyle.

Although a consummate couturiere, Chanel is known for the simplicity of her designs as characterised by the 'garconne-style' outfits. She made jersey-wear fashionable, was instrumental in gaining social acceptance for women to wear trousers and is credited with creating the immortal 'little black dress', introduced in 1926. At the time *Vogue* saw the significance of her black dress, comparing its likely uniform appeal to the new and popular Ford motor-car. In 1921 she launched Chanel No. 5, which was her first perfume. Gabrielle Chanel died in 1971 and her house was re-invigorated by Karl Lagerfeld, who took over as artistic director of Chanel in 1983, designing both couture and RTW collections from 1984. Today Chanel is still known for its classic suits and tweed fabric; it is one of the few large couture businesses to be privately owned.

Yves Saint Laurent

Described by Suzy Menkes (2001) as having 'invented the way modern women dressed in the second half of the 20th Century', Yves Saint Laurent is one of the few living legends in fashion, having begun his career as assistant to Christian Dior, taking over designing for the house on Dior's death in 1957. In 1962 he set up his own business with partner Pierre Berge. The YSL label is now owned by the Gucci Group, which bought the RTW and beauty products businesses in 1999. Tom Ford rejuvenated the YSL RTW collections. Yves Saint Laurent showed his last couture collection for the brand in January 2002, with his spring–summer 02 designs. His famous 'le smoking' designs made it popular for women to dress in sharply tailored trouser-suits.

Madeleine Vionnet

Madeleine Vionnet is best known for having 'invented' the bias cut and the distinctive dress designs arising from it. Having worked as a designer with Jacques Doucet, she set up her own house in Paris in 1912. In common with Chanel, Vionnet never relied on paper designs, preferring instead to mould the dress on a body. She famously developed all her designs using wooden dolls as mannequins to mimic the contours of the body. Typically, her dresses were made from single pieces of fabric and she ordered fabrics 2 yards wider than normal in order to cut them on the bias. A feature of the bias cut was that a Vionnet dress could be slipped on over the head and worn without fastenings or underpinnings.

What is successful fashion design?

There are many points of view about what represents *good* fashion design, just as there are numerous debates about the definition of 'fashion'. Some see fashion as art and the designer as a sculptor who crafts fabrics and trimmings into a beautiful creation worthy of exhibition. Indeed, designers such as Giorgio Armani and Vivienne Westwood have exhibited their clothing and accessories at museums and galleries around the world. Others see fashion as a purely commercial activity in which products are created and sold to the various markets. Such a juxtaposition of fashion as art and fashion as a purely commercial enterprise might be represented by the designs of Hussein Chalayan on the one hand and 'New Look' products on the other. One could debate which one is successful. Clearly 'New Look' is the more successful financially, particularly as Chalayan has been bankrupt in the past, but the latter is a global name and respected as a highly talented designer by the fashion world. Similarly Prada uses Miuccia Prada's association with art as an element in the brand's positioning.

Commercial reality?

At the beginning of the pragmatic twenty-first century, success in fashion design is more likely to be judged on how it contributes to the bottom line of a balance sheet as opposed to the hemline of a garment. Even the saviour of Gucci, Tom Ford, is quoted as saying: 'In fact, for me the ultimate test for a product is sales. If I design something that doesn't sell, it means I have failed – failed to create the right product failed to judge the mood of the customer, or perhaps I just made something really ugly' (Ford 2001: from a conference speech).

While it is true that sales and profits are key to any fashion business that wants to survive, volume sales of clothing is not the only measure of success. Volume sales and increased profit margins are key performance indicators for mass-market fashion brands, but critical acclaim, creative innovation and celebrity profile are as important for luxury brands. Many luxury fashion brands rely on their image and designer association to sell their mass-market perfumes and cosmetics and make profits.

National competences/stereotypes

There is a commonly accepted understanding of what is meant when people talk of 'Italian style', 'French elegance' and 'British creativity'. Such descriptions satisfy people's need to sum things up simply, to present a snap-shot view of an issue, and are as much about feelings as they are metaphors for real national capabilities. However, as with all generalisations there is an element of truth about them relating to each country's history and industrial development, which lends credibility to the statements.

Paris was and is the home of haute couture, while the British have a reputation for inventiveness and creativity that is regrettably unsupported by domestic government investment. Although 'Italian style' is believed to have achieved real international status after the Florence show of 1951 (White and Griffiths 2000), Italy has long held a reputation for intricate handwork on fabrics and exquisite craftsmanship. However, even in 1947 US *Vogue* was covering Italian fashion, holding the view that 'Italian clothes are inclined to be as extrovert as the people who wear them – gay, charming, sometimes dramatic' (Mannes 1947: 119).

Brit style

Britain is generally considered to be the training ground for talented and innovative fashion designers who are free thinking radicals. Vivienne Westwood, Hussein Chalayan, Alexander McQueen and John Galliano have all been regarded both as anarchic and as possessing genius. While there is little doubt about the creative talent of British fashion designers, concern exists over an inability to capitalise on their talent and achieve commercial success. However, exactly what British style is remains a mystery for many. The eclectic nature of 'Brit style' can be found anywhere on a continuum between Savile Row tailoring and George at ASDA making it difficult to identify a distinctive 'quintissentially English' look. A few brands such as Paul Smith, Burberry, and Gieves & Hawkes are strongly associated with Englishness – although Hackett is probably a good contemporary example of traditional English style.

Today the increased casualisation of dress owes more to American and Australian influences than those of closer European countries. Although the Savile Row genre of tailoring is clearly evident, especially in The City, most high-street fashion is casual as people dress less formally for special occasions. For many people there is no longer a social expectation to dress formally for work, significant family occasions such as weddings or 'nights out' to the theatre. The majority of British fashion consumers prefer to buy the diffusion lines of designers, such as those available in Debenhams and the Autograph Collection in M&S, or low-priced imitations of designer styles produced and sold through retailers like Top Shop and Zara. There may be many reasons for this, including a general lack of interest in heritage or traditional style, through to the higher prices charged by many brands in the UK for all sorts of products, including fashion.

In most European cultures it appears that there is very much an acceptance of one style as the norm during any fashion season: there is a great reluctance to stand out in the crowd. This unusual feature of the UK fashion season makes London a top destination for international designers looking for that something different.

Design skills

Many fashion designers have been criticised for creating unwearable collections. To some extent this is disingenuous, as such designs inevitably appear on runways in shows at fashion weeks with the primary purpose of courting publicity. However, there is also criticism of the 'all-roundedness' of many young designers who leave college or university and find it difficult to succeed commercially.

As this book is focused on fashion so the discussion around the subject of successful design is concerned with apparel and textile products. Although a designer must be multi-skilled, capable of a range of tasks including communication, costing and interpretation, the abilities required of a fashion designer can be broadly divided into those which are *creative* and those which are *technical*. By creative we mean the capacity to conceptualise original designs or even interpret fashion trends so as to produce something new and distinctive. When talking about technical ability we mean the 'know-how' associated with fabric construction and performance, and the manufacture of garments from patterns through to finishing processes.

Role and tasks of a designer

The role of a designer varies across different fashion businesses. A designer for a high-street retailer is commonly aiming to create lower-priced versions of the latest catwalk, celebrity or street trends. This normally involves working to a profitable *formula* which can be repeated across seasons, such as repeating a successful silhouette and changing the fabric or simply changing the colourway of a stripe print. A more expensive and focused fashion business would still be interested in monitoring trends but more likely to interpret them in a distinctive way to ensure a degree of exclusivity and brand differentiation.

By contrast, a designer for a leading luxury brand will be more interested in setting trends than following them. A number of international designers working with luxury brands, including John Galliano at Christian Dior, see themselves as artistic or creative directors rather than simply designers, as they are responsible for the overall brand image of their businesses. Centralised creative control over store design and advertising has been key to the successful communication of rejuvenated images for luxury labels such as Gucci and Yves Saint Laurent.

Key tasks of a designer

The term 'fashion designer' conjures up glamorous images of models, catwalk shows and exotically designed fashion garments. However, the reality of the job for many designers is one of working under commercial pressure and within tight budgets for a leading fashion retailer brand or one of their suppliers. The work is fast paced and, some may argue, lacking in creative satisfaction as interpretation of trends rather than innovation and originality are what mass-market fashion businesses often want.

It is worth noting at this point that there are many different textiles and apparel design roles in the fashion industry. Some examples are:

- established designer of international brand (e.g. Paul Smith);
- textile designer for fabric manufacturer;
- designer for multiple fashion retailer brand (e.g. Top Shop, Arcadia Group);
- designer for small fashion mail order business (e.g. Bowden); and
- designer for fashion manufacturer (selling designs to retailers).

In each of these cases the roles of the fashion designers will be slightly different, according to the level of autonomy enjoyed and customers' needs. A designer working with Giorgio Armani will need to be creative but must also understand that Mr Armani has the final say over a design. At a recent conference he said, 'I also must say that when I take decisions, the work of others becomes easier; it is much easier to come and ask what I want, instead of doing things that maybe I don't like. My teams are rather autonomous but the last word – yes or no, white or black, long or short – is unfortunately my responsibility' (Armani 2005).

However, the generic fashion design process is phased and includes a common series of steps involving research, design development and manufacture (Sinha 2001: 174). But as there is significant diversity in the role of a fashion designer according to the nature of their business it is important to review tasks, which are common to most product designers involved in fashion. Readers should appreciate that not all designers necessarily engage in all steps, as some steps maybe the responsibility of others in the supply chain (e.g. sampling is often undertaken by the supplier or manufacturer).

The generic fashion design process

Stages in the fashion design process

1 Review the best and worst selling designs from the current and previous seasons
2 Research new trends in colour, fabric, shape and print
3 Plan and select fabric and styles to reflect fashion direction of the season
4 Test base fabric
5 Confirmation of range by directors and buyers
6 Development of product specification sheets and patterns for sampling
7 Liaison with manufacturer and amendments to fit samples
8 Bulk fabric approval
9 Garment grading
10 Manufacture

Review best and worst

Although fashion is primarily about change and inevitably implies something new, many fashion businesses recognise that their customers expect to buy core items each season. Consequently most ranges will have a range of *basics* which can be made to reflect a season's trend through changes in colour and minor amendments to styling. In the same season a *range* will include more directional designs, some of which will sell better than others. Effective monitoring of sales can enable fast-selling lines to be modified or repeated quickly, usually within a few weeks. At the end of a season most fashion businesses will undertake a 'post mortem', analysing which styles sold well and which did not. Where a trend is still going to be strong for next season, styles can be continued with minor changes. Although these are design issues, buyers and merchandisers will conduct this process with the designers.

Research new trends

It is common for all fashion designers to seek inspiration for new collections. Where the business is more exclusive there is an expectation of greater innovation and originality. By contrast high-street and mass-market fashion is aimed at a much wider market. Sources of inspiration therefore can vary tremendously according to the nature of the market that the designer is working in.

Common early stages in the research for fashion direction will include textile trade shows, which provide insights to colours, fabrics and prints. It is also common for designers in some fashion retailers to accompany buyers on international shopping trips to buy products and take photographs to inspire new looks in their own product ranges. Good ideas about product presentation and sales promotions are also noted. Other sources of information include trend forecasting services, which are discussed on p. 55, and designers' own observations from the world around them.

Plan and select fabrics and styles for the season

Fabrics frequently dictate the theme to a group of designs, for example jersey-wear. Such a group of designs may commonly include a dress, t-shirt and pants for a relaxing 'at home' capsule range. Denim is always a popular fashion story, and has become more so over the last few years with developments in the fabric such as twisted denim. Seasonal trends in jeans and denim skirts make it a fabric which is frequently central to any new range. The two-pocket western jacket was restyled by designers such as Marc Jacobs and Phoebe Philo for Chloe to become a hot fashion item. Where a particular fashion business is well known for its fabric, such as Zandra Rhodes's or Laura Ashley's prints, then fabric has a more significant role in the range than a business that sells polyester blouses. The designer is responsible for creating a fashion look which balances considerations of garment performance and fashionability with cost and delivery.

Test base fabric

Fabric testing is something that would probably be carried out by the manufacturer. Nevertheless, it is important for readers to realise that fabric undergoes tests at different stages, depending on the structure of the supply chain. Some retailers are happy to let trusted manufacturers carry out testing, whereas others will seek independent testing. Base fabric tests are those which ensure that the fabric is fit for its intended purpose, for example its tensile strength, the stability of the fabric when cleaned or washed, and the extent of pilling or wear and tear. If the fabric fails at this stage there is no point dyeing it or cutting it for manufacture at a later date.

Confirmation of the range

Although the designer is responsible for creating the collection, others, including buyers and the company directors, generally authorise the spending of budgets that ultimately pay for the ranges. Decisions over numbers of units per style and colour option are also likely to be made by people other than designers, in particular buyers and merchandisers.

Development of and amendments to samples

There are a number of different kinds of samples, ranging from 'prototypes' of new garments to production samples, that are photographed for publicity before the ranges arrive in stores. Early development samples are often called *toiles* and are used by designers to determine basic fit measurements. In a typical fashion retailer the buyers and garment technologists see 'fit samples', which are the manufacturer's first attempt at producing the required design from a 2D specification sheet. These are tried on models to assess fit, and it is normal at this stage for the samples to require some amendment.

Bulk fabric approval

Bulk fabric is the finished fabric to be used in manufacture. By this stage the fabric may well include a print and will need to be tested for colour fastness. Failure at this stage would present a business with significant problems as the production space will have been booked and the lead-times for delivery will be shorter. This is especially true for high-street younger fashion for which production is very close to the selling season. Once again, although this is an issue relating to the design and manufacture of garments, it is likely that the testing would be done by someone other than the designer.

Grading and manufacture

Grading refers to the process of creating sizes, which are smaller or larger than a base size. In general size 12 is used as the base size for high-street womenswear and size 10 is used for designer-wear to be modelled on the catwalk. Once samples have been approved they are 'sealed' and production takes place.

Design processes for mass-market apparel and designer-wear

Differences in the design process exist between those fashion businesses which produce mass-market fashion apparel and those houses that produce exclusive designer-wear. One of the more significant is that mass-market fashion is produced first and sold to consumers through a retail distribution network that is typically owned and controlled by the brand. This is inherently risky as it is difficult for fashion businesses to know exactly which items will sell and which will not. However, many top designers sell their new collections through the bi-annual fashion weeks, often using RTW shows to attract the interest of international buyers. Orders are taken following the shows and then production begins.

Allegra Hicks is a designer who uses this approach, preferring to sell to buyers who have attended shows of her collections. Orders are then taken at the show rooms and production takes place on receipt of orders. This approach reduces the risk of unsold stock faced by most high-street fashion retailers, but limits demand to specific selling periods.

Another internationally known British designer, Katherine Hamnett, used to show her collections on fashion runways having moved between London and Paris in the 1990s before withdrawing from the fashion weeks altogether in 1997. The label is now owned by a Japanese company, and so the design process at Katharine Hamnett has to take into account the involvement and decision making of the Japanese owners. The typical design process followed by the designer Dilys Williams, for an autumn–winter season, is displayed.

Designing for the autumn–winter season:
DILYS WILLIAMS FOR KATHARINE HAMNETT

1   In January Dilys will begin work on autumn–winter collections with an evaluation of the best and worst fabrics, colours and styles from the previous season. This is followed by research into a concept for the next fashion season. Originality and creativity have to be balanced with the essence of the brand and its heritage. The designer Katharine Hamnett has always been

concerned with ecological issues in fashion, as evidenced by her 'Stop Acid Rain' and 'Preserve the Rainforests' slogans on her t-shirts in 1983. Such a strong brand identity provides both direction and constraints for design ideas each season.

2   Once Dilys has the central direction for the season she can plan the fabrics and styles that are to be used across the various groups of designs. As the brand is ecologically focused the fabrics must be as environmentally friendly as possible. There is a tendency towards natural fibres, such as wool, and to modern synthetics that are biodegradable, such as Tencel. A balance is always struck between fabric performance, quality, appearance and cost.

3   By February Dilys has a clear idea of the range concepts and fabrics she wants. Although there is a good choice of textiles trade fares to visit, Dilys still prefers Première Vision (PV), a fair that has experienced significant competition from new shows such as Texworld and Tissu Premier over recent years. In her opinion PV exhibits a better selection of mills than elsewhere. Dilys may see more fabrics from mills whose collections are not complete by February at her office in London. Although the PV March fair is strictly for the spring–summer season of the following year, it can still provide ideas for autumn ranges. This is consistent with a general trend in fashion of making some design decisions nearer the season.

4   By March designs are being finalised as sketches and fabrics have been selected. As the owners have to approve everything, the fabrics' details are sent off to Japan. Once confirmation is provided the fabrics can be tested and booked with textile manufacturers. Substitute fabrics may need to be sourced if the originals are too expensive or unavailable.

5   Once the fabrics are agreed, Dilys liaises with the pattern-cutters based in the Japanese manufacturers. They cut the fabric according to the garment specification she has designed for each style and the production of a first sample, or *toile*. Required amendments to the toile are discussed between Dilys and the pattern-cutters using email with photographic attachments.

The lead time for the sampling process is approximately six weeks.

Textiles

Key to most fashion trends and product developments are the fibres and fabrics that form the garments. New fibres have produced dynamic properties in fabric performance, ranging from increased stretch capacity to dirt-resistant finishings. Clothing has always featured fabrics that have been woven or knitted from natural fibres derived from animals and plants. However, in the twentieth century, man-made fibres such as nylon, polyester and elastane created a revolution in textiles which transformed what could be done in clothing design. Today many garments are a mix of natural and synthetic fibres as designers aim to produce the best balance of fabric benefits, including feel, durability and ease of care. The key stages in the development of a textile are fibre, yarn, fabric and finish.

Fibres

Fabrics used in fashion clothing are made from yarns that have been spun from single fibres or a blend of fibres. Fibres can be categorised into either *staple* or *continuous filament* forms and may be selected according to their particular characteristics, including length, thickness, strength, lustre, elasticity, handle and colour. Staple fibres are short strands which form naturally such as animal hair, wool, or plant fibres, like cotton and linen. Individual strands can be of varying lengths and degrees of quality. Most natural fibres are in the staple form, with the exception of silk, which is a continuous filament or thread. Man-made fibres are produced as continuous filaments and then cut into the lengths required for manufacture.

Traditionally fibres have been categorised into *animal* and *vegetable*. Animal fibres include silk (from silkworms), wool from sheep and hair from assorted animals, including goats (cashmere) and camels. Vegetable fibres include more sub-categories as indicated in the box below.

Categories of vegetable fibre

Cotton and flax (linen) are by far the most commonly used vegetable fibres for clothing fabric, although hemp is used in workwear because of its durability, natural strength and lack of elasticity. Cotton is the most common in clothing, and is produced in varying lengths and qualities. In the early 1990s strains of coloured cotton were developed in USA under the name Fox Fibre. This cotton grows naturally in shades of green and brown, as opposed to the more commonly produced off-white colour. Although Fox Fibre does not need to be dyed, it is grown in only small volume and so is expensive.

Vegetable fibres

Category	Fibre(s)
Bast	Flax, hemp, jute, ramie
Seed	Cotton
Leaf	Sisal, banana, pineapple, coir

Man-made fibres

Man-made fibres were the result of attempts in the late nineteenth century to make an artificial silk, as a substitute for the scarce and expensive real silk. The first artificial silk filaments were based on cellulose, and were the forerunners of rayon and viscose. A more modern version of a cellulose-based fibre is lyocell (Tencel), produced by Courtaulds and Lenzig Lyocell. As with elastane (Lycra), Tencel blends effectively with other fibres to provide enhanced fabric benefits such as improved softness, drape and crease recovery.

Nylon first emerged as a commercial fibre in the late 1930s and was widely used from the 1940s in women's stockings. Polyester was discovered after nylon and was used widely from the 1950s onwards. These are still two of the most commonly used synthetic fibres in fashion, although more so now in blends, as mass production of cotton and wool has brought down the price of 100 per cent natural fabrics. Ease of care and lower cost are two of the more obvious benefits of fabrics containing polyester.

Fabrics

The selection of a fabric is a decision made early on by any designer when planning a new range because its appearance and performance reflect changing fashion trends. Designers need to be aware of the practical capabilities of the fabrics to be used, especially where a garment is constructed of a combination of differently weighted fabrics. Designers at the exclusive designer end of the fashion market frequently attempt the impossible in order to achieve a distinctive design or look. One such designer has attempted to combine canvas with chiffon in a garment, an experiment which failed due to the considerable difference in the weights of the fabrics.

Most high-street fashion multiple retailers have sophisticated procedures for textile selection and testing which eliminate any serious fabric problems in their garment ranges. Designers and buyers are also supported by garment technologists who are expert in fabric performance and garment construction. A big issue for all kinds of designers, though, is the consistency of colour across a single garment comprising different fabrics made by different suppliers. Pantone references and lab-dip testing are methods used to achieve colour consistency, although the latter depends on human judgement.

Colour can be introduced to a fabric in a variety of ways: the fibres could be naturally coloured or dyed; the yarn could be dyed; or the fabric itself could be dyed. Each method has its pros and cons linked to cost, dye penetration and responsiveness to customers' needs.

Fabrics are produced from yarns and are mostly either woven or knitted, with each method of manufacture requiring different equipment.

New technologies in textiles

Advances in technology have affected the fashion apparel industry in many ways, some of which are discussed in Chapter 5. However, it is in the areas of fibres and finishings that some of the more exciting developments have occurred. Waterproof garments are common and involve either treating fabric with oil, as with Barbour jackets, or sophisticated fabric construction as in the case of GORE-TEX. It is important to note that unless a garment is treated with specific waterproofing or is made from the unique GORE-TEX fabric it is probably only showerproof.

Cutting-edge fibre and fabric developments have now introduced a range of health- and cosmetic-related benefits into clothing. Antibacterial qualities can be built into fibres or treated onto fabrics and offer a number of benefits, including odour reduction. Microban and Amicor are two brands used in a range of products, including sportswear, socks and underwear.

Other textiles benefits include the ability to release vitamins into the skin to moisturise the skin (specific brands of hosiery), to release scent and to interact with consumers electronically. Philips has produced garments that contain 'wearable electronics' with applications for sportswear, allowing users to monitor their performance and childrenswear that incorporates tracking technology.

Developments can occur at all levels of textiles. The box below provides some examples of technological developments at each stage.

Examples of developments in textiles

Level	Technological development
Fibre	Lyocell (Tencel): a synthetic cellulosic fibre that is strong, soft to handle, and biodegradable, and is an easily blended fibre produced by Courtaulds and Lenzig Lyocell
Yarn	Chitopoly: an anti-allergenic blend of Chitosan and polyester which has been used in babywear and underwear by M&S
Fabric	GORE-TEX: a fabric which uses a membrane sandwiched between two other layers of fabric, allowing the skin to breathe but fully water-proofing the wearer
Finish	Various finishes producing anti-static, glow-in-the-dark and dirt-resistant benefits in clothing
Colour	Naturally coloured cotton (Fox Fibre) and 'golden' coloured silk from silkworms; chromatic dyes which change colour in response to changes in temperature, light and moisture

Sizing survey

The fit of a garment is as crucial a factor in the decision to buy as is the fashion look. However, the problem of getting clothes to fit has become progressively worse for consumers as people have become larger and fashion brands have not all adjusted their product specifications. On top of a general change in shape and an increase in the size of women since the 1950s (when the last major sizing survey was undertaken), there is the problem of size variations between fashion brands. The average woman today is size 14 according to the research undertaken by M&S 6 years ago. However, exactly what specifications represent a size 14 varies among fashion brands and retailers, as there has been no industry norm. Many women have experienced buying a size 12 in one store only to find that they need a size 14 in a garment from another store. This problem does not affect men in the same way as they tend to buy garments either by identifiable waist and chest measurements, which can be altered, or by a broad brush S, M, L, XL. A further problem associated with the 'out of date' sizing of British women is the increased demand for larger sizes, as stores often buy in the incorrect size ratios. This is evident during the 'sale' periods as small- and large-sized garments are generally available in large quantities.

In summer 2001 the National Sizing Survey was launched, funded between the Department of Trade and Industry and a consortium of retailers including Arcadia, Bhs, the John Lewis Partnership and Great Universal Stores. The survey measured 10,000 men and women of all ages and ethnic groups using a 3D body scanner; the results should inform participating fashion retailers and brands about appropriate sizing for their clothing products.

Fashion seasons

A concept central to all fashion is the 'season', defined as a period of time during which fashion products are sold. Most people recognise this when new fashion clothing and accessories appear in the shops. Seasonality is not purely a fashion phenomenon as many products, such as food and gifts, experience variations in patterns of demand according to the time of year. However, within fashion there are traditionally two distinctive periods – spring–summer and autumn–winter – which have directed fashion designs and ranges. These have been based around the four annual seasons and the lifestyle activities people have associated with each. However as peoples' lifestyles have changed, becoming busier and more heterogeneous, so fashion brands and retailers have had to segment their ranges to take account of sub-seasons instead of buying to satisfy two large periods of demand.

There is the issue of *when* exactly a season begins. To some extent the question is similar to 'How long is a piece of string?' It depends on where your business is in the supply chain. For example, to a textiles manufacturer selling spring–summer 2007 fabrics to retailers at a trade show such as Tissu Premier, the selling season is underway in January 2006, a whole year before the 2007 spring–summer stock hits the shops. Similarly, London Fashion Week will show spring–summer 2007 during September 2006. The one constant to which everyone works is the timing of spring–summer merchandise in the shops for consumers. To that end the box below identifies the months of the major seasons and possible sub-seasons.

The box indicates how the traditional four seasons of the year can be further broken down to accommodate consumers' fashion needs more accurately. However, some fashion retailers are introducing new lines every 4–6 weeks within these 'core sub-seasons' to keep their look fresh and to persuade customers to maintain their spending. The new lines will frequently be a variation on successful styles that season. This might

Changing spring–summer and autumn–winter seasons in the UK

Fashion seasons and sub-seasons	Months
Early spring	January–February
Spring (events – e.g. Valentine's Day)	February–March
Early summer (holiday)	April–May
Summer	May–June
High summer	June
Summer SALE	June–July
Transitional autumn	July–August
Back-to-school (where appropriate)	August
Autumn	September–October
Party wear	November
Christmas presents/transitional spring	December
Winter SALE	December–January

be a styling detail such as a different neckline or a minor change to print, for example a new colourway in a successful stripe. The speed and wider accessibility of trend information is having a big impact on the diversity of looks being sold in a season. This issue is investigated in relation to trade shows and, later in the chapter, fashion forecasting.

There is an interesting point emerging about the value of seasons, particularly the notion of spring–summer and autumn–winter. It is difficult to see why these terms are still being used to segment the fashion year, other than the fact that they are so deeply ingrained in our culture. Fashion 'looks' frequently transcend 'seasons' and have little to do with the weather associated with a particular season. In fact milder winters and wet summers go against the traditional view of what consumers should be wearing: it rains every June and July in the UK but it is quite difficult to buy a raincoat then. Similarly, warm autumns are occurring regularly in the UK although many fashion brands are caught out with clothing that is too heavy/wintry. This issue of predicting trends ahead of a season is discussed later under fashion forecasting.

Table 3.2 shows the typical sales' contribution that each calendar month represents in the retailing of fashion products.

Table 3.2 Monthly sales' contributions in fashion retailing, 2003

Month	% sales
January	7.8
February	6.8
March	7.5
April	7.8
May	8.9
June	7.8
July	8.0
August	7.6
September	7.5
October	8.6
November	10.3
December	11.4

Source: Fashion Trak (2004).

Trade shows

Fashion shows are events at which buyers and sellers meet to trade a variety of fashion components, ranging from textiles to finished garments. The word 'show' refers generally to the diverse range of organised events that facilitate the selling process; these could range from a yarn fair through to a designer RTW show. There is in fact much more of a 'show' element to the apparel events: CPD (Germany) and Pitti Immagine Uomo include scheduled catwalk shows at regular intervals throughout their duration. However, all trade shows consist mainly of manufacturers' stands at which business is conducted with visiting buyers.

The sequence of shows mirrors the development of fashion apparel as fabric shows follow yarn shows, and then designer garment and accessory collections are shown much closer to the start of the season.

Figure 3.1 Sequence of fashion shows/development of apparel

Pitti Immagine Filatti

Pitti Filatti is one of the more influential yarn shows, which are held prior to the fabric shows. It is held in Florence, Italy; in February 2006 for the spring–summer season of 2007 and July for the ensuing autumn–winter season. As trade shows go it is small with approximately ninety exhibitors a season, most of which are Italian. Many visitors, including designers and buyers, use the show to source specialist knitwear suppliers, but for many others it is one of the earliest credible trend indicators. Trends in colour and in yarn development can be discerned, enabling early decisions on range designs to be evaluated before the forthcoming fabric shows.

Première Vision (PV)

PV is the largest of the European textiles trade shows. Once regarded as the key show for early indications of colour, fabric and print trends, ten months ahead of a season, it is now seen by many in the design world as being equalled by competitors including Texworld and Tissu Premier. The show is nevertheless very important and is held twice a year in Paris: in February for the following spring–summer and in September for autumn–winter. Although numbers of exhibitors vary from year to year, around 780 European textiles companies present their fabric collections at the two shows. Exhibitors are selected on the basis of their creativity and quality of manufacturing, and the shows attract approximately 40,000 visitors from around the world over the four days of each season.

PV, in common with all fashion trade fairs, has a dual role: it is primarily a business event where orders are placed for fabric; but it is also an important guide to future fashion trends. As such the organisers hold a preview before the show is officially open to buyers, enabling journalists to communicate reports of key trends early on, stimulating interest in the show. Online fashion forecaster Worth Global Style Network (WGSN) provides preview summaries of the trends about ten days prior to the official opening.

Decisions about the key trends to be shown in PV are the result of the combined views of the European Concertation, a body of sixty-five fashion experts who identify the current international fashion trends, and the PV fashion team. The Concertation brings together weavers' spokesmen and style bureaux to gather and exchange data about the trends which will be significant in the coming season.

The colour palette, for the season showing, is signposted around the vast exhibition and an audio-visual show provides conceptual background to the trends at intervals throughout the day. Well before the 'salon' opens, and based on forecasts made by the Observatory, PV's fashion department applies a lighting which involves making sense of everything being heard, seen, done and analysed.

Texworld

This is an increasingly important trade fair, now in its eighth year, which runs parallel to PV, starting and ending one day earlier. The emphasis of the fair is normally on non-European countries. In 2004, the show hosted around 651 exhibitors, a year-on-year increase of 21, from 43 different countries, including Asian countries, Turkey, Brazil and Eastern Europe – with new exhibitors from Romania and Poland – but also some European countries, notably Italy with about 20 exhibitors. Visitor numbers totalled 17,305 from 111 countries, with several coming from new EU members in an attempt to find new suppliers (WGSN). Just as production tends to follow price around the globe, so new trade shows are reflecting the increase in scope of global sources of production. Texworld is particularly attractive to buyers who source a portfolio of suppliers from locations as diverse as South America, Central Asia, India and North Africa. It is also increasingly featuring manufacturers from the developing Eastern European countries where labour rates are low and quality of production is high. Some designers and buyers will attend PV for trend information and go to Texworld to place fabric orders.

Tissu Premier

Tissu has been operating on a small scale since 1980, when it started with only twelve French jersey manufactures (WGSN-edu.com). However it has grown in stature since 1999 and is now regarded as the first important fabrics fair of the season. Smaller than PV, it hosts approximately 420 exhibitors at the exhibition centre in Lille. Although it is common for fabrics shows to go in and out of favour with buyers, for some fashion retailers and brands Tissu has a real advantage over its larger rivals: it shows nearly a whole month earlier, in February for spring–summer and early September for autumn–winter. This compares favourably with PV, which shows spring–summer in March and autumn–winter in October. To the untrained eye this subtle difference may not seem important, but the extra month provided by Tissu allows buyers to react within the current trading season, in addition to planning for next year.

It is clear from the display that the timing of Tissu enables buyers to order fabrics in February and arrange production in sufficient time to still have fashion clothing

PV and Tissu Premier season–date comparison

Date	Show	Season showing	Retail season's dates
January	Tissu	S–S following year	Spring–summer: January–July
February	PV	S–S following year	
September	Tissu	A–W following year	Autumn–winter: August–December
September	PV	A–W following year	

delivered for the latter part of spring–summer (the season ending in June). The extra month delay until PV does not afford buyers a similar opportunity. For many the spring–summer shows are useful for different reasons:

- Tissu Premier for very late 'on-trend' replenishment of current spring–summer stock;
- Première Vision for confirmation of next spring–summer's trend; and
- Texworld for placing fabric orders with less costly non-European manufacturers – having confirmed trends at PV.

An additional benefit of Tissu compared with PV is that buyers can navigate it simply and quickly as it is smaller. An interesting development in the continuing trend to have information much closer to a season is the move, in 2004, of the yarn show Expofil to join PV.

Fashion weeks

The term 'fashion weeks' normally refers to the designer RTW shows that are held twice a year in the major fashion cities of New York, London, Milan and Paris. The events enable leading designers to showcase their collections for the next season. However the value of the shows is as much about international publicity as it is about selling the designers' collections.

The display below gives the timings of the various shows and the seasons to which they relate. RTW collections are shown further away from the season than the couture shows and are used by many fashion commentators to predict trends for the forthcoming season.

Timings of shows and related seasons

Month, year	Show	Associated fashion season
January 07	Couture (Paris)	Spring–summer 07
February 07	All RTW	Fall–winter 07
July 07	Couture (Paris)	Fall–winter 07
September–October 07	All RTW	Spring–summer 08

The longer lead-time for the RTW shows, typically three months before the season starts, differs from the couture shows. This is to allow sufficient time because RTW has to sell, manufacture and distribute to international buyers soon after the shows. As couture is custom-made for individuals, the shows can occur during the early part of the season. In addition to the principal RTW fashion weeks, other cities are showing designer fashion. These include the Brazil and the New Zealand Fashion Weeks and the more established Mercedes Australian Fashion Week (MAFW).

London Fashion Week (LFW)

British fashion is paraded twice a year at LFW. Organised by the British Fashion Council (BFC), the event was sponsored for many years by Vidal Sassoon, with P&G Beauty taking over in September 2002. The shows have an international audience of tens of thousands, which includes 3,000 fashion buyers, journalists and photographers. Typically there are between 50 and 60 catwalk shows across the 6 days, which are a mixture of both official on- and off-schedule and unofficial off-schedule events. Scheduled shows are held at the LWF location which fluctuates between the Duke of York's Headquarters on the King's Road in Chelsea, and the Natural History Museum, both of which are in London. Designers also use the off-schedule shows, which are located elsewhere in London. In addition to the shows, there is the exhibition tent featuring approximately 150 exhibitors over 4 of the days. The exhibition contains stands representing designers and brands, and is used to sell ranges to overseas buyers.

There is always a great deal of press speculation and debate about which city a fashion designer chooses 'to show' in. As a result of their international interests, and in some cases European employers, it is easy for some designers to show in any of the big four cities. Recently, some high profile designers have deserted London Fashion Week and the fact has generated a good deal of heat and debate about the snobbery and opportunities linked to fashion weeks in the leading cities.

Just prior to the February 2002 autumn–winter shows a debate about the operation and significance of LFW took place in the press between Nicholas Coleridge, then chairman of the British Fashion Council, and Colin McDowell, fashion historian and journalist. The debate followed the poor attendance of the previous September's LFW, which had been inevitably disrupted in the aftermath of the 11 September outrage. Superficially the focus was poor attendance but underlying the difference of opinions was the question of how British designers are seen by the rest of the world and how Britain sees fashion design. Coleridge acknowledges that British designers go abroad once recognised: 'There's been a trend – which is both irritating and flattering to London – in that they (Italian and French design houses) tend to take British designers when they reach a certain point of fame and appoint them world head of fashion houses' (Chittenden and Elliott 2002).

Britain has a history of producing highly creative and innovative design talent, but not using it to support its domestic economy. The list of designers who have left to join European fashion houses grows every year and includes John Galliano, Alexander McQueen, Stella McCartney, Matthew Williamson and Julien McDonald. This 'desertion' to work abroad was also criticised at the same time by Paul Smith who attacked fellow designers for earning their reputation in Britain and then leaving to work or show abroad. Matthew Williamson and Luella Bartley were other designers to go abroad, showing in New York as opposed to London, during the autumn–winter round of RTW shows February 2002.

Coleridge argued strongly that London is very relevant as it is the 'crucible of cutting-edge design and new talent', offering more drama and surprise than competing cities such as Milan and New York. This is the reason why so many foreign designers show at LFW: they recognise London as the 'cutting-edge fashion capital'. His views reinforce the commonly held belief that Britain, and London in particular, encourages a more radical and less conformist approach to fashion and design. However, McDowell's view reflects that of many struggling small fashion businesses in this country, which is that the BFC needs to do much more to support evolving fashion designers and businesses. This view is also supported by Alexander McQueen who believes that the Government should do more to support the British fashion industry (McQueen 2002: 22):

> London is an important artistic platform and offers designers the scope to grow creatively. Beyond that however, there is little support for the industry itself. Other European governments have the foresight to realise that fashion is an incredibly lucrative industry, not simply a promotional tool. It is about time the British Government made that same commitment.

Further, McDowell believes that weaknesses in LFW have been tolerated in the past (by foreign journalists and buyers) due to the extraordinary talent of individual designers, such as those who have now gone abroad. However, while there is currently a shortage of high-profile British fashion design talent LFW is in danger of losing key journalists and buyers from abroad, especially from the USA. To combat this the BFC launched New Gen (New Generation), sponsored by Top Shop, to support fledgling designers, and recently appointed a new chief executive to strengthen the British fashion industry.

Fashion forecasting

Being aware of trends and understanding how to interpret them for a specific market is a critical success factor for a modern fashion business. As society has become more complex and has focused increasingly on the individual, so businesses need to consider a variety of trend information concerned with lifestyle and fashion. The business of trend prediction has developed since its evolution in the 1970s. Today there is a range of services that range from simply reporting information on shows through to offering very customised advice to specific fashion companies. Fashion forecasters, trend-prediction businesses and cool hunters are all trying to achieve a similar result, namely an advantage for their clients. Some of the better-known fashion-forecasting businesses are Trend Union, Peclers, Sacha Pacha and Promostyl.

Promostyl is an international design agency that researches trends for its clients. Founded in 1967 it provides a consulting service to clients and produces trend books, which include analysis of the design influences on trends and predictions for colour, street wear, and clothing for men, women and children. The agency provides detailed predictions of garment designs and styling eighteen months ahead of, as well as very close to, a season, enabling clients to capitalise on the latest looks. Since the late 1990s trend prediction has moved online. It began with www.wgsn.com, and other companies have emerged more recently, including fashionsnoops.com and stylesight.com.

Worth Global Style Network (www.wgsn.com)

WGSN is arguably the largest UK trend agency, describing itself as 'the world's leading online research, trend analysis and news service for the fashion and style industries'. Launched in 1998, it is relatively new compared to the established and mostly French-owned forecasting services. Nevertheless it has a huge client base, reflecting the diversity of businesses which use trend-forecasting services. Its UK fashion retailer clients include Arcadia Group, ASDA, Harrods, Next and New Look, among many others. WGSN provides trend information globally from brands as diverse as Armani, GAP, H&M, Bulgari, Levi's and Versace.

It provides a unique blend of visual fashion information and text-based industry reportage and analysis, aiming to be a one-stop-shop for its clients. The site combines elements of fashion-trend prediction, design and style information, news and business journalism, and fashion market data. The company provides mostly qualitative data through its unique online subscription service.

All major yarns, textiles, product and designer fashion shows are covered in detail through a blend of written analysis and comprehensive photographic coverage. In common with many traditional fashion-forecasting businesses such as Promostyl, Perclers and Trend Union, WGSN provides views of the future through its 'think-tank', a standardised facility in contrast to the more customised service that other 'forecasting' companies typically provide for their clients.

The company employs approximately 150 people, 90 of whom are based in the London office, with further offices in New York and Hong Kong. However, it is only the London office that generates creative content as the other global offices are concerned with reporting. The company is quite unique in employing both designers and journalists (approximately 80 of its employees work on site content – 30 in design and 50 in journalism/research). Its team of creative and editorial staff travels extensively on behalf of subscribers and works with a network of experienced writers, photographers, researchers, analysts and trend scouts in cities around the world, tracking the latest stores, designers, brands, trends and business innovations.

Categories of information provided by WGSN include:

- 'Catwalks': detailed reviews of runway shows from global fashion weeks;
- trade show reviews;
- trends information: reviews of major trends, product and consumer;
- city-by-city guides and visual coverage of store windows in key locations;
- think-tank: prediction of future macro and product-specific trends; and
- news on the global fashion business.

Further content includes youth market, what's in store?, business resource, retail talk, *The Magazine*, beauty, active market, and graphics.

Conclusion

A Moschino advert in 1999 proclaimed: 'Fashion without passion is just another business.' In a world of increasing standardisation, where the same brands are sold in Europe, Asia and the USA, and designers all have access to the same information, there is a danger of losing innovation and originality. Further, large multi-brand groups and multiple fashion retailers must be aware of the dangers of risk-avoidance in a misguided attempt to generate profits, as consumers look for originality as opposed to bland brands. The fashion clothing markets are becoming polarised between the bland but cheap seasonal fashion products, which are ultimately disposable, and the super-expensive and customised real luxury items. Fashion needs to be commercial and profitable, but it also needs to be innovative and risky, otherwise where are all the new fashion breakthroughs going to come from? 'Fashion comes from a dream and the dream is an escape from reality' (Christian Dior).

4 Global luxury brands

Tim Jackson and Carmen Haid

T his chapter examines the concept of luxury and its relationship with fashion, and provides an analysis of the global luxury goods industry. It identifies the majority of the large multi-brand groups and illustrates a number of contemporary luxury themes through a case study of Burberry plc. There is a misconception held by some people that the luxury industry is not a significant one compared to other sectors of global fashion and in particular the UK fashion industry. This misconception is based on the view that luxury goods are bought by a minority of consumers and that the distribution of luxury brands' products in the UK is small by comparison with mass-market fashion. While the latter is true, however, the overall belief is not. The luxury goods industry operates globally and was valued at some US$70 billion at the end of 2003 – a conservative estimate as it does not reflect the retail value of wholesale and licence sales (Mintel 2004a). This figure is set to reach US$100 billion by 2008 as global tourism increases, supported by the expected strong growth of the Asian markets (China in particular). It is further interesting to note that the market capitalisation (mcap) of LVMH, admittedly the largest of the luxury multi-brand groups, is double that of the combined mcaps of Marks & Spencer (Britain's largest clothing retailer) and Next plc at the time of this publication.

What is luxury?

The modern word 'luxury' has its origins in the Latin words *lux*, meaning light, *luxus*, meaning excess, and *luxuria*, meaning extravagance. The term 'luxury' is capable of wide usage, being applied these days to an increasing range of fashion products and businesses. Contemporary understanding of the term relates to notions of the exclusivity, rarity and indulgence of products and experiences not accessible to everyone. Luxury goods are normally defined as those that are restricted in supply, expensive and of high quality. In many cases they also possess a significant heritage that gives integrity to a brand. A luxury product confers a particular image and status on the owner, making the product desirable for reasons other than mere functionality. MSDW (Morgan Stanley Dean Witter) identifies seven key ingredients of a luxury brand (MSDW 2000). These are: global recognition; critical mass; core competence; high product quality and innovation; powerful advertising; immaculate store presentation; and superb customer service.

However, as Western economies have become wealthier so each generation of consumers has an interpretation of luxury different from the previous one. The products and brands that were out of reach for one generation quickly become normal consumer items, even necessities, for the next generation. Such growth in wealth and consumerism expands the boundaries of 'luxury' and of luxury goods as mass-market consumers are able to afford them. The term 'five star', which was the principal signifier of best quality and exclusivity in hotels twenty years ago, represents a premium-priced experience that is accessible to the majority of people. An overnight suite at the Ritz hotel in London is within the reach of a significant number of working people, should they wish to splash out. However, the consequential gradual disaffection of the wealthier consumer with the loss of exclusivity has brought about a shift towards new measures of luxury. For example, hotels with notional 'seven star' ratings have emerged such as the Burj Al Arab, in Dubai, in order to differentiate themselves. Such hotels operate a pricing structure that is unappealing to the mass market consumer.

Some industry definitions of luxury

Although there are plenty of conventional definitions of what luxury and luxury goods are, it is worth reflecting on some views of those whose work influences the industry. For example Ralph Lauren regards the term 'luxury' as outdated: 'The word luxury is almost old-fashioned. I have a very different philosophy on luxury – to me it is the right pair of jeans that fit well and could be any brand. I call it design-led quality' (Lauren 2002). This view is very product-oriented and focused on a mass market. The husband of Miuccia Prada and CEO of the Prada Group regards luxury as a blend: luxury = care, innovation and identity (Bertelli 2002). This is a more esoteric and brand-focused view, one that is consistent with Prada's image. The architects Rem Koolhaas, who worked on the rebranding of Prada in 2001 through *Projects for Prada Part 1*, define luxury in an even more abstract way: 'In a world where everything is shopping . . . and shopping is everything . . . what is luxury? Luxury is NOT shopping. Luxury = Attention, "Rough" Intelligence, "Waste", "Stability"' (Koolhaas 2001a). This view is skewed towards the specific project of redesigning Prada stores, each element of the statement representing a particular focus for the new design concept.

The democratisation of luxury

Since 2002 there has been considerable debate about the democratisation of luxury or 'luxury overload', as Paul Smith refers to it (Smith 2002). Luxury should be about scarcity if it is to retain a sense of something that is rarely experienced and is exclusive. Concern over the dilution of the luxury concept and ambiguity over what exactly represents a luxury product or brand remains a live issue. The problem seems to stem from the overuse of the word to refer to premium-priced brands and products that are no longer 'exclusive' due to distribution strategies that have made them more widely accessible to consumers. Serge Weinberg reinforces the importance of exclusivity: 'you have to be very exclusive and no way can you justify the image if you don't have a very strong brand. It's about managing expansion in a disciplined way and it's a delicate balance' (Menkes 2002). The recent involvements of Stella

McCartney and Karl Lagerfeld in the Hennes and Mauritz (H&M) fashion businesses are indicative of how accessible designer branded products have become to the mass market. Lagerfeld is famous for his long-established role designing for Chanel; he also designs for Fendi (LVMH) and he produces his own collection. A few years ago the prospect of Lagerfeld designing for a low-priced fast-fashion brand would have been unthinkable. However, it is likely that there will be further forays by designers and celebrities into designing capsule collections or diffusion lines for mass-market fashion brands in the future. David Beckham's DB7 range, Jade Jagger's line of jewellery for Asprey and Kelly Brooke for New Look are further examples. The recent M&S advertising slogan 'Luxury for less' illustrates perfectly the wide variation in the use of the term 'luxury' and the inevitable dilution in meaning, as the brand has been running a large price-cutting strategy at the same time.

Dangers of aggressive growth

Michael Zaoui, managing director and head of European mergers and acquisitions at Morgan Stanley, warned of the dangers that luxury brands face from aggressively targeting a broader and less-affluent consumer market: 'The great upside of reaching out to broader consumer segments and making luxury affordable to more people has an opposite face. That is that in hard times, those segments of the population are hardest hit and they will refrain from making what they consider less critical purchases' (Zaoui 2002).

This view mirrors that of Umberto Angeloni, CEI of Brioni:

In my view, the downside of the more aggressive version of such 'global brand strategy' has been:

- growing dilution, both of a brand's customer base (no longer only affluent) and of its essence (no longer related to the core product or to its cultural identity)
- diminishing loyalty on the part of the consumer (brand substitution).

The rather extensive sales' declines experienced by some global brands during the past 12 months may be explained by these factors. In other words, it would seem that a good portion of what was sold in the last ten years was 'aspirational demand' of 'quasi-luxury' products by 'mainstream consumers'. This demand is intrinsically more volatile in times of recession (Angeloni 2001).

Different types of consumer

Today's consumers of luxury goods are quite different from those of the past. The mid-twentieth century consumers of luxury goods were mainly the super-rich and wealthy tourists. Now the market comprises a more diverse population of consumers, as luxury products are pitched at all levels. At the top end are the very wealthy who are referred to by analysts as 'high net worth individuals' (HNWIs) – those with more than US$1 million in financial assets at their disposal. However, the amount of wealth in this segment is on average much higher: 'According to research by Ernst & Young, at the end of 2000 there were 7.2 million consumers with an average of $3.8 million in financial assets. Together they owned $27 trillion in liquidity, and when compared with the total annual turnover of the luxury industry ($80 billion, or

0.3 per cent) one can begin to perceive this group's purchasing power' (Angeloni 2001). This is consistent with the figure of 7.2m HNWIs in 2000, produced by Merrill Lynch (2002). In addition, Morgan Stanley refer to a super class of HNWIs, which it describes as 'ultra-high net worth individuals' (U-HNWIs) and are individuals who have liquid financial assets of US$30 million or more. In 2001, there were approximately 55,000 U-HNWIs globally (MSDW 2001: 7).

Individuals' cash-rich but time-poor lifestyles have encouraged some luxury brands such as Bulgari, Giorgio Armani and Versace to diversify into hotels and Givenchy and Guerlain into spas, focusing on service experiences as opposed to mere products. This is addressing a Western trend and interest in 'well-being' which has afforded many companies brand-extension opportunities. Further definitions of luxury in terms of 'time', 'peace' and 'independence' reflect the views of some Western consumers who are wealthy and already own conventional luxury goods. However, not everyone is convinced of the value of such extended and abstract definitions of luxury brands. The view of Bernard Arnault, chairman and CEO of LVMH, is: 'I know they (consumers) say this. But what do they do? They buy. Louis Vuitton's business in the US is bigger than ever. Dior is bigger than ever. To me, this is just talk. It's a snob thing, it means nothing' (quoted, Kalt 2004: 10). This widening reference of 'luxury' is relative to differences in global, cultural interpretations and experiences of luxury products. For example, Western consumers are already familiar with brands such as Louis Vuitton and Gucci and are able to purchase them at varying levels according to disposable income, most commonly at the low-price or 'entry-level' product categories that include accessories. However, this is not the case in the emerging economies of Russia, China, India and Latin America (including Brazil), where ownership of luxury products is relatively low and where luxury is still directly linked to the conspicuous use and display of products from Western brands. Each of these markets is expected to grow significantly over the next ten years. Robert Polet, CEO and chairman of the Gucci Group, believes that consumers of luxury products are becoming more knowledgeable and often know more about fashion than brands know about their customers. He also perceives consumers as being 'educated' by fast fashion retailers who offer new products every six weeks, creating a fast shopping rhythm (Polet 2005).

Luxury and fashion

The terms 'fashion' and 'luxury' are uneasy partners and represent a potential dichotomy when combined to reference 'high-end fashion', or luxury goods. The concepts are not necessarily complementary since the ubiquity and perishability of fashion items may be at odds with the rarity and timelessness of luxury items. Although some luxury brands have a strong fashion heritage, including Chanel and Yves Saint Laurent, modern mass-market interpretations of fashion do not always equate to fashion references of the early to mid-twentieth century. Seasonal mass-market fashion is disposable, instant and available to everyone, which is the antithesis of luxury. A so called 'democratisation of luxury' (Menkes 2002) has occurred as many luxury brands have targeted a broader consumer base and redefined 'pure luxury' as 'accessible luxury'. The original clientele of designers such as Chanel and other French *maisons* were the elite in society, many of whom were on personal terms with the designers. Such an intimate understanding between artisan and customer is not reflected in today's faster mass marketplace. Many consumers buy into luxury brands through seasonal and low-priced 'entry-level' products (typically accessories) or even worse through counterfeit goods. The strong association with fashion that underpins the demand for luxury products is reinforced through runway shows in fashion weeks, which are widely reported and the designs interpreted by low-priced mass-market fashion brands. The increased dissemination of the designs and styles of luxury brands through editorial 'cheap-version-of designer-label' features, further erodes the mystery surrounding exclusive labels. This is the inevitable outcome of a strategy to seek wider audiences, which many luxury brands have adopted. Luxury brands have gone from being fashionable to being in fashion, with all the accompanying dangers and investment required to stop them going out of fashion.

The convergence arises from the repositioning of old luxury businesses using a strong fashion identity. Examples of this strategy include brands such as Louis Vuitton, Gucci and Burberry, all of which have become highly desirable as leading fashion designers have used a blend of brand heritage and contemporary design to deliver creative identity and direction for the businesses. However, whereas the LVMH group and Gucci Group NV have employed high-profile external designers in their businesses, including John Galliano, Marc Jacobs, Oswald Boateng, Alexander McQueen and Tom Ford (now departed), Prada has retained family control of its creative and business strategies.

Many of these designers also produce their own collections including John Galliano, Marc Jacobs, Oswald Boateng, Karl Lagerfeld and Matthew Williamson (Table 4.1). Fashion clothing, footwear and accessories have always been used by people to convey an identity. The added dimension of symbolism, which is communicated through the ownership of specific brands and products, enhances identity. It enables an individual greater self-expression and group association.

Table 4.1 Fashion designers and their relationship with luxury brands 2005

Designer	Luxury brand/group	Designer collection(s)
Miuccia Prada	Prada	Prada, Miu Miu
John Galliano	LVMH	Christian Dior
Marc Jacobs	LVMH	Louis Vuitton
Oswald Boateng	LVMH	Givenchy Men's
Ricardo Tisci	LVMH	Givenchy Women's
Matthew Williamson	LVMH	Emilio Pucci
Karl Lagerfeld	LVMH, Chanel	Fendi, Chanel
Alexander McQueen	Gucci Group NV	Alexander McQueen
Stella McCartney	Gucci Group NV	Stella McCartney
Nicolas Ghesquière	Gucci Group NV	Balenciaga

National identity

The fashion labels that are paraded twice a year on RTW runway shows in New York, London, Milan and Paris often benefit from a perceived national identity integral to the cities involved. Italian style, British creativity and French chic are all clichés that emerge from stereotyping national heritage, culture and values. French fashion is built on the great heritage of the fashion 'maisons' that emerged from the early couturiers of the late nineteenth century and iconic designers of the early and mid-twentieth century. The names of Chanel, Dior, and Yves Saint Laurent are now dominant brands in modern luxury goods markets. The association of fashion with France is reinforced by the bi-annual haute couture shows held in Paris, which are still considered to represent the pinnacle of fashion design. Many luxury brands benefit from such associations with National Identity. For example, France is regarded as the fashion capital of the world by the Chinese, and English fashion brands such as Paul Smith and Burberry are hugely popular in Japan. In fact 40 per cent of Burberry's brand sales by global region are in Japan (Cartwright 2004). Italian fashion that emerged from Rome and Florence is now centred in Milan, which itself has become a metaphor for Italian style. The impact of fashion in Italy is significant as it gave strength to Italian design in general, according to Santo Versace (2004).

Table 4.2 lists the perceived national images linked with countries according to research undertaken for Morgan Stanley in 2000. It is interesting to note that British identity was linked to a 'country living' image that is rarely reflected in the branding of contemporary British fashion. However the perceptions of art and culture linked to France and Italy are less surprising. French haute couture, which is widely regarded as unprofitable, survives because it provides designers with an opportunity to go to extreme limits and develop ideas as well as products.

Table 4.2 National image perceptions

Country	Associated image
France	Art, culture
Italy	Art, culture
USA	Bigger, better, cheaper
Switzerland	Reliability, quality, chic
Germany	Efficiency, engineering
Japan	Aesthetic, tradition, modernity
Britain	Country living

Source: MSDW (2000).

The links between France and luxury goods are strong. The largest multi-brand group is the French-owned LVMH, and France's heritage of artisan skills in dressmaking and leather-goods production is valued by French society. Sadly, such skills have been declining in other European countries as many source cheap overseas suppliers to produce mass-market fashion casual wear. The influential French organisations La Chambre Syndicale de la Haute Couture and Comité Colbert lie at the heart of the French haute couture and luxury-goods industries.

Le Chambre Syndicale de la Haute Couture was created in 1868. It was a union to exchange, develop and promote haute couture fashion designers and specialist artisans and skills in fashion manufacturing within the Paris region. In 1973, both the Chambre Syndicale du Prêt-à-Porter et des Createurs de Mode and the Chambre Syndicale de la Mode Masculine were founded in addition. They have the same duties as the Chambre Syndicale de la Haute Couture, except for women's RTW and men's RTW; for the former the president is Ralph Toledano and the vice presidents are Laura Ungaro and Jean-Charles de Castelbajac, while the latter the president is Simon Burstein, the honorary president is Pierre Cardin and the vice president is Stephane Wargnier. In 1975 another organisation was founded: L'Union Nationale Artisanale de la Couture et des Activités Connexes. Today, it is all called La Chambre Syndicale de la Mode and diversifies in the categories mentioned above, all headed by president Didier Grumbach. Its activity is to organise the presentation of the collections, schedules, timings, press lists, participation and promotion of cultural French fashion activities, develop relationships with press and media. Equivalents in Italy and the UK would be Camera Nazionale (Italy) or the BFC.

The French luxury-goods association Comité Colbert helps to promote the interests of its member companies and brands through the world. There are currently (2006) sixty-eight French companies that are members including Boucheron, Céline, Chanel, Christian Dior, Givenchy, Hermes, Lanvin, Léonard, Louis Vuitton, and Yves Saint Laurent. Today, the French luxury-goods industry employs 200,000 people in France and is responsible for providing the second-largest surplus in their balance of payments.

Artisan skills, quality and heritage

Product quality, heritage and prestige are the key characteristics that have traditionally defined luxury brands, some of which are hundreds of years old. Several luxury brands such as Louis Vuitton, Burberry and Chanel were launched in the nineteenth and early twentieth centuries when a strict social class system defined society, and royalty and aristocracy reigned supreme. During this period, designers like Christian Dior, Louis Vuitton and Guccio Gucci designed clothes, luggage and leather goods exclusively for the nobility. Their products were art forms, involving special artisan skills, that took several weeks and sometimes months to make – and this was all a part of the 'luxury and prestige' experience. During this period, it was the norm to dress from head to toe in a single brand. Perceived value through quality of design, materials and manufacture is a key component of the luxury-goods equation. Today markets are increasingly competitive, and so quality is paramount. The enduring quality and heritage of a particular luxury product is a key part of its appeal. A luxury fashion brand must preserve its aspirational quality and heritage while maintaining its relevance to people's daily lives. There is a real art in defining the relevance of a luxury brand while keeping its heritage alive: it is a matter of catering to existing clients while attracting new customers, which involves an ongoing assessment of the appropriate balance between a product's form and function and how they fit with the way people live today. A vigorous debate is underway about the importance of country of manufacture to luxury goods sales. Prada recognise that not all Italian luxury goods will continue to be made in Italy and have stated that some products made outside Italy may be labelled 'Made by Prada'.

The business of luxury

The 1970s and 1980s were periods of expansion for a number of luxury brands that were achieved mainly through licensing agreements with manufacturers and distributors. Licensing was a convenient distribution strategy in many ways as it generated large incomes, from royalties, and provided low-cost global distribution for luxury brands. It also raised awareness of the brands in foreign markets, which was important for the domestic tourist business (tourists are more likely to buy brands they have heard of when shopping abroad). However, the over-use of licensing resulted in agreements with unsuitable distributors who did not maintain quality standards and began to undermine the reputation of many luxury brands in the process: Gucci,

Burberry, Yves Saint Laurent and Pierre Cardin are brands that suffered from this problem of brand dilution in the past.

Throughout the 1990s a different model emerged in which luxury brands moved more towards directly operated stores (DOS) in order to control the overall brand identity and customer shopping experience. It coincided with a trend for the role of artistic or creative director as a replacement for the traditional designer role. Tom Ford was the creative director for the Gucci Group, including Gucci and Yves Saint Laurent brands, and was personally responsible for the design of all products at both houses and for all advertising, store design, visual display, fashion communication, and image activities. His view was simply that the product could not be separated from the selling environment:

> I realised a long time ago that one can either design a dress or design a brand: a dress does not exist in a void, it exists in a world, and its context can radically alter its effect, or its success, or its appropriateness for that matter. In order for my message to be clear, it is imperative that I complete the design. A world for that dress to live in. A store is that world (Ford 2001).

However, while there are strong and obvious marketing benefits to owning flagship and other DOS their method of distribution is not without its dangers. Umberto Angeloni of the Brioni Group identified three categories of problem associated with DOS:

> *Conceptually*: A sector naturally geared towards a tailored, innovative and 'one-of-a-kind' approach (to design, production, service, distribution and communication) ended up operating on a basic, standard model. A culture of promoting lifestyle, provenance and iconic products has in effect been substituted by the mere promotion of the brand and of its cult, mass products (i.e. the accessories). *Economically*: An industry that was relatively low-capital-intensive and with a flexible cost structure is today financially burdened with high inventories and fixed rental charges. As the majority of their stores are today over five years' old, soon companies will be faced with a massive wave of restructuring charges (and temporary loss of business). *Image-wise*: The brand status could be severely curtailed whenever a company is forced to cut back on stores or relocate them to less glamorous locations. The necessity to create Outlets for the disposal of stocks, has further reduced the mystique and exclusivity of the brands (Angeloni 2004).

Hard and soft luxury goods

'Hard' and 'soft' are terms used to distinguish particular categories of luxury products: hard goods include jewellery and watches, whereas soft goods include fashion clothing, leather goods and cosmetics. Traditionally brands that have sold hard goods have preferred to use wholesale as the method of distribution and those selling soft goods have used DOS. There are many reasons for this, including the extensive network of independent jewellers and watch retailers. However, more luxury brands have moved over to selling their jewellery via DOS.

In the early 1980s, the industry was dominated by a small number of highly recognised established brands, such as Armani, Yves Saint Laurent, Chanel, Hermes and Louis Vuitton. LVMH did not exist, nor did Prada Group, and Gucci was a busted brand that had declined into a licensor of cheap and tasteless products.

A changing model

Table 4.3 Key success factors in distribution, 1970s–present

1970s and 1980s	*1990s*	*2000 onwards*
Licensing	Vertical integration into retailing and manufacturing	Targeted brand management

Source: Merrill Lynch (2002).

In the last ten years a significant number of fashion houses and luxury goods brands have been sold to large multi-brand conglomerates to ensure their survival. Rapid growth in demand for luxury goods in the 1990s encouraged larger groups to buy smaller brands to broaden their product and brand portfolios. There are various motivations for merger and acquisition (M&A) activity most of which are concerned with improving market share and profitability. Some include adding to core competences, buying heritage, securing talent and buying-in product extensions (through the acquired brand), which is important if current products and brands are plateauing. An example of securing talent would be when the Gucci Group bought Alexander McQueen's label and Nicolas Ghesquière at Balenciaga. Further motivations for M&A would be to secure growth and market share through a joint partnership (as in the case of LVMH–De Beers) and access to advanced technology (as illustrated by Gucci's takeover of Sergio Rossi in order to access its manufacturing facilities).

A new landscape has developed: a plethora of exciting brands has emerged, as have new ownership structures led by the likes of LVMH, new styles of management turned into an art form by Tom Ford and Domenico De Sole (ex-Gucci Group), and new kinds of products that are now recognised categories such as new technology, furniture and eyewear. A vast amount of wealth has been created globally and that has turned millions of individuals into potential customers for premium and super-premium goods and services. The consequences of this wealth creation and the thirst for products are reflected in the turnover across the luxury industry. The impact of the 'Tom and Dom' partnership at Gucci was fundamental to the new marketing approaches adopted by other luxury brands. Their departure followed the takeover of the Gucci Group by PPR and for many months speculation was rife over whether or not Ford would resurface as a fashion designer. Now Tom Ford has re-emerged, back in partnership with Domenico De Sole, having formed a new company carrying Ford's name and marketing ultra-premium products to compete at the price level occupied by Chanel, Hermès and Louis Vuitton. The company is to be based in Los Angeles (USA) but will operate a design studio in London. It will work with Estée Lauder on a Tom Ford collection for Estée Lauder, which is to be followed by a comprehensive Tom Ford beauty brand. The first fragrance from the new range is expected in autumn 2006 (WGSN). There will also be a separate deal with Marcolin, for which Tom Ford will design a range of eyewear. In the longer term the Ford–De Sole pairing is believed to be planning fashion ranges for sale in their own brand boutiques (WGSN).

Who owns what?

The so-called 'multi-brand' group of luxury branded business, or conglomerates, emerged in the 1990s following the lead of LVMH. Many heritage luxury and fashion businesses have been absorbed into large groups, which are listed in Tables 4.4–9. However there are a number of privately owned brands that include Armani, Chanel, Dolce & Gabbana (D&G), Ferragmo, Missoni and Prada Group (subject to change).

Other brands that are in private hands include those listed in Table 4.4.

Table 4.4 Luxury brands in private ownership

Brand	Owner
Bally	Texas Pacific Group
Ballantyne Cashmere	Charme Investments
Escada	HMD Partners
Asprey and Garrard	Lawrence Stroll and Silas Chou
Christian Lacroix	Falic Group
Jimmy Choo	Hicks, Muse, Tate and Furst
Bruno Magli	Opera Fund
Chanel, Holland & Holland, Bourgeois, Eres	Wertheimer family

The brands in Table 4.5 are owned by large industrial groups which are manufacturing businesses as opposed to dedicated multi-brand luxury groups.

Table 4.5 Luxury brands owned by large industrial groups

Brand	Owner
Calvin Klein, Michael Kors	Phillips–Van Heusen
Keneth Cole, Geoffery Beene	Phillips–Van Heusen
Moschino, Alberta Ferretti, Pollini, Narchiso Rodriguez, Jean Paul Gaultier, Velmar	Aeffe
Hugo Boss, Valentino	Marzotto
Cerruti	Fin.Part
Karl Lagerfeld, KL Gallery, Tommy Hilfiger, 7L	Tommy Hilfiger Group

Multi-brand groups (luxury)

The majority of the large groups are considered to be public companies even though in the case of LVMH–Christian Dior, Bernard Arnault has a large personal investment. The Prada Group is not publicly owned as it has not managed to undertake an Initial Public Offer (IPO) and so ordinary shareholders cannot buy into the company. The Prada Group has sold its Jil Sander and Helmut Lang brands, with Prada and Miu Miu now representing 99% of the Group's revenue.

LVMH Louis Vuitton–Moët Hennessy

LVMH is the world's largest luxury goods multi-brand group and is owned through a complex arrangement between Christian Dior and Group Arnault involving differing levels of equity stakes and voting rights. Group Arnault owns a 34.1 per cent stake in LVMH and Group Arnault holding companies have a 68.6 per cent equity stake in

Christian Dior. Christian Dior Couture is a separate company that is fully owned by Christian Dior. The brands and business groups of LVMH are listed in Table 4.6 below.

Table 4.6 LVMH business groups and brands 2005

Wines, spirits	Fashion, leather goods	Perfumes, cosmetics	Watches, jewellery	Selective retailing	Other activities
Moët & Chandon	Louis Vuitton	Parfums Christian Dior	Tag Heuer	DFS	Tajan
Dom Pérignon	Loewe	Guerlain	Ebel	Miami Cruiseline Services	DI Group
Mercier	Céline	Parfums Givenchy	Zenith	Sephora	Connaissance des Arts
Ruinart	Berluti	Kenzo Parfums	Christian Dior	Le Bon Marché	Art & Auction
Veuve Clicquot	Kenzo	Laflachère	Fred	La Samaritaine	sephora.com
Canard-Duchêne	Givenchy	Bliss	Chaumet		eLuxury
Krug	Christian Dior	BeneFit Cosmetics	Omas		
Château d'Yquem	Fendi	Fresh	LVMH–De Beers		
Hine	Stefano Bi	Make Up For Ever	(joint venture)		
Newton	Emilio Pucci	Acquadi Parma			
Cape Mentelle	Thomas Pink	Marc Jacobs Fragrances			
Chandon Estates	Marc Jacobs	Kenneth Cole Fragrances			
Cloudy Bay	Donna Karan				
Hennessy					
Mount Adam					

Pinault Printemps Redoute (PPR)

PPR is not traditionally a luxury business and only entered the luxury market after its takeover of the Gucci Group NV in 2003. Its activities prior to the takeover of Gucci were primarily retailing, ranging from departments stores to mail order, selling a wide range of products including electrical goods, markets in which it still operates. However, through ownership of the Gucci Group (developed by Domenico De Sole and Tom Ford) it now also owns the luxury brands shown in Table 4.7.

Table 4.7 PPR luxury business groups and brands

Fashion, leather goods	Perfumes, cosmetics	Watches	Jewellery
Gucci	YSL Beaute	Boucheron	Boucheron
Yves Saint Laurent	Roget & Gallet	Gucci	
Sergio Rossi	Oscar de la Renta	YSL	
Bottega Veneta	Van Cleef & Arpels	Bedat & Co.	
Alexander McQueen	Fendi		
Stella McCartney	Boucheron		
Balenciaga	Alexander McQueen		
	Ermengildo Zegna		

Compagnie Financière Richemont

Richemont is the world's second-largest luxury goods group and the world leader in what is referred to as 'hard' luxury products, including watches, jewellery and writing instruments (Table 4.8). Richemont also owns Purdey, which is famous for its English Best shotguns; anyone who watched the film *Lock, Stock and Two Smoking Barrels* will be aware of their value as a luxury item.

Table 4.8 Richemont business groups and brands

Jewellery	Accessories	Watches	Clothing
Cartier	Cartier	Cartier	Chloé
Van Cleef & Arpels	Montblanc	Piaget	Hackett
Piaget	Dunhill	A. Lange & Sohne	Dunhill
	Lancel	Vacheron Constantin	Old England
	Chloé	Jaeger–LeCoultre	Purdey
	Hackett	Panerai	Shanghai Tang
	Old England	Baume & Mercier	
	Purdey	IWC	
	Shanghai Tan	Dunhill	
	Montegrappa	Montblanc	
		Van Cleef & Arpels	

The Prada Group

The name Prada is closely associated with the cool elite of the fashion world. It is a brand that has managed to retain a sense of exclusivity that one can argue is diluted in peer luxury brands such as Gucci and Louis Vuitton. Prada is a luxury brand that has evolved from a small leather goods business into one of the world's leading fashion signatures and multi-brand luxury goods groups, Prada Group NV. The first Prada store was opened by Miuccia Prada's paternal grandfather in the Victor Emmanuel Galleria in Milan in 1913. Today the business is run by Miuccia Prada and her husband, the CEO, Patrizio Bertelli. Throughout the late 1990s Prada undertook an aggressive expansion strategy along with its peer luxury groups LVMH and the Gucci Group. However this was at a time when global markets were growing. Today the Prada Group is still family-owned, having attempted on a number of occasions to undertake an IPO, which has been postponed until 2007 at the earliest (WGSN 2005).

Table 4.9 Prada Group brands and their contribution to group revenue

Brand	Contribution %
Prada	90
Miu Miu	9
Azzedine Alaia	<1
Car Shoe	<1

Source: Company data.

Luxury brands' valuation comparisons

Table 4.10 shows the relative market capitalisations of many luxury brands and multi-brand groups for 2003 expressed in US dollars (billions).

Table 4.10 Comparisons of company valuations

Company	Market capitalisation ($ Bn)
Bulgari	2.67
Christian Dior	11.95
Coach	6.70
Gucci	8.77
GUS	14.36
Hermes	7.23
LVMH	37.13
Polo Ralph Lauren	2.77
PPR	12.79
Richemont (Luxury)	7.25
Richemont (Group)	13.79
Swatch	7.23
Tiffany	5.92

Source: Datastream, Research estimates, Goldman Sachs (2004).

It is often difficult to assess such valuations due to currency fluctuations. Sometimes the valuations are expressed in euros and sometimes in US dollars, making comparison among companies and across years difficult. A recently published comparison of the market capitalisation of LVMH across three years is expressed in euros (millions) in Table 4.11 (LVMH 2004).

Table 4.11 LVMH market capitalisations 2002–4

Year	Euros (millions)
June 30, 2002	24,987
June 30, 2003	21,160
June 30, 2004	29,127

Source: LVMH (2004).

Breakdown of global markets

Table 4.12 represents the global regions in which luxury goods are sold and their relative percentage contributions. It is important to note that tourists buy significant amounts of luxury goods outside of their domestic markets.

Table 4.12 Sales of luxury goods by region

Country/region	%
Europe	35
USA	25
Japan	20
Rest of world	20

Source: MSDW (2000).

Table 4.13 Global sales (%) by selected brands

	Armani	LVMH (fashion and leather goods)	Hermes	Gucci	Prada
Asia (ex-Japan)	5	16	16	11	26
Japan	19	32	30	20	–
Rest of world	3	2	3	4	–
Americas	22	24	14	21	23
Europe	52	26	37	44	51
Total sales[a]	1,255	2,023	1,230	2,587	1,360

Note
a Total sales are in euros (millions).

Source: IHT (2004).

Since 2004, countries such as China, India and Russia are starting to move into the growth phase of luxury goods consumption, whereas the vanguard of the luxury marketplace – Western Europe and the USA – has moved on to the maturity phase. The consequences are significant for luxury brands and can demand entirely different strategies to satisfy the varying tastes in Eastern and Western markets.

The importance of Asia

The Far East has been a significant region for the fashion industry for many years. Mass-market fashion brands have sourced manufacturing production from many countries, including Hong Kong, Taiwan and Singapore for over twenty years. China has been an equally popular location for fashion production over the last ten years and is expected to become the largest source of clothing production in the world. By contrast, luxury brands have tried to retain their production within domestic markets as volumes have been small and specialist artisan skills are located there, particularly in respect of French and Italian luxury brands. However, this is changing as more luxury brands are making products in Asia.

Japanese consumers

The Far East is a significant consumer market for luxury goods. The Japanese consumers are an important market, accounting for 41 per cent of global luxury goods' sales (Goldman Sachs 2004). There may be a number of contributing factors which explain the enthusiasm of Japanese consumers for luxury goods. Prices for these products tend to be 40 per cent more expensive in Japan than they are in the typical Japanese tourist destinations (Goldman Sachs 2003). Japanese consumers often build in time for shopping when they travel (*ibid.*). There is a Japanese custom called *Omiyage* requiring a traveller to return with a gift for family, relatives and close friends (*ibid.*). Further, the Japanese consumers regard European products as superior to those in the East (MSDW 2000). Traditionally Japanese consumers have spent more when travelling abroad although the global uncertainties linked to 9/11, Sars and the Iraq war badly affected air travel and thus Japanese tourism throughout 2002 and 2003. The 41 per cent of global luxury goods' sales that Japanese consumers account for is broken down into 24 per cent from purchases made in Japan and 17 per cent from those ravelling overseas. This difference can be explained in partly by reduction (although business is recovering) in air travel and in part by an increase in the presence of luxury brands in the domestic Japanese market. Japanese consumption is expected to increase as the economy improves and international air travel returns to pre-9/11 levels.

Chinese consumers

The significant political, social and economic changes that have occurred in China, including its entry into the World Trade Organization (WTO) have resulted in it becoming a major economy. China is also now a significant market for luxury goods, with Chinese consumers believed to account for 12 per cent of total global luxury goods' sales in 2004, of which 10 per cent was from Chinese consumers buying abroad (including Hong Kong) and 2 per cent from purchases in mainland China (Goldman Sachs 2004). Hong Kong is seen as a 'shop window' for the latest luxury brands and products by mainland Chinese consumers. Increased Chinese tourism is expected to benefit luxury brands, in particular those brands that already enjoy brand recognition and have a presence in China. Luxury goods' sales are expected to increase on the mainland in particular, as brands have had targeted specific shopping districts with new store openings and promotional activity to raise brand awareness among indigenous Chinese consumers. Many European countries now have Authorised Destination Status (ADS) from the Chinese Government, which is likely to stimulate significantly greater tourism.

Segmentation

The mainland Chinese market can be segmented into four *tiers* of cities, which represent market segments, according to 'Access Asia' (IHT 2004).

Chinese tiers of cities/market segments

- The *first-tier cities* include 4 municipalities: Beijing, Chongqing, Shanghai, Tianjin, between them representing total retail sales of more than RMB[a]30 billion, with an annual per capita income of RMB11,000 and high per-capita retail sales as a proportion of income. The municipalities contain 10 provincial capitals: Changchun (Jilin), Chengdu (Sichuan), Guangzhou (Guangdong), Hangzhou (Zhejiang), Harbin (Heilongjiang), Jinan (Shandong), Nanjing, (Jiangsu), Shenyang (Liaoning), Wuhan (Hubei), Xi'an (Shaanxi), and 4 leading cities: Dalian, Qingdao, Shenzhen, Xiamen.
- The *second-tier cities* are the 17 provincial capitals: Changsha (Hunan), Fuzhou (Fujian), Guiyang (Guizhou), Haikou (Hainan), Hefei (Anhui), Hohhot (Inner Mongolia), Kunming (Yunnan), Lanzhou (Gansu), Lhasa (Tibet), Nanchang (Jiangxi), Nanning (Guangxi), Shijiazhuang (Hebei), Taiyuan (Shanxi), Urumqi (Xinjiang), Xining (Qinghai), Yinchuan (Ningxia), Zhengzhou (Henan); the 50 prefecture-level cities, including, Ningbo, Suzhou and Wuxi; plus 15 more cities with populations of between 500,000 and 2 million.
- About 200 county-level cities account for the *third-tier cities*.
- The *fourth-tier cities* are the 400 or so capitals of county towns.

Note
a *RMB = Renminbi* (people's money), the currency of China.

Source: Access Asia (2004).

Case study | Burberry

Burberry is a good example of a brand that was in decline and heading towards fashion obscurity in 1997. Rose Marie Bravo was appointed chief executive and developed a strategy that turned the company into a hugely successful premium fashion brand with high global recognition and brand equity. She was able to do this because Burberry already possessed a strong heritage: 'In order to restore something to its past glory, one must have something worth saving and reviving to begin with' (Bravo 2002). Burberry sees itself as the original British luxury brand (*ibid.*) although some commentators believe that this position has been diluted by its 'accessible luxury strategy'.

BACKGROUND

The company was founded in 1856 by 21-year-old Thomas Burberry, who opened a small shop in Basingstoke, Hampshire, to provide outerwear for the local farmers, sportsmen and landed gentry. His business thrived, and by 1870 Burberry had become an 'emporium' with an increased focus on the development of outdoor wear for local residents and visiting sportsmen.

By 1880 Thomas Burberry had developed waterproof gabardine, taking out a patent in 1888. Gabardine is a breathable fabric produced using an innovative process in which the yarn is waterproofed before weaving, making the fabric water-resistant and durable. In 1895 Burberry designed a coat for the British military which became the prototype for the now world famous Burberry trench coat, using the unique gabardine fabric. In 1891 Thomas Burberry opened his first shop in London at the Haymarket, and in 1901 the company was commissioned by the Government to design a new service uniform for British officers.

Burberry's famous check, which was designed in 1920 and is registered as a trademark, was introduced as a lining into the trench coat in 1924. In the 1940s and 1950s, Burberry was popularised by Hollywood as stars, including Humphrey Bogart in *Casablanca* and Peter Sellers in *The Pink Panther*, wore the famous trench coat. Burberry obtained its royal warrant in 1955. In 1967 the trademark check was transferred onto umbrellas, luggage and scarves having mainly been used on coat linings prior to that time. In 1970 Burberry broke into the US market through the opening of a flagship store in New York. This was followed by a much bigger expansion throughout the USA in the 1980s, including new store openings in San Francisco, Chicago, Boston, Washington, DC, Philadelphia and California.

PROBLEMS FACED BY BURBERRY

By the late 1990s Burberry was facing a number of strategic and structural issues, despite being profitable. Its business was reliant on a small base of core products and the company had made only limited investments in its infrastructure, including design, marketing, merchandising, distribution and support functions. Its distribution strategy was unfocused, with stores often located in unsuitable locations, and inconsistent wholesale distribution policies had resulted in Burberry products being sold across an extensive range of environments of varying quality. In particular, its products were being sold by wholesale customers to other distributors over which Burberry had no direct control – a practice referred to as parallel trading and also as a gray market. Similarly the brand did not control its licensees effectively, resulting in price, design and product quality varying across markets.

THE NEW MANAGEMENT TEAM AND STRATEGY

In 1997, Great Universal Stores plc (GUS) began recruitment of a new management team to address these issues. The management team under Rose Marie Bravo inherited a brand that had existed for many years as part of GUS plc, and which was an international business in its own right. Burberry was widely recognised and profitable although becoming less relevant in terms of its fashionability in the global marketplace. Its product portfolio was under-developed and the business was over-dependent on licences, making it difficult to control its brand image. The business model that Bravo developed required major changes to its product portfolio, design ethos and distribution channels. The first 6–9 months of the restoration process were spent understanding the brand's heritage and DNA, and drawing on a number of the values associated with the innovative trench coat fabric. Christopher Bailey was brought in to provide the brand with a new creative direction and strategy.

ROSE MARIE BRAVO

The rejuvenation of the Burberry brand has been credited to the efforts largely of Rose Marie Bravo, the CEO. What is undeniable is that she brought a change of approach to business and culture to the Burberry organisation, which badly needed Bravo's merchandising and distribution talents. Quintessentially British, the company had become unbalanced by the mid-1990s as the Far East accounted for approximately 75 per cent of Burberry's sales. This was the result of management awarding a master licence for Japan to the Mitsui trading company in the 1970s. Bravo believed it had become a virtually Asian brand (Heller 2000).

Bravo stated: 'Our objective was to distil what the Burberry brand stood for and determine how to make it relevant for today's consumer'. (Alderman 2002). The result has been the creation of an 'accessible luxury' status icon that has succeeded in tapping a broader clientele at a time when most other labels are struggling.

CHRISTOPHER BAILEY

Burberry's turnaround should not be attributed only to the widely acclaimed advertising campaign instigated by Bravo, but to the vision and creativity of creative director Christopher Bailey. In common with many others who lead the design team in a luxury brands business, Bailey's original position of chief designer was adapted to take on a broader focus, ensuring that the vision for the products is in keeping with the whole brand. Christopher Bailey had worked at both Donna Karan and Gucci, with Tom Ford, prior to joining Burberry.

Bailey's collections are inspired by British traditions and culture. The influences are interpreted and updated with contemporary silhouettes, fabrics and finishes. Bailey is reported as having said:

> What attracted me to Burberry was the richness of the brand. Not just its archives, but also the mentality. The founder Thomas Burberry was a brilliantly innovative designer. He was the guy who invented gabardine as a weave. In his day motorcars were becoming important, so he pioneered a whole series of clothes for cars that changed the way people dressed. He was also able to design an incredibly broad choice of clothes, everything from coats for the Antarctic to dresses for a London cocktail party (Deeny 2002).

REPOSITIONING OF THE BURBERRY BRAND

Bravo's team worked to reposition Burberry as a distinctive luxury brand with a clear corporate strategy aiming to broaden its appeal to new customers while retaining its traditional clientele. The central elements of the 1998 repositioning included:

- a highly distinctive advertising campaign;
- change of name from Burberrys to Burberry;
- a strong in-house design team and the launch of Prorsum;
- closure of unprofitable and non-core retail stores in Europe;
- opening of a flagship store in London – New Bond Street;

- elimination of inappropriate wholesale accounts including the termination of distribution to known parallel traders;
- upgrading of the international Burberry London product range, including the restructuring of its sourcing and pricing, and the elimination of unnecessary product variation;
- renegotiation of Japanese licences;
- acquisition of Spanish licensee.

Burberry's objective is the continued development and global growth of its distinctive luxury business through the execution of a strategy to:

- nurture and evolve the brand;
- promote the Burberry brand and image;
- continue to develop and expand the product portfolio;
- expand the directly operated store network;
- selectively build wholesale distribution;
- enhance operational capabilities.

When Bravo arrived at the brand, she regarded it as a niche at the convergence of fashion apparel and pure luxury. Her approach was to make the brand accessible to a broader market and to 'be accessible yet aspirational and to have friendly prices yet be luxurious; to be inclusive yet special' (Bravo 2002).

DESIGN

The London-based design teams are directly responsible for the Burberry Prorsum and Burberry London ranges, and they oversee the design direction of all other ranges and lines. In Spain and Japan, local design teams are in regular contact with their London counterparts to coordinate the design directions. All designers have access to their archives, which are a valuable resource for new product concepts. Christopher Bailey, the creative director, focuses on the Prorsum range but provides creative direction for the Burberry brand as a whole. In addition to their main responsibility for designing products, the teams are also responsible for product and prototype development, and have significant input to technical specifications, supplier selection and quality assurance.

TRADEMARK/INTELLECTUAL PROPERTY

The Burberry check is an instantly recognisable trademark which personifies the brand. This has been both a strength and a weakness, enabling the brand to broaden its product range very simply but also making the brand vulnerable to counterfeiting. More so than many other fashion businesses, Burberry products can be identified, making for conspicuous ownership, which is popular with consumers. By the same token, the check can be copied and imitated, resulting in the unauthorised widespread distribution of imitation checked products in discount shops and market stalls throughout the country. The check is registered throughout the world, together with the Burberry name, the equestrian knight insignia and the various labels (Prorsum, Thomas Burberry, etc.).

THE PRODUCT

For many people Burberry's products are instantly recognisable by the check. However, the product range is considerably more diverse than the narrow range of products that carries the check.

Table 4.14 Turnover by product category, year ended 31 March 2002

	2000		2001		2002	
	£m	%	£m	%	£m	%
Womenswear	63.4	28.1	134.7	31.5	165.2	33.1
Menswear	73.8	32.7	142.4	33.3	149.4	29.9
Accessories	50.2	22.2	98.0	22.9	125.8	25.2
Licence	30.8	13.7	45.8	10.7	53.5	10.7
Other[a]	7.5	3.3	6.9	1.6	5.3	1.1
Total	225.7		427.8		499.2	

Note

a Includes their fabric-weaving operation and 'miscellaneous' products such as childrens wear.

Source: Anon 2: Burberry IPO report (2002).

Table 4.15 Percentage contribution by product category (first half 2004)

Category	% contribution
Womenswear	34
Menswear	27
Accessories	25
Licence	11
Other[a]	3
Total	100

Note
a Includes Childrenswear.

Source: Cartwright (2004).

Table 4.16 Burberry brand sales by global region 2003–4

Region	% contribution
Japan	40
Europe	38
USA	13
Asia	9

Estimated brand sales at retail value 2003–04: £2.5 billion.

Source: Cartwright (2004).

Burberry positions itself as the authentic British lifestyle brand. The company's heritage is in apparel and soft accessories, but it has established a heritage for fabric innovation and outerwear. The repositioning of the brand has enabled the business to offer a wider range of products in both apparel and accessories. Products include women's, men's and children's apparel, including outerwear, knitwear, dresses, jackets, skirts, suits, shirts, trousers, casual wear, swimwear and underwear, and both 'soft' and 'hard' accessories – the former include such products as scarves and ties, the latter small leather goods, handbags, eyewear and time-pieces.

Asia represents 49 per cent of estimated brand sales value (at retail) for 2003–04 or approximately £1.25 billion, of which Japan accounts for 80 per cent (Cartwright 2004).

The products reflect the brand's attributes through their sophisticated and classic styling with fashion influences and high-quality standards. Burberry designs draw on the constantly evolving influences of the trench coat, the Burberry check and Prorsum's equestrian knight.

Burberry seeks control over the creation of its products from design to sourcing, manufacturing and distribution. Where specific expertise is required the company works with product licensees. For example, fragrance, eyewear, time-pieces, childrenswear and men's tailored clothing are currently manufactured and distributed by third parties under licence agreement. Product coherence in a growing global marketplace is achieved through the central coordination of design and merchandising for all product categories by the London-based design and merchandising teams.

FASHION CLOTHING RANGES

Burberry perceives its products within the hierarchy of a pyramid structure, with Prorsum at the top, followed by London and Thomas Burberry.

PRORSUM

Burberry's high-fashion range designed to reinforce the brand's luxury proposition, Prorsum provides design direction for other collections and serves as a focus for editorial interest, image and positioning. The range features hand-tailoring, innovative fabrics and couture details. It is produced in limited quantities and is targeted at 'affluent fashion-involved' customers. Burberry Prorsum for men and women is featured bi-annually at the Milan Fashion Week, alongside other luxury brands, and is distributed through its own stores as well as in prestigious stores such as Barney's (New York), Club 21 (Singapore) and Harrods.

BURBERRY LONDON

Burberry London is the core collection and reflects the brand's lifestyle positioning, with products that are both classical and fashion-influenced, while having cross-generational appeal. Two principal collections are produced each year, autumn–winter, spring–summer (A–W, S–S), products that are predominantly Europe-sourced. Burberry London lines have been developed for domestic markets in Japan and Spain.

WOMEN'S APPAREL

Women's apparel has been the focal point for the repositioning strategy with an emphasis on broadening the brand's appeal to a younger, more contemporary customer. The ranges include outerwear, knitwear, casualwear, tailored garments, swimwear and underwear. There were (2002) between 450 and 500 styles per season on offer. Traditionally the products have been focused on the A–W season due to the company's heritage in outerwear, but recently Burberry has included a broader range of products suitable for warmer climates. For example, in the S–S 2000 collection, the brand launched a bikini in the Burberry check to editorial acclaim and commercial success. The success of the bikini was built on by extending the swimwear collection to include a wider selection of swimsuit styles, as well as outerwear and sportswear in fabric types and weights suitable for warmer weather. Such products add to the seasonal offering.

MEN'S APPAREL

Menswear builds on the masculine heritage and associations of the Burberry brand. The offer includes products which address more traditional customer needs, such as tailored suits, raincoats, trousers and shirts, as well as a wide assortment of more fashion-influenced apparel including sportswear and a ski collection. There are currently between 330 and 350 styles per season.

THOMAS BURBERRY

This is a contemporary casual range designed to appeal to a younger (15–25 years) and more fashion-conscious customer. It is sold exclusively in Spain (launched in 1997) and Portugal (2002). The collection, comprising outerwear, casualwear, shirts, trousers, jeans and sweaters, is being redesigned to emphasise a British sensibility, and is supported by a new logo and advertising campaign. The Thomas Burberry range is differentiated from Burberry London in terms of design, marketing, distribution and pricing management.

BURBERRY BLUE AND BLACK LABELS

In conjunction with its primary licensees, Burberry offers two lines of clothing and accessories exclusively in Japan, which are targeted at the young customer. The Burberry Blue Label product range was introduced in 1996 and is principally a casual range targeted at younger women. Burberry Black Label was launched in 1998 and is a clothing line for young male professionals, providing tailored clothing and sportswear. Both lines have lower price points and higher fashion content relative to the Burberry London range, and are marketed separately. The ranges are designed in Japan in collaboration with the London design and merchandising teams which retain approval authority over the designs of all products.

ACCESSORIES

Accessories were central to the repositioning of the Burberry. They are key drivers of growth and profit due to their low prices, enabling mass-market consumers to buy into the brand. Accessories normally have a higher profit margin relative to clothing, partly because of the higher proportion of continuity products and lack of size differences. Handbags are featured in the traditional check, trench and Prorsum. In 2002, they represented the largest accessories product category by turnover in both the retail and wholesale divisions. Other accessories include shoes, scarves, belts, wallets, umbrellas and luggage.

PRODUCT LICENCES AND DISTRIBUTION

Burberry has reduced the number of licences it operates as a means of exerting greater control over its own brand image. It withdrew licences that it believed were inconsistent with its repositioned image, limiting licences to those companies which produce specialised products such as fragrances, eyewear, time-pieces and childrenswear. Those licensees that do exist have to be consistent with Burberry's brand image.

Burberry distributes its products through both retail and wholesale channels. The company has a website, but it is not transactional and is used primarily for product and brand promotion. Retail distribution is through DOS (comprising flagship and regular-price stores), concessions, designer outlets and factory shops. The wholesale channels include independent retailers (department and speciality stores, duty-free retailers and free-standing Burberry stores operated by wholesale customers). Licensees distribute through their own channels.

The flagship stores are important since they act as a showcase for the brand, creating a sense of theatre through which Burberry can promote a lifestyle and its product ranges. The stores are also used to trial new products and concepts, and they carry exclusive lines. Burberry flagship stores normally require upwards of 10,000 square feet of space and are specifically located in exclusive areas of key cities around the world. The first flagship store was opened in 2000 in New Bond Street (London) with others in Tokyo, Barcelona and New York. As part of its repositioning a number of stores were closed, renovated or relocated, according to image and performance. The product mix for regular price retail stores is broadly similar across different geographical regions, allowing for variation in retail space availability and consumer requirements. Merchandise is, however, tailored to the local climate and reflects the local variations in Burberry product ranges. For example, the Beverly Hills store carries a greater proportion of light-weight products compared to their retail stores in the US. Many of the brand's most recent store openings have been concentrated in warm-weather markets like Boca Raton, Orlando and Coral Gables in Florida, Scottsdale in Arizona and Houston in Texas.

The wholesale customers include leading department stores and speciality stores, including duty-free retailers and (in selected markets) free-standing Burberry stores operated by wholesale customers. Burberry selects wholesale customers on the basis of reputation and market positioning. It also works with wholesale customers on a store-by-store basis to ensure the right product mix. Burberry engages in joint marketing (promotion) activity with key customers and services them through showrooms in London, Milan, New York, Paris, Düsseldorf, Barcelona and Hong Kong.

THE BURBERRY BRAND

Burberry believes that its active marketing and management of the brand has been critical to its success. Marketing initiatives including advertising and fashion shows, and editorial placements are intended to generate editorial coverage and achieve a high profile and consistent visibility in domestic and international markets. The advertising has articulated the brand values through innovative visuals that have helped formulate a merchandise strategy and provided inspiration for what Burberry could stand for in a contemporary market (Bravo 2002). Marketing activities are centralised and coordinated in London. The marketing team is responsible for ensuring a consistent brand image around the world. Local marketing activities follow the direction determined by London and revolve around advertising, special events and visual merchandising.

In common with most luxury brands, where average advertising spend is as high as 10 per cent of sales, Burberry sees advertising as key in strengthening its brand name and image. In 1998, the company began its successful advertising strategy to re-launch and reposition its brand. It hired advertising agency Baron & Baron and celebrity photographer Mario Testino, using models Kate Moss and Stella Tennant, among others, to inject contemporary sophistication and excitement into what had become a tired traditional brand. Mario Testino helped to visualise the brand. Kate Moss has arguably been the most high-profile face associated with the campaign, although other celebrities have been involved in its publicity, including Jerry Hall, Nicole Appleton, Jarvis Cocker and the Beckhams. The powerful black and white images of Moss in a bikini were key in capturing the attention and imagination of the public. According to Rose Marie Bravo, putting Kate Moss in a bikini was a last-minute suggestion made by Anna Winter (*ibid.*). Concern has been voiced by many fashion commentators that the brand exposure, especially the check, has gone too far, as lower-list celebrities have readily adopted the look. For example, the widely published photographs of Daniella Westbrook dressed head-to-toe in the check pushing her baby, also covered in the check, reinforce the image of a mass-market rather than an accessible luxury brand. Similarly the recent UK 'chav' phenomenon, which is so strongly associated with the Burberry check, is believed to be undermining the brand's luxury image.

FUTURE GROWTH

Asia represents significant growth opportunities for Burberry, as it does for other luxury brands. Japan is the brand's most advanced consumer market in Asia and its initial point of entry into the region, having been operating there since 1920. The core Burberry men's and women's lines have been extended to more fashion-forward youth-orientated collections – Blue Label for women and Black Label for men – both aimed at the under-25 age-group. This group has also proved particularly receptive to the Prorsum international runway collection, so much so that the Prorsum runway show moved from Milan to Tokyo in 2004 (Cartwright 2004).

Outside of Japan, Burberry has consolidated its distribution in Hong Kong, Singapore and Korea having acquired distributorships in 2002. Since 2002 the brand has added 40 stores and concessions, increased sales by 40 per cent and now has 190 points of distribution in the region (*ibid.*). It has new childrens-wear business in Korea, has opened new prestige stores in Hong Kong and undertaken new marketing initiatives in Singapore, including Christopher Bailey interviewed in front of a live audience in Singapore as part of the Singapore Fashion Week. Burberry's position in China was re-established in 1993 by its Hong Kong distributor and today the partnership has a network of 33 locations in 23 cities in China. Greater China now represents approximately 5 per cent of the brand's revenue (*ibid.*). Following the success of its first perfume 'Brit' in 2002, Burberry has launched 'Brit Red', a new addition to its Brit fragrance line, in China.

Burberry has continued to grow and generate large profits since its successful stockmarket listing (IPO) in 2002. It has followed an *accessible luxury* positioning that has enabled it to achieve its global growth. The flip side of its democratisation has been the hijacking of its distinctive check by untypical Burberry customers who have been able to buy into the brand at the low-priced accessories' level. The problem is more visible for Burberry as its check is that much more readily identifiable than the small logos of peer luxury brands. The brand has a significant and growing presence in Asia and many of the characteristics of a global luxury brand, including: iconic recognition, a global presence, a strong heritage informing its creative direction, cross-generational and cultural appeal.

THE INTERNATIONAL HERALD TRIBUNE LUXURY CONFERENCES

In 2001, the *IHT* newspaper staged its first conference on the luxury goods industry at the George V Hotel in Paris. The conference was entitled 'Fashion 2001 – the business and the brand' and was hosted by Suzy Menkes. Since then it has hosted a conference each year, the latest in 2005 in Dubai. Menkes identified the key aim of the first conference as being to gather an audience of some 250 participants from more than 25 countries for discussion and exchange of ideas. The major strength of each conference has been the high calibre of speakers and delegates, who have created a unique forum for insightful discussion and exposition of facts, figures and issues (on the luxury industry) not replicated elsewhere in such diversity or depth. A sample of those who have contributed to the four conferences is displayed below. The quality of speakers is also matched by that of the delegates, as the conferences target the most senior executives and professionals across the luxury world.

A selection of the speakers at the annual IHT luxury conferences 2001–5

Giorgio Armani	Laudomia Pucci
Bernard Arnault	Dixon Poon
Umberto Angeloni	Vittorio Radice

continued

Patritzio Bertelli	Robert Polet
Chritian Blanckaert	Paul Smith
Rose Marie Bravo	Nadja Swarvoski
Ferruccio Ferragamo	David Tang
Tom Ford	Ralph Toledano
Ralph Lauren	Daniel Tribouillard
Suzy Menkes	Santo Versace
Rosita Missoni	Jennifer Woo

Conclusion

The luxury goods industry has grown by a significant amount since the early 1990s and is expected to grow still further in this decade as a result of the fast-developing Asian markets, China in particular. The industry is truly global as the products of luxury brands are distributed and sold throughout the world both to domestic consumers and to tourists buying in European and American markets. However, the huge expansion of luxury markets, the aggressive marketing of brands and products, and the emergence of powerful multi-brand groups have created a quandary. How can luxury exist if it is everywhere? Although one can intellectualise about the subject and redefine the word in abstract terms, most people have an intuitive understanding of luxury as something special, rarely experienced and which is all the more delightful for those reasons. When luxury brands move from being aspirational to accessible one can argue that they lose their integrity. The formulas used by luxury brands to grow during the 1990s are now regarded with scepticism by many. The post-9/11 and post-no-logo world is beginning to see a change from overt product branding in European markets towards greater customisation and individual personalisation – both of product and service. Western consumers are also seeking new ways to express luxury, including one-off experiences as opposed to simply buying more clothes, shoes and bags. Personalisation is as important in customer service as it is in product design. However, there is a potential schism emerging as Eastern markets desire Western branded fashion, leather goods and accessories in large quantities, whereas many Western consumers are seeking something different. Luxury cannot be unlimited as limits are an inherent quality of a brand, which provide strong consistency and integrity.

5 Fashion clothing manufacture

David Shaw

This chapter outlines the complex processes required to turn yarn into garments. The vast majority of us wear clothes, yet few people consider the complex processes involved in the making of them. In this age of universally available fashion, the path of woollen clothing from sheep to shop involves many processes at which Britain once excelled. This chapter considers the UK garment and textile industries and potential strategies for their survival against global competition.

Introduction

'The perfect yarn is yet to be spun, the perfect cloth yet to be woven and the perfect garment yet to be made' – this used to be quoted by my father, who spent his life as a travelling salesman selling fashion fabrics, if a client found fault with an order. The many hundreds of processes required to manufacture yarn, fabric and finally a fashion garment, render it almost impossible for a perfect garment to exist. The varied natural sources of fibres, especially wool and cotton, suffer from naturally occurring imperfections. The man-made machines that spin, weave and/or knit fashion fabrics are also prone to breakdown or can suffer poor human management, leading to more imperfections. On top of these variables, we now have the multitude of processes that occur when the fabric is cut and sewn together to make the final garment. It is unlikely that the average person considers the hundreds of processes that a garment has gone through during manufacture, as they go about their daily routine of dressing. What appears to be a simple consumer product is in fact a hugely complex and labour-intensive item. This chapter outlines these processes, although the complexity of garments in the modern wardrobe precludes it from covering every conceivable type of process and fashion product.

The start of the garment: THE DESIGN PROCESS

The design process with its famous designers and designer names described in Chapter 3, is to the general public, the most glamorous side of the fashion industry. Design creativity is the driving force behind every fashion garment, as it is at this first point of the garment manufacturing process that the designer envisages the initial idea of shape, colour and fabric. Throughout history, as described in Chapter 2, fashion has continually evolved, putting endless demands for newer and more innovative garments and styles on fashion designers. Their role and influence on fashion has never been higher, as the world of fast fashion, typified by Top Shop and Zara, demands that real and immediate fashion is made available to all who can afford to shop. UK fashion retailers have evolved over the past ten to fifteen years from simply providing clothing as a necessity to supplying fashion products in line with the demands and wants of an increasingly sophisticated fashion consumer. The 20% decrease in clothing prices in real terms over the past five years now puts all but the most luxurious designer brands within the reach of a majority of the population. This democratisation of fashion has created a chain reaction driving an increasing demand for more creative fashion design. The huge number of fashion design courses available at UK colleges and universities are a by-product of this new demand. The UK has become the world's hothouse of graduate and postgraduate fashion design, and is universally envied. The huge impact of young British fashion designers on the famous French couture and design houses is an indicator of its strength.

The role of the designer is to translate inspirations and ideas into two-dimensional pictures which ultimately become three-dimensional garments or accessories. This three-stage process sounds so simple, yet is the essence of all fashion designers' work. The secret is to create designs that translate into garments that sell, not simply garments that amuse and arrest. After an idea is committed to paper, the designer will create an initial sample of the garment, sometimes in a light linen fabric, to give an overall impression of the garment's shape and suitability. This also allows adjustments to be made, before a paper or fibre-card pattern is created, which then acts as a template for cutting out the different fabric panels of the garment. To use the proposed fabric at this early stage of the design process might lead to enormous costs and wastage if things went wrong! These simplified initial design processes are the same for a designer working individually for a personal client, as well as for one designing for a high-street fashion chain. However, the final judge of garment design suitability will be the consumer, immediately the garment arrives for sale in store.

The creation of patterns from prototype garments is a skilled and complex process. Most initial sample garments are made in a standard size (usually a UK size 10 or 12), to ensure that the garment looks balanced and normal when worn. Once the first standard size has been agreed, patterns will need to be produced for every size garment that is proposed to be stocked. The grading of patterns is a skilled process, as different component parts and panels of a garment do not increase proportionately as the overall garment size increases. All garments, once unstitched, look like pieces of a large jigsaw, all of them having to fit together perfectly. This process is where art and geometry come together, although pattern grading today, once a manual process, is speeded up through the use of computer-aided design (CAD) and manufacture (CAM). Many designers and clothing factories use the services of external pattern-making agencies which create paper or card patterns, or in some instances send the pattern designs and dimensions electronically to another country where the physical patterns are actually made locally.

One of the leading manufacturers of systems and software to support fashion CAD/CAM is Gerber, whose systems are to be found in most fashion colleges and factories around the globe. The Gerber product portfolio spans virtually every aspect of clothing design and manufacture. Key products include management, design and development, as well plotting, spreading, labelling, cutting and matching. See Gerber's website, http://www.gerbertechnology.com, for more information.

Fabrics

After the designer has created the original garment concept, design and initial sample, the important next step is to decide the most suitable fabric to be used. Designers usually start the design process with a specific fabric in mind. Fabrics are made of yarns, which in turn are made from fibres. Originally most fabrics were made from fibres and yarns that occurred naturally such as cotton or wool. These two basic fibres are still important today, although now we have many other man-made fibres. There are literally thousands of different yarns and fabrics available, and often natural and man-made yarns are blended together to give fabrics varying qualities of physical performance and feel, for example, wool and its man-made substitute acrylic fibre have a warm, soft feel, ideal for colder climates, while the lightness of cotton, sometimes blended with man-made polyester fibres, is ideally suited to warmer climates.

The huge variations in weights and textures of fabrics and their associated fibres are beyond the scope of this book, although for more detailed insight into fabric and fibres, readers are referred to *The Encyclopedia of Textiles, Fibers and Non-woven Fabrics* (Grayson 1984), one of the most complete works ever written on this specialised area of fashion. The ways in which fibres can be used are endless but normally fabrics are designated into three major fabric genres – woven, knitted and non-woven. The sequential processes through which fibres pass before becoming woven or knitted fabrics are generally similar.

Yarns

Yarns are made up, or 'spun' by combining together staple fibres or continuous yarns. Fibres such as cotton or wool naturally occur in staples of various lengths, with cotton usually having one of 2 5cms. Generally, the longer the staple, the better the quality of cotton yarn and ultimately the fabric. Man-made continuous filament yarns are usually made by a process of extruding chemicals through a fine nozzle, and then winding the filament ready for spinning or cutting up into smaller staple lengths. In nature only silk is created as a continuous fibre and is derived by unwinding the cocoon of the silkworm. The decision to use either continuous or staple yarn fabrics is made depending on the type of garment and its style. Shinier fabrics are often made from continuous filament yarns, while warmer and more comfortable fabrics tend to be made from staple yarns. Colour can be added to a fabric in several ways. Sometimes yarn is dyed before it is knitted or woven, in a process called yarn dyeing, though sometimes cloth is woven in a natural state and then the complete bale of cloth is dyed in a vat. This process is known as piece dyeing and it avoids the requirement of forecasting colour requirements too early in the fashion cycle by allowing colour decisions to be made later on. Another alternative is called garment dyeing: garments are made up first in un-dyed fabric, and then dyed as a whole garment shortly before delivery to stores. This process enables colour decisions to be made shortly ahead of the product being required in store, thus reducing buying risk. Modern consumers are spoiled for colour choice, with fashion colour demand now changing almost on a weekly basis. The right-styled garment in the wrong colour is useless and will ulti-mately reduce sales profitability when it has to have its price reduced. The fast-fashion retailers are continually attempting to cut down dyeing times to shorten lead-time to market.

The stages from fibre to fabric

Fibre – natural, man-made or blend
Spinning of yarn – using either continuous filament or staple fibres
Knitting or weaving of yarn – using loom or knitting machine
Fabric finishing – dyeing or printing

The choice of fibre or fabric type depends on the properties required of the finished garment. Some fabrics drape and mould to the body, e.g. velvets are naturally suit-able for ladies' evening wear, whereas a closely woven waxed cotton fabric would be ideal for hardwearing waterproof outer wear. Fabrics appear to appeal to people's tactile sense, with consumers usually touching a garment before trying it on. The properties of fabrics are often enhanced by the use of blends, e.g. linen on its own creases in wearing at very low temperature, but when mixed with man-made viscose will retain its shape longer. Soft yarns such as cashmere are wonderful to the touch, but wear very badly unless strengthened and mixed with other fibres. Some fabrics will consist of up to five to six different types of fibre, each constituent part performing a specific function. The options are endless, with most fashion fabrics performing well in wear. Fabric is becoming more consistent and reliable as a result of ever-improving manufacturing technologies. The look and feel of fashion fabrics are the key drivers when fashion buyers make decisions as well as for the final consumer.

Key yarn properties

Capacity of the yarn to absorb dye
Elasticity and ability to recover from creasing
Fine or coarse feel
Weight and/or durability
Current availability and cost
Flexibility and ease of making into garments
Protection properties against staining

Today's fashion consumers have high-performance expectations of the garments they purchase. Fabrics need to be durable and easy-care, so that clothing may be thrown into a washing-machine, tumble-dried and come out crease-free, ready for immediate wear. The more casual style of modern dress, together with a disposable approach to clothes purchasing, means that fibres and fabrics have to perform under pressure. Prior to the mass availability of the washing-machine, clothes' care was an arduous process, especially in the days when clothing was more formal. Formal fabrics tend to require more specialist care and attention than casual ones, with dry-cleaning the normal option. Although not researched or proven, it may well be that the international shift towards casual dressing is a result of time-starved workers having little time to look after formal clothes. The changing role of women into full-time employment (historically the family launderer) must also be a powerful driver of the movement towards ease of care. Non-woven fabrics are not widely used in fashion garments, although they are sometimes used for unseen garment applications, such as the stiffening of formal shirt collars. Despite many attempts to develop non-woven fabrics, the results have never been as good as, or an acceptable alternative to, traditionally knitted or woven ones.

Woven fabrics

The weaving loom is used for interlacing two sets of yarns that ultimately form a cloth fabric. The warp yarn or thread runs vertically down the fabric and the weft yarn runs horizontally across it, weaving backwards and forwards across the loom, with the help of the shuttle. The first looms were hand- or foot-powered, but as a result of the Industrial Revolution and its associated inventions, the power loom harnessed water, steam and finally electrical power to dramatically increase productivity. The choice of yarn types that can be woven together fundamentally changes the physical and visual properties of a fabric. For example, elastic fibres used in one direction will give a one-way stretch, while tightly woven, fine, hard-wearing fibres produce a tough, hard-wearing cloth. The fabric options available are endless when considering the qualities of touch, colour, texture, weave design and weight. The way in which the weaving process is carried out can change the surface appearance of a cloth. For example, 'twill' refers to the surface appearance of a fabric rather than its component fibres: where the weft thread passes alternatively over and under warp threads, to create a diagonal pattern on the surface of the fabric. The variable weaving methods and effects available are too numerous to cover in this chapter, but Adanaur (2005) explains most in great detail.

A main breakthrough in weaving was made by Joseph-Marie Jacquard (1752–1834), the inventor of the automated jacquard loom attachment, which enabled intricate weaves to be made on the surface of brocade and damask cloths. This invention revolutionised the decorative weaving of fabric on automatic power looms. Until the invention of the jacquard machine, complex weaving was done by hand, making it expensive to produce and limiting supply. Every fibre and fabric will undergo many varied and complex processes, involving physical and chemical processes before it is ready to be used in a garment. The complex processes undergone by wool, prior to it becoming a fabric, are displayed in the box that follows.

The processes that turn wool into a fabric

Sorting – fibre is sorted according to its length and fineness; different sheep breeds produce different qualities of wool

continued

Scouring – wool from sheep is covered with naturally occurring lanolin oils; the grease is removed through a sequence of chemical processes

Rinsing and drying – once scoured, the chemicals need to be washed off and the staples dried

Carbonising – wool naturally catches seeds and burrs that need to be removed; this is done using acids that do not destroy the wool

Blending – different qualities of wool are blended together, depending on the end use of the fabric

Carding – the cleaned wool is passed through large spiked rollers to straighten out the staples into longer threads in readiness for spinning

Spinning – the carded wool is now spun into the yarn (this complex process holds the staples together and gives the wool intrinsic strength and stability during the process) and the long threads are wound onto bobbins in readiness for their placement on the loom

Weaving – the yarn is woven using a warp and weft thread; the fabric can be woven plain or with surface effect

Printing – plain fabric can be machine-printed or hand-printed using a wide variety of printing processes, e.g. screen or roller printing

The versatility and scope of available fashion fabrics have never been greater, although sadly, as outlined in Chapter 1, the remaining UK textiles-manufacturing sector is trying to survive against immense global price and technological competition. Textile-weaving is a capital- rather than labour-intensive enterprise, in which leading-edge technology is crucial to profitable survival and expansion. The UK's involvement in two world wars has been blamed for a lack in textile machinery investment, leading ultimately to the UK's textile industry being left with inefficient and worn-out equipment. The speed, reliability and versatility of weaving looms are the critical drivers of success and profitability. Modern textiles machinery requires very little labour, with some US factories having worked 1,000 looms in a single factory, run and managed by a handful of workers. Loom reliability combined with consistent yarn quality means that there are few yarn breakages or loom stoppages, leading to high worker productivity and ultimately keener pricing. Unlike garment production, where dexterous hands using sewing-machines cannot be replaced, textiles manufacturing is much easier to automate. There have been several attempts to introduce robotic garment machinists, but the variable physical properties of fabrics make it hard to replace human hands.

Knitting

Knitting by hand can be traced back to the early Egyptians, but today most modern knitting is done by machine. Knitted fabrics are normally made from a single yarn using automatic knitting-machines. If the fabric is knitted from a single yarn, this known as weft knitting, although if several yarns are knitted together at the same time it is known as warp knitting. Machine knitting became established in the UK in the early 1900s, reputedly as result of a health fad for wool at the end of the nineteenth century which extolled the virtues of wearing wool next to the skin. Dr Jaeger of the famous Jaeger brand was a main proponent of this idea. Knitting is an extremely versatile process, as knitted fabric by its very nature, has the physical properties of stretch and give. Its looser construction allows air to be trapped, thus making it warm to wear, unlike tightly woven fabrics. Almost any combination of fibre and yarn can be knitted together. The complexity of knitting stitches that can be achieved allows for wonderful designs and effects. Generally the more intricate patterns in knitted fabrics are achieved by using warp-knitting machines. Knitted fabrics are ideally suited to leisure, casual and sporting activities where garments must have give, be able to breathe and wash easily. A great deal of modern casual fashion apparel is made using knitted fabrics, with woven fabrics tending by their very nature to look stiffer and more formal. Knitting-machines come under two major genres: flat-bed machines and circular knitting-machines. The development of knitting yarns together to form a circular tube of fabric has its origins in hosiery knitting, although circular knitted fabrics are often used for garments that are not knitted as whole, but made of fabric pieces which are then sewn together. This is called cut-and-sewn knitwear, as opposed to fully fashioned knitwear that is made more to the shape of the garment, generally on flat-bed machines. There are countless different types and sizes or gauges of knitting stitches. The Leicester area was traditionally the most important knitting area of the UK, but now only a few factories survive from its heyday in the 1930s. The Borders region of Scotland still produces high quality cashmere garments, although other famous knitting areas such as the Shetland Islands are finding it increasingly hard to survive against massive global competition.

The making of garments

From earliest times humans made clothes from animal skins to protect them from their hostile environment, although it was not until the Industrial Revolution (1750–1850) that woven cloth, could be manufactured in large enough quantities to come within economic reach of the masses. Historical figures are often depicted dressed in sumptuous garb, giving rise to the mistaken belief that everyone in the past was as elegantly dressed: in reality the average person probably possessed few changes of clothes, often owning no more than a handful of garments. People in modern developed societies generally admit to having far too many clothes, as is evident from the huge levels of recycled clothing being sold in the UK's 6,000 plus charity shops. The actual processes involved in the making of fabrics and garments are many and varied – in essence there are hundreds of different types of cloth that can be woven or knitted, these being made up from natural, man-made or fibre blends. Similarly, there is a multitude of different garment types, styles and fashions into which these fabrics can be made. The choices available to the fashion consumer have never been so great. Prior to the Industrial Revolution, when only hand-spun and hand-loomed fabric was available, clothes were high-value items and as such were treated with respect, often being handed down or used as work-wear once exhibiting signs of wear. The rich could afford personal tailors and seamstresses to make their garments, although home sewing and making was often the norm for the masses.

The development of ready-made clothes

The concept of productive specialisation, resulting from the Industrial Revolution, was first used for factory-produced clothing by the French tailor Barthélémy Thimonnier. In 1830 he invented the first sewing-machine, which was used successfully for the production of army uniforms. Unfortunately in 1841, disgruntled Parisian tailors and seamstresses, believing their livelihoods to be threatened, destroyed his factory during machinery riots. It is interesting to note that throughout textiles history, hand-craft workers often rioted when machines were used to speed up production, their introduction being seen as a threat to employment. Earlier, in 1811, the fictitious leader of the Luddites, General Ned Ludd, reputedly led an uprising of lace and hosiery machine-wreckers in Nottingham who were complaining at lowered wages and declining product quality as a result of the introduction of machine-made goods. As a result of the Luddites, many manufacturers moved away from Nottingham and set up elsewhere in the UK, for example John Heathcoat & Co., a surviving current textile manufacturer who moved to Tiverton, Devon, in 1816 and still manufactures there today.

Thimonnier came to London and patented his machine in 1848, although it was not until 1851, when Isaac Merritt Singer patented his version, that the industrial potential of the sewing-machine was realised. Shown in Figure 5.1 is a modern factory sewing machine in use.

The speeding up of sewing processes created the need for faster pattern- and cloth-cutting, which was solved by the invention of the mechanical cloth-cutting band knife. Hand-cutting with shears was slow, but now, using the band knife, up to fifty thicknesses of cloth could be cut at one time. The ready-made clothing industry was in its infancy, with further developments of the sewing-machine helping the

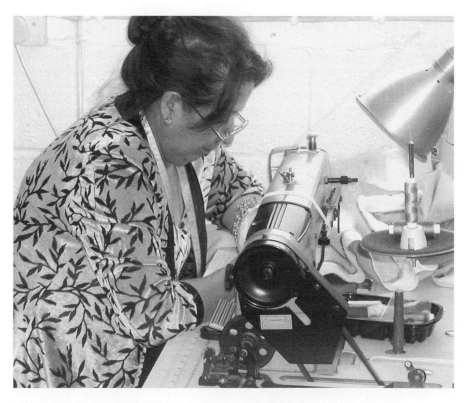

Figure 5.1 The modern factory sewing machine in use

component parts of a garment to be sewn together faster. Felling-machines were able to turn over cut and frayed edges, stitching as they went to stop further fraying. Sleeving-machines allowed the easier insertion and stitching of curved seams on shoulders and sleeves. Buttonhole-making and stitching-machines soon followed, speeding up a once-laborious hand process. Soon followed machines to mark out fabric from patterns, which thankfully speeded up one of the slowest of all manufacturing processes. The early sewing-machines were hand- or foot-driven, so that with the introduction of powered machines, productivity dramatically improved further. Factory production, with its sectionalised production and specialisation, now meant that a coat might go through fifty different hands before arriving at the end of the production line. Subdivision of labour allows the skilled and less-skilled operatives to work together to best effect. In most other manufacturing industries (particularly over the period since the 1970s), the labour cost of traditional assembly industries has dropped from over 25 per cent to between 10 per cent and 5 per cent of total production costs, mainly as result of increasing automation. Unfortunately, the apparel industry has not been able (as yet) to benefit from such large savings as result of the high level of product-handling and skill input required to make the average garment. This is despite great efforts by the Japanese, who are the masters of robotic manufacture. Displayed below are the basic stages of the garment making process and the people involved.

Basic stages of the fashion garment production process

Garment design and selection by designer and buyer

Fabric and trimmings selection by cloth buyer

Patterns designed and cut by pattern designer

Lay plan created by pattern designer

Fabric cut by cutter

Garment assembly by garment machinists and operatives

Garment finishing by finishing operatives

At the start of the garment manufacturing process, the base fabric is laid flat into several thicknesses and then the pattern, or lay, is marked onto the fabric in readiness for cutting it into the individual panels that constitute the garment. Patterns are arranged into a 'lay', to ensure that there is as little wastage as possible between each part. This process used to be undertaken manually and required high skill levels, with the best pattern-layers able to ensure minimal fabric wastage during the cutting process. Today's CAD–CAM software enables this process to be achieved automatically, thus ensuring the absolute minimum wastage of fabric. Laser cutters and other technological advances are being developed to further speed up and improve garment production processes. After the fabric is cut up, the pieces are numbered, bound together and moved around the factory, on a conveyor system, to each machinist or process point. Here, the relevant pieces or panels are assembled into the final garment. The time taken to make – and hence the manufacturing cost – of each garment depends on the design and construction complexity of the garment.

One of the most complex garments to manufacture is the man's three-piece suit, which, including all buttons, linings, pockets and other accessories, requires around 200 separate operations during manufacture. At the other end of the scale would be a simple sleeveless ladies' summer top, which might consist of two panels of fabric, requiring only a few stitching and finishing operations. The level of sewing and making skills required vary according to both the intricacy of the garment and to the price being charged. The famous couture houses and bespoke tailors of Savile Row still hand-stitch much of their work, with the associated hand-making costs reflected in their high prices. Garments vary so dramatically in the complexity of their design and the amount of fabric used, that garment factories need to undertake very detailed time/cost calculations to ensure that they are manufacturing at a profit. Standard times are used for the more basic making operations, which list the time involved in each type of garment manufacturing operation. This enables manufacturers to accurately cost the making time of each garment.

Once garments have been made, there is normally a need for a final finishing process. Under old manufacturing and quality-control systems, quality was often checked *towards* or, more often, *at* the end of the manufacturing process. In the days when labour and materials were cheap, and when competition may have been weak or even non-existent, examination at the end of the process was cost effective, but now it is usual for clothing factories to undertake production using total quality management (TQM) processes. Using TQM techniques, production is checked at *all* stages of the manufacturing process, by everyone involved. Simplified, this means that everyone in the manufacturing process is equally responsible for the final quality of a garment. The development of TQM production methods (while Japanese in origin) was strongly boosted by the introduction of British Standard 5750 (BS), and its European successor ISO 9000. Both were key drivers in the field of improving service and product quality across many sectors. Garment finishing ensures that garments arrive on the shopfloor in pristine condition. The way a garment is first perceived by a customer is important in giving them the confidence with which to start and complete their purchase.

It is important to be aware that, in general, the quality levels of manufactured goods have been rising steadily since the 1950s. As the average consumer's affluence level and standard of living have inexorably risen over the past decade, consumer expectations of quality and prestige have risen accordingly. There is simply no room at any level of the clothing market for the manufacture of sub-standard or 'shoddy' products.

The quality of fabrics, linings, trimmings, accessories used in garment manufacture, as well as the machines used to make them, continues to rise. The international consumer has the basic expectation that a garment will wear well, wash well and last for the required time. At the lower end of the mass fashion market, it is normal to use cheaper fabrics, although the consumer still expects these to stand up to reasonable levels of wear and tear. High-fashion garments are not in principle required to last for many years, and therefore the younger and more fashionable a garment is, the stronger the likelihood is that a low/medium quality fabric will be acceptable, although this is not always the case. Young + trendy = short lived fashion + lesser quality fabrics is not the mantra of all retailers of young fashion!

This is not the case with most of the luxury brands that have been adopted by the young where quality fabrics still prevail. However, there is no direct correlation between a brand's retail price level and the quality of the fabric and the making-up process. Fabric quality is hard to measure objectively, although laboratory measurement of such dimensions as durability and washability can now be precisely measured. The quality levels of many so-called middle-market brands, in the authors' experience, is often quite mediocre. It is only the more knowledgeable customers who can, at a glance, make accurate and objective observations about fabric quality, the construction quality and hence the overall suitability of the garment in question. Many middle-market brands rely on a lack of consumer product knowledge to offer what can only be described as a very average or mediocre product. In the longer term, the customer will eventually catch on, and in good time the inevitable product life cycle (PLC) will lead to the demise of the brand which fails to deliver good quality garments. Customers deserve and eventually always demand value and quality of any reputable brand.

The more simplistic designs of many modern fashion garments may be driven partially by profit and the practicality of production costs, rather than by aesthetic considerations. As garment worker costs are around ten times cheaper in China and India than in the developed world, it is evident that more intricate garments are now increasingly being sourced from them. Even the manufacture of simple garments only just makes economic sense in high-cost economies.

The use of cheap labour in clothing manufacturer

The global garment industry has tended to use cheap or sweated labour, with the UK garment industry being historically built on immigrant labour, who escaped persecution to London – the original centre of the UK garment-making industry – in the late nineteenth and early twentieth century. Sweated labour remains an international issue, with many countries still using child and female labour at extremely low rates of pay. From time to time, the UK media uncovers the excesses of international sweated labour, though once aired they tend to be quickly forgotten. Although not acceptable by modern standards, garment workers have always tended to be low paid. The move in the developed world towards more acceptable employment standards has encouraged many large UK retailers to publish their policies of corporate social responsibility; Fair Trade products are now an integral part of the 2006 M&S and Top Shop fashion ranges. However, despite the worthy nature of such documents, sweated labour is still an issue in countries where any pay is better than none. Marks & Spencer (M&S) was instrumental as the first retailer to try to improve the conditions of UK garment workers in the factories from which it purchased. M&S gained great admiration for its stance, which also ensured that the product ordered was of the highest quality. By insisting on basic factory working conditions, this is in itself a means of motivating workers and productivity. Unfortunately the decline of M&S's UK sourcing programme (due to international global pricing pressure) means that much of their sourcing is now foreign. While still maintaining its stance on basic factory working conditions, it is in practice more difficult to police the working conditions in other countries. Even as late as 1909, the Trade Board highlighted that in bespoke tailoring, 'rates of wages were exceptionally low as compared with those in other employment'. Recent visits to remaining London sweatshops in early 2006 found that wages are still very low and immigrant workers are still being exploited – little has changed.

The plight of immigrant workers still continues in many European capitals, where they provide the cheapest labour (Rath 2002). New immigrants are usually pleased to have any form of paid work. For them a sewing-machine represents a relatively small capital investment that can become an immediate cash generator. Machinists will most probably be female, for whom becoming a 'home worker' can often fit in with other domestic responsibilities, as well as not requiring high language proficiency. Home-workers, or out-workers, are paid for the number of pieces or garments sewn, the work usually being delivered to their homes as ready-cut pieces of material to be sewn together etc. Finished garments are then collected at a scheduled time, normally to be sent back to a central factory or warehouse for inspection, pressing and pre-retailing.

The main advantage of using out-workers is that they can provide production flexibility for a local factory, which at key times may be unable to cope with the high levels of demand. The seasonal patterns of fashion retail trading generally puts very heavy early season requirements on the garment-manufacturing sector. Manufacturers can 'switch to' extra production simply by calling up out-workers, who may be short of work, to fulfil new seasonal demand peaks or to respond to early repeat orders of best-selling lines. For the manufacturer, the control of out-workers can be difficult, especially over issues relating to quality control: it is very easy for the unsupervised home-worker to allow standards to slip. In general garment manufacturers employ only those out-workers whose work quality is consistent, although at busier times of year there can be a tendency to use less-skilled workers in order to meet production targets.

The home- or out-worker industry is still active in the traditional garment-manufacturing areas of the UK. However, the possibility that many of these workers are illegal immigrants or are working for cash payment outside of the tax system makes this a shadier part of the manufacturing sector that is hard to find or measure without being 'in the know'. Many out-workers are now aged over 50 and are a fast-vanishing breed. Government legislation has driven many sweatshop factories underground, where they do not come under the direct scrutiny of the factory inspectors. The few remaining mainstream factories working legally within the economy are now much better working environments than they were even twenty years ago. The author's personal experience of visiting UK factories and comparing them to factories throughout the world has revealed that many foreign manufacturers still expect their workers to produce garments in very poor factory environments.

When looking at pristine well-made garments on the rails of European shops and stores, it is hard for the average customer to realise that many will have been made in filthy, unsafe and unhygienic work environments. Clothing manufacture often involves the use of sharp needles, knives and shears, used at speed in confined spaces. Modern electric band knives used for cutting fabric can amputate a finger or two in a second if the operative fails to wear the correct protective chain-mail glove. Factory safety is often very poor in certain countries.

There is now a growing ethical trading movement, that is slowly alerting consumers to the level of exploitation being suffered by textiles and garment workers in developing countries. Ethical practice is now rising up the agenda, as the world's consumers become more aware of the way in which brands are made. However, anecdotally it is only a small percentage of consumers who take affirmative action to seek out ethically produced garments.

Why Britain historically developed a powerful textiles industry

In most developing countries, after agriculture and mining, the development of a textiles industry is often seen as the next logical stage in overall economic development. The huge growth of the cotton industry in the UK had several important drivers that initially gave Britain a unique but eventually unsustainable competitive advantage over its rivals of the time. The key drivers have been variously identified as:

*   *plentiful resources* – the availability of fuel and energy in terms of natural coal resources and plentiful water;
*   *climatic advantage* – ideal wet and damp climate for handling cotton during spinning and weaving processes;
*   *British inventiveness* – the key development of steam engines and the development of efficient factory production;
*   *advanced technology* – the unique state of technological development of the UK's spinning and weaving industries;
*   *plentiful cheap labour* – thousands of workers no longer needed on the land following technological improvements and developments in farming;
*   *captive and easy markets* – the developing markets of the British Empire led to trade dominance and world's largest merchant fleet for many years; lack of serious competition – many developing countries were simply slow off the mark to develop their textiles industry.

Improved communications, advances in technology, changing geo-politics and economics have all conspired to act against the once mighty UK textile industry. Whether or not the new manufacturing nations will be able to sustain their new positions of global dominance remains to be seen.

Famous manufacturing areas of London, past and present

Many streets and areas of London have had longstanding associations with the manufacture and selling of specific types of fabrics and garments. For example, the tradition of the bespoke tailor making clothes for individual clients still lives on in London's famous Savile Row, where are to be found some of the world's best tailors, shirt-makers, designers and couturiers, who once again make mainly for the rich (and famous). Savile Row suits are totally reliant on hand-making processes, with clients often being required to attend their tailors three or four times to be fitted at the various stages of production. At current pricing levels, it is unlikely that any customer, either male or female, would come away with a good bespoke Savile Row suit with much change out of £3,000. Nevertheless, the unique experience of personal tailoring has been described as 'a rite of passage into manhood'. Many top female executives also find their way to Savile Row, but the small numbers of female tailors (historically a male preserve) still makes tailoring for women a rarity.

Gieves & Hawkes is one of the most famous tailoring houses in Savile Row, and is the holder of at least three current royal warrants. On their premises at 1 Savile

Row, customers are able to select their preferred fabric and style of tailoring with the help of experienced and well-trained staff. The various fittings required, together with the actual making-up of the final garment, are all carried out on the premises. Gieves & Hawkes is also probably the best-known military tailor in the UK, tailoring dress and ceremonial uniforms for the three British armed services. The varying regimental styles and types of dress and ceremonial uniform, together with the correct application of military decorations and ribbons, properly ordered, makes military tailoring very demanding. Recently Savile Row has enjoyed a renaissance, with new, younger, targeted tailors such as Oswald Boateng and Richard James now trading in the area. Their sharp and modern styling, like that of the late Tommy Nutter, has managed to revive and refresh the street, keeping it in the sights of the fashion media. Savile Row, so favoured by the famous dandy Beau Brummel and James Bond 007, still maintains its rather old-fashioned image.

Garments labelled 'Made in Britain' once had considerable international cache, although in this age of global sourcing, consumers seem less interested in the country of origin, and more in the brand name. Modern consumers no longer expect clothes to be made for them, although for the mega-rich, the personal tailor and the couturier have never gone away. Some of the best-quality hand-produced clothing and shoes in the world are being made still in London. Apart from Savile Row, London also has Jermyn Street, the centre of bespoke shirt-making. There the more affluent customers are able to select fabrics and designs to have shirts made to their own size specification. London, in common with many capital cities, has quarters/streets/groups of streets, specialising in specific clothing/fashion or garment offers.

Famous London streets/areas with fashion, textiles and clothing connections

Oxford Street	Leading department stores and national and international clothing multiples
Regent Street	Leading department stores and specialist fabric shops; national and international clothing multiples
Jermyn Street	Bespoke shirt-makers
Savile Row	Bespoke men's and ladies tailoring and shirt-makers
Carnaby Street	Young fashions, developed in 1960s, are reviving again
Kings Road	High-fashion and clothing multiples
Covent Garden	Young fashion since 1980s
Hatton Garden and Clerkenwell	Fashion and precious jewellery-makers, designers and craftsmen
Sloane Street	Luxury brands and international brands
Bond Street	Luxury brand flagship stores and boutiques

In the past, some of these fashion-related areas were often full of workshops and houses belonging to weavers, tailors, seamstresses and other artisans. Today they are mainly retail outlets, with their workshops situated in cheaper outlying areas. The reasons for their location were plentiful supplies of original raw materials and/or cheap immigrant labour. The Spittalfields and Brick Lane areas of east London were once home to the Huguenot silk-weavers and lace-makers who, having been driven out of France in the middle of the sixteenth century, settled in England to become a key part of the textiles industry. Famous above all was the Huguenot Samuel Courtauld, who founded the once-mighty Courtauld's textiles company, for many years one of the UK's largest fabric- and garment-manufacturing businesses. Originally based on the business of important silk weaving, Courtauld's diversified over the years, although as a result of increasing textile and garment import penetration it is no longer a pillar of the British economy, having now been taken over by the US Sara Lee organisation.

Although London was the historic garment-making centre, a great deal of ready-made tailoring moved towards Leeds and the West Riding of Yorkshire, the natural sources of the best woollen and worsted cloths. The largest ready-made tailoring factory was built and operated by Montague Burton at Hudson Road Mills; in its day, during the 1930s, it was probably the best tailoring factory in the world. Burton was a Jewish immigrant, whose manufacturing business has ceased, although his name lives on as the Burton menswear brand of Arcadia.

The regional distribution of the UK's clothing and textiles industry has not remained constant in proportional terms, with many historic production centres experiencing huge size reductions in numbers employed. The four traditionally important English centres of the south-east, Yorkshire and Humberside, the North and the North-East have taken the brunt of job losses over the past 30 years, with over 200,000 jobs having gone (Jones 2002). In Table 5.1 were the major players in

Table 5.1 Comparison of the involvement of major UK manufacturers 1996–7 and 2005

Company	Sales (£ millions) 1996–97	Believed still manufacturing in UK in 2006
Courtaulds Textiles plc	1,006	No – taken over by Sara Lee
Pentland Group plc	890	Yes
Baird Textile Holdings plc	595	Limited
Coats–Viyella Clothing	342	No
Dawson International	297	Yes
River Island Clothing Co	285	Yes
Laura Ashley	250	No
Levi Strauss (UK)	205	No
Claremont Garment plc	186	Yes
Burberry	175	Yes
Sherwood Group	166	Yes
Dewhirst (Ladies wear)	146	Limited
Umbro	133	Uncertain
Alexon	119	No
Stirling Group	102	Uncertain
Wrangler	100	Uncertain
Austin Reed	78	No
SR Gent	74	No
Aquascutum	45	No
Slimma plc	23	Yes

Source: Adapted from Jones (2002) p. 62 and author's conversations with the Industry Forum.

UK garment manufacturing in 1996/7 (*ibid.*). By 2005 many of these companies had withdrawn or substantially reduced their UK manufacturing base. Shown below in Table 5.1 is a summary of their currently known UK manufacturing involvement.

There has been a continued withdrawal from apparel manufacturing in the UK between 1997 and 2006, with some famous names now maintaining only a token level of production. At the time of writing, many of these businesses have withdrawn from full-scale manufacturing in the UK. Some are importing made-up but unfinished garments into the UK, where they are finished off and processed, before being sent out to stores. The remaining production lines are normally reserved for high-value products or for fulfilling QR orders.

It is likely that many more of the UK-based businesses shown in Table 5.1 will further withdraw from all manufacturing in the near future. Due to this rapid change, it is difficult to accurately assess the scope and scale of the remaining garment manufacturing sector.

Can anything be done to protect the UK's remaining clothing and textile industry?

The outlook for UK textiles and garment manufacturing looks difficult, despite the efforts of the Government, the manufacturers and the unions to develop a sustainable business strategy that will halt its decline.

From Figure 5.2 the massive decline in the UK textiles and clothing manufacturing sectors can be seen continuing at a dramatically fast rate. Between 1998 and 2004 employment has halved from 280,000 to 125,000. This breathtaking collapse can be ascribed to a combination of factors:

- Impossible price competition – an inability of the UK's high wage economy to compete with low-wage economies, particularly those in Asia.

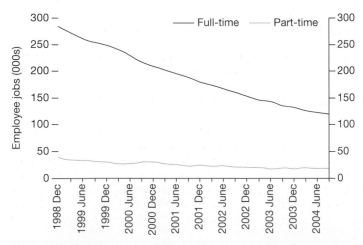

Figure 5.2 Employee jobs in the textiles, clothing and footwear manufacturing sector, thousands, 1998–2004

Source: ONS employee jobs series, 1998–2004, GB.

- An over-strong pound – the high value of sterling makes imports appear cheap and our exports appear expensive.
- Poor internal communication between retailers and manufacturers – in other countries buyer–seller relationships are less adversarial than in Britain.
- Poor investment in training and little re-investment in textiles and clothing machinery.

In November 1998, as a result of a meeting between already established textiles and clothing trade associations and unions with Department of Trade and Industry (DTI) ministers, the Textiles and Clothing Strategy Group was formed. The main objective of the group was to 'improve substantially the ability of the textiles and clothing industry to compete successfully in world markets'. To this end a seminal document was produced in June 2000 entitled 'A National Strategy for the UK Textiles and Clothing Industry'. This concerted effort by the Government and industry made fifty-five recommendations, some of which were to be tackled by the Government, but the majority by the industry itself. The report was both clear and pragmatic, with the steering committee ably supported by Government, business unions and relevant academia.

The working party has continued meeting since that time, and April 2002 saw the release of a follow-up document entitled 'A National Strategy for the UK Textiles and Clothing Industry – Making it Happen'. The aim of this subsequent publication was to clearly record the progress to date being made by the members of the group, as well as to give an update regarding the first tranche of recommendations made in the original report. The second report is very well illustrated with solid examples of business generated as well as benefits derived from both local and national government initiatives.

The Industry Forum

The support generated by the Textiles and Clothing Strategy Group's initiative is unparalleled in the history of the British clothing and textiles industry; additional support has come through the work of the Industry Forum, an organisation aimed at improving the overall supply chain.

An interview with Ken Watson of the Industry Forum concerning the general issues of the whole UK trade is summarised as follows.

Q: Is the Forum having an impact in getting UK retailers to focus on trying to buy in the UK?

A: The DTI insists that our Forum must have an impact as a key fundamental, specifically aimed at getting small manufacturers to adopt best practice, mainly through workshops. However, with such a fragmented sector it is sometimes difficult to get smaller companies to become fully involved. Our Forum's impact is pretty effective in relation to the funds put into the project. Much more money has been put into other, similar, Government–industry projects, such as the car industry which is a significantly larger part of the economy and larger exporter than we are.

Q: Britain educates and produces a huge number of designers, yet British manu-facturers and retailers do not seem to excel in developing world-beating brands themselves. Can you explain this?

A: This may well be a direct result of the large size of the major clothing retail chains and the relatively small size of the independent retailing sector in the UK. As an island, we do not have pan-European distribution as do many of the Continent-based brand houses. It is difficult because of the fact that we are simply a smaller market; but, secondly, the consumer has historically been much more price-conscious as a result of the multiple's dominance; and, thirdly, there is a lack of major design houses in the UK – our young designers simply rarely have the opportunity to learn from a 'maestro', hence those wanting their own labels are trying to set up early in their careers and generally experiencing fairly high failure rates. Hopefully the young designers who are going abroad will eventually return to the UK, having gained experience abroad, to open up their own labels. Finally, the remaining manufacturing base of better-quality manufacturers has been aimed mainly at supplying the more mainstream companies, who again were focusing their marketing at the larger middle-market.

Q: Might one of the major problems of getting British retail buyers to consider buying from the UK simply be a lack of knowledge as to what is actually available in their own country? Going abroad always seems to be a first reaction, from my own buying experience.

A: There is a definite knowledge gap that we have identified in a recent buyers' forum. Our retail sector experiences a high level of staff turnover, leading to a seepage of knowledge out of organisations, with manufacturers tending to follow the relationship rather than staying with the original company.

Q: Can you explain why there is such a large turnover of fashion buying personnel in the UK?

A: Not really. There does, however, seem to be far less buyer change in the department store sector, probably because of their generally greater level of trading stability. We also have a very American style hire-and-fire mentality, as well as not spending much on staff training or on research and development. In any business you get what you pay for – we simply do not give our buyers time to learn, usually making all their decisions more on a short-term basis.

Q: How do you feel British buyers compare with those of other countries?

A: Some European buyers are comparable with those of the UK, although American buyers are much better rewarded and much better trained, and in the main have much better support systems, especially in terms of information technology. American buyers also enjoy a considerably higher status than those in the UK, as well as usually working with well-established brands rather than having to undertake the buying of unknown in-house brands – brand buying, or selection, is a much easier form of retail buying.

Q: Do you think that there is a way to stop a further decline of the UK's clothing and textiles sector, or is this process inevitable?

A: Most importantly we need a higher quality of management throughout the manufacturing sector, but in terms of a magic bullet, yes, there may be. As overall buying quantities decline and buyers buy less of more lines, we see SKU (stock keeping unit) proliferation as an end result, throughout all sector products. This is happening worldwide. Line width demand increases as people's lifestyles start to fragment. Forecasting is becoming a much harder thing to do as customers' tastes change at an ever-increasing rate. Volatility of demand means that the ratio between stock-holding and return becomes more critical, needing a much faster response time to ensure that lower overall stock levels are kept in stock at all times. Coping with the stocking of fringe sizes and colours is particularly problematic as range width increases.

Q: Is there any magic bullet that could be applied to the entire UK clothing and textile industries to arrest any further decline?

A: Yes, it is really for manufacturers to respond lightning fast to any changes in consumer demand and to innovate at a faster rate. Foreign manufacturers are simply not able to work at such a speed as a result of the physical and cultural distance. About 20 per cent of current fashion-buying depends more on proximity and consumer understanding, rather than simply on the issue of low price. This is where British producers will always win hands down. Understanding the market and interpreting trends quickly into tangible products, as well as understanding what motivates people to buy and wear certain products is critical for success. This is really all about using marketing and marketing research better. Giving the customers exactly what they want is essential if the UK clothing and textiles industries are to continue and thrive.

Q: What is your view about the increasing number of foreign retailers coming into the UK marketplace? Should we fear or welcome this increase?

A: If you look at some of the new entrants, they often are simply taking other people's designs and re-issuing them to the market. This works while they are a small-scale business, but cannot work if a company is to become a major player in the UK marketplace. Some of the best UK retailers are themselves becoming very innovative and will make the highly competitive UK marketplace a tough one for new entrants. We also have a new genre of smaller and more innovative UK retailers who are creating a meaningful and understandable presence within the marketplace. The greatest threat may actually come from the complete cessation of the MFA, when there will be no controls or quotas on products coming into the UK. We could be faced with situations where huge international retail groups (such as those in the US) are now able to divert production, with their immense buying power, directly into the UK market, further undercutting UK garment makers and buyers. Possibly this type of threat may also come from other large European value-proposition retailers, which might divert their own cheap non-quota production into the UK. Finally, finding good locations and creating good management and staffing structures are not easy within the UK. This can still present a considerable barrier to any would-be foreign retailer trying to enter this market.

Q: Why do you think UK retailers have such a poor record of running foreign-based retail businesses?

A: Some UK retailers are still enjoying international retail success. In general this is because they take the franchise route into foreign markets, using a good franchise partner. When UK retailers try to apply direct UK retailing and management techniques to foreign outlets, this generally does not appear to work very well. They forget 'think global, act local' is the most important mantra. UK retailers can often suffer from brand arrogance, usually having too much faith in their UK nurtured brand's international appeal. It is so important to understand what will work in different retail environments. There is also a severe shortage of well-trained and effective international retail managers within the UK retail scene – shortage of calibre international management is severe. Possibly there is a lack of strategic forethought, as well as a shortage with strong UK retail brands with strong international appeal.

Q: What do you think are the key issues facing the work of the Industry Forum and the Textiles and Clothing Strategy Group?

A: The problem is that the industry is very fragmented and relatively small-scale in parts. However, there are some world-class companies working in the UK. Niche sectors such as outdoor and golf clothing are still producing some of the best products in the world. Often we miss some of the cleverest and most innovative manufacturers who are working with the multiples to deliver fast response fashion brands. They are often small and unknown, but are still world-beating. Because of the nature and structure of our retail sector, good small manufacturers have often found it difficult to grow and become large producers.

Q: Why is there such a lack of knowledge and understanding about the potential of UK clothing and textiles manufacturers as that displayed by certain UK retailers?

A: Firstly the problem of fragmentation is a major issue, as well as the lack of a knowledge-transfer mechanism. People are often simply unaware of what is available or, sometimes, simply too busy to find out.

Although the Industry Forum is a positive step in the right direction, and while several initiatives are underway, with some small levels of Government investment being put into skills and technology, the bottom line appears to be that such initiatives are too little and too late. Whether this view could be deemed to express an innate British cynicism in manufacturing industries remains to be seen – as most investments take time to fully deliver dividends. However, in a typical British way, the huge number of bodies, committees and other interested parties involved in trying to sort out what should be a fairly simple management issue for Government seems to be clogging up the process, with more intellectual effort being expended on taking minutes and making strategic decisions, rather than taking direct action and measuring the results. Not enough direct and firm action has, or is currently being taken, to defend the last vestiges of the UK's once great clothing and textile industries. The whole issue of central government support for the textiles and clothing industry is under review, with plans to extend support to the regions. The future of the remaining British Textile and Clothing industry is in the balance.

   It is argued that direct protectionism is no longer either an acceptable nor an economically sensible way to defend an industry from foreign competition. It should, however, be possible for governments and interested parties to work together to ensure that any industry is working efficiently and effectively. A nation with no manufacturing base at all must surely put itself ultimately at great strategic economic risk. Paradoxically, despite the attraction for UK retailers to buying from foreign manufacturers, the consistent receipt of timely deliveries from foreign manufacturers is still of major concern. The UK may soon become almost completely dependent on sourcing garments from abroad. The lower costs of buying abroad can easily be negated in lost sales as a result of late delivery. Other hidden costs are often involved with purchasing from abroad that are not immediately obvious to the retail buyer. These have been well documented and analysed by Hines (in Jackson and Shaw 2001). Foreign fashion buying and related issues and problems are dealt with in depth in Chapter 7.

Potential strategies to retain the UK textiles and garment industry

In one of the most recent and probably most comprehensive reviews of the UK apparel industry (the older, but American preferred term for clothing), R. M. Jones (2002) concludes, after his well-written review of its rise and decline, that its best chance of surviving will hinge on it quickly developing and implementing a range of strategies against the ever-increasing wave of cheap, well-designed, imports. These suggestions were categorised and have been re-interpreted by the author as follows.

1 *Importation of a successful domestic clothing strategy from elsewhere.* Italy has continued producing clothing and textiles despite being a high-wage economy – there are several other similar examples. To study and understand the Italian model might give us clues how to hold our remaining manufacturing capabilities.

2 *Use niche marketing more effectively.* A focus, for example, on high-value items with a unique design or product propositions – e.g. cashmere knitwear, English outdoor country apparel such as Barbour – could be developed.

3 *Develop added value, QR and/or lean manufacturing principles.* These are ideal in today's fast-moving and fragmented fashion market, where quick, small runs from small to medium-size manufacturing units have an advantage over larger and generally less flexible units.

4 *Develop external solutions.* For example, move all manufacturing to cheaper off shore areas, while repatriating profits and retaining a certain level of key personnel employment in the UK. As trade barriers have dropped away, this seems a one of the better alternatives.

It is of interest that textiles and clothing has probably enjoyed a higher level of protection than almost any other form of international manufacturing, even though since the mid-1970s, their manufacture has constituted only a very small percentage of traded manufactured goods in Europe and the USA. The emotional and psychological links with the old industries can probably be the only explanation for such protectionism. While in general it appears beneficial to protect any developed industry, fashion-related or otherwise, to enable an orderly retreat into new types of manufacturing, there is some evidence that consumers and the economy as whole have not benefited from high-cost manufacturing operations being offered quota protection. In general De La Torre (1986: 220) argues that there is evidence to show that 'the job preservation strategy actually proved to be extremely costly and ineffective in maintaining employment'.

Conclusion

It is unlikely that the UK will retain anything but a small vestige of its former mighty textiles and clothing manufacturing sector. The forces of the world economy are so powerful that to attempt to save it may prove even more expensive in the long term. Whether that will be to the long-term economic and social benefit of the nation as a whole remains to be seen.

6 Fashion retailing

Bill Webb

Buying clothes is unlike any other form of retail. It is not about the acquisition of objects, but about the transformation of the self (Linda Grant, *Guardian*, 21 September 2004).

Introduction

This chapter aims to introduce the reader to the principles and characteristics of the retail distribution of fashion. Discussion is grounded in the UK market, but makes reference as appropriate to international markets and businesses.

To a visiting Martian it might not immediately be apparent why an Earthling should be prepared to pay up to ten times more for a simple garment to cover his or her body than it costs to make it in the factory. The rationale for the evolution of a distinct distribution sector to transfer products and services from producer to consumer depends on the retail sector's ability to provide additional 'value' that justifies the cost and resultant price mark-up. In practice this so-called 'value-chain' can include a series of other intermediaries such as agents, wholesalers and buying groups who perform part of the process of getting a fashion product from the producer to the consumer. They are not covered in this chapter.

Traditionally, a number of retailer 'added-value' benefits have been identified which together validate the retailing function.

How shops add value

- Pre-selecting and editing product ranges
- Negotiating value-for-money prices
- Breaking down bulk orders
- Providing time and location shopping convenience
- Holding stock
- Providing information for customers
- Providing product support, service and refunds
- Providing consumer credit

Nevertheless, it is a characteristic of a developed economy that, as it expands, the retail sector grows at a slower rate than the economy generally and more slowly than consumer expenditure overall. In other words, as people get richer they choose to spend proportionally less in the shops. In 2005 retail sales in the UK will probably dip below 30 per cent of consumer expenditure for the first time – twenty-five years ago, in 1980, they accounted for 47 per cent. A quick glance at government consumer expenditure figures will indicate why – things like housing, health care, motoring, communications, meals out and recreation are all growing at a faster rate than retail sales. Within the retail sector, clothing sales are especially weak. From 7.7 per cent of UK household expenditure in 1980, clothing and footwear sales have dropped to 5.3 per cent in 2003. This is a reflection of a number of factors from both the demand side, such as an ageing population with saturated needs and having to save money to finance other purchases, and the supply side, most especially falling prices for textile goods.

It is true to say that by the end of the twentieth century the UK fashion retail sector looked pretty sick. It was dominated by bloated, mature businesses with traditional cultures and values. The sector had endured twenty years of the progressive displacement of 'merchant' skills by cost-saving IT solutions with a consequent lack of investment in human resources. First-mover advantage from its relatively early development and sector concentration had afforded it temporary protection from global competition. Ownership of freeholds and long leaseholds supported high prices and margins. The growth of multi-brand conglomerates like UDS, Sears, Storehouse and Fascia (all subsequently broken up), the rapid growth of new identikit shopping centres and the spread of sourcing strategies, interior design schemes and other management skills among the main players all encouraged a convergence among fashion brands that were intended to be distinct. The consequence for the fashion shopper was a retail experience that was too expensive, too uninspired and too much like hard work – and too often ended in failure.

As if this was not enough, technology in the form of the internet has produced a new 'route to market' for fashion brands which, despite initial misgivings, is estimated to have generated fast-growing sales of £1 billion of clothing and footwear in the UK in 2004.

Against this backdrop, most shops, and especially those selling fashion, have had to rediscover their purpose for the new century. Some, such as Allders or C&A no longer exist, having faced the consequences of failing to do so. Others, such as Selfridges, Top Shop and Burberry, have emerged from the process re-invigorated. Some additional opportunities for fashion retailers to provide added-value are displayed below.

New roles for fashion shops

Shops can:
- be a centre for enjoyment and entertainment
- provide therapy and enhance personal well-being
- showcase brands and build consumer awareness and loyalty
- allow customers to interact with brands and give feedback
- provide a trial and service facility for products.

For a fuller discussion of the retail 'Concept Cube' model for contemporary shop concepts see Webb (2001). These roles are heavily dependent on human relationships and skills. They lie at the heart of any strategy to build brand loyalty through retail stores. Shops are expensive and inflexible assets for a business to operate, and without the development of these skills it is doubtful whether the current provision of retail selling space will be sustainable in the long term. This chapter will explore the main characteristics and trends of the UK retail market in more detail, but it begins with a brief look at the historical background.

Historical perspectives

The earliest beginnings of organised commercial distribution of clothing can be traced back to the mediaeval livery companies such as the Merchant Taylors, cloth-workers and skinners who organised and regulated trade as early as the fourteenth century. Craftsmen and itinerant hawkers gradually took to stabilising their business through selling from small shops specialising in their own wares – clothiers, hatters, shoemakers, drapers and so forth. Elizabethan London, and other major cities, were characterised by a wealth of such outlets, as well as regular fairs and markets. Old prints of London show, for example, the original London Bridge covered end to end in shops and houses. The first organised market was Inigo Jones's Piazza (later to become Covent Garden), opened in 1631 (Dennis *et al.* 2005). Much of this infrastructure in the capital was swept away by the Great Fire in 1666. Shopping provision speeded up rapidly during the elegant regency period, with the Burlington Arcade opening in 1818 and early department-store companies having their origins during this time. The growth of the middle classes, improved transportation, better building materials and international product sourcing all fuelled the growth of department stores in the nineteenth century. Harrods, Whiteleys, John Lewis, Debenhams, Kendal Milne and Bainbridges are some of the many stores whose origins date back to the 1830–70 period (Adburgham 1989). Emile Zola's famous novel *Au Bonheur des Dames* (Ladies' Paradise), still a classic of department-store vision, appeared in 1883 based on the famous Parisian store Au Bon Marché, which had opened in 1852.

At the end of the nineteenth century the famous brands that characterise today's high streets and shopping centres began to emerge. Examples include Marks & Spencer, opened as a market stall in Leeds in 1884, and Jaeger (1883). The larger mail-order companies such as GUS also date from around 1900. After the end of the Second World War, demand for civilian wear, and especially for affordable suits for job interviews from returning demobbed soldiers, fuelled the rapid growth of companies like Montague Burton, Jackson the Tailor, John Collier, Irvine Sellars, Hepworth and Alexandre – mostly based in the textiles heartland of Yorkshire, but with rapidly growing national networks of stores. Other chains such as Saxone, Manfield, Lilly & Skinner and Freeman, Hardy & Willis sold shoes, while still more began to cater for the growing demands of the female consumer (Richard Shops, Van Allen, Bambers, Peter Robinson, Paige, Martin Ford, Werff). A growing number of retail entrepreneurs like Sir Charles Clore (Sears), Sir Isaac Wolfson (GUS) and Murray Gordon (Combined English Stores) built significant retail empires by combining and developing these chains. Sadly, the majority of these businesses and brands no longer exist.

The large and significant 'baby-boomer' generation consisting of those born between 1945 and 1964 first made its presence felt in supporting the growth of brands such as Mothercare. By the early 1960s they were buying Beatles, and Rolling Stones' records and shopping in new so-called 'boutiques' like Snob, Bus Stop, Top Shop, Chelsea Girl, Jean Machine, Lord John and Biba. The King's Road was a confrontation zone for 'Mods' and 'Rockers', each with their own dress code. Harrods opened its famous Way-In department in 1967. This generation continued to influence the retail fashion scene as its members grew older. By 1981 10.6 million women were working in the UK. The same year J. Hepworth acquired the ailing Kendal's ladies' rainwear chain, re-launching it the following year amid a blaze of publicity as Next, closely modelled on the growing US career womenswear chains such as Ann Taylor and Paul Harris.

The first UK shopping centre proper is thought to have been the original Bullring in Birmingham, opened in 1964. This was notably followed by Brent Cross in 1976 and a proliferation of 'Arndales' throughout the 1970s. Growing car ownership and a better road network spurred the growth of ever-bigger out-of-town shopping centres, with regional shopping centres of over 1 million square feet opening in Merry Hill (Dudley – West Midlands) in 1984, Gateshead (Metro Centre – enlarged in 2004 to make it the largest UK shopping centre) in 1986, and Lakeside, Thurrock, and Meadowhall, Sheffield, in 1990. The development of these vast regional shopping malls culminated with the opening of the 1.4 million square foot Bluewater, south east of London in 1999. This centre has 3 department stores and some 360, mostly fashion, specialist stores from around the world. The rise of the shopping centre put pressure on traditional high streets, and especially on high-cost department stores with poor facilities and no parking. In London, once-famous names like Whiteleys, Daniel Neal, Marshall & Snelgrove, Swan & Edgar and Bourne and Hollingsworth were converted to shopping centres or put to new uses. Around the country, the largest groups, Debenhams, House of Fraser and the John Lewis Partnership, swallowed up the best local stores, such as Browns of Chester and Corders of Norwich.

Towards the end of the twentieth century changing public policy and consumer demand patterns have worked in favour of new types of shopping centre, notably 'factory outlet' centres selling famous brands and city-centre schemes to encourage urban renewal. Examples of the former include Bicester Village, near Oxford, and Gunwharf Quays in Portsmouth, and, of the latter, The Oracle in Reading and Festival Place in Basingstoke.

Another important trend which should be noted is the rise in 'corporate' discounters and low-price stores. Previously inexpensive clothing was of poor quality and was sold in unattractive environments such as street markets. Companies like Primark, Peacocks, Matalan and TK Maxx revolutionised this. Supermarkets are also of growing importance. In fact, Carrefour and Tesco had attempted to build a UK clothing business in the 1970s but failed due to the poor quality of the real estate, unsuitable corporate brand positioning and lack of supply-chain skills. Having developed the high-margin home-meal replacement market and seen it mature, they have now turned back to clothing as a means of securing growth in sales and profits. ASDA, with the George brand, has led the way, closely followed by Tesco with Florence & Fred and Cherokee, and more recently Sainsbury with Tu. Finally, the growing importance of sport stores such as JJB and Sports Soccer in clothing and footwear sales should be noted. Changing market shares are illustrated in Table 6.2.

The last thirty years has seen successive waves of attempted retail brand-building in the fashion sector. However, apart from the corporate mono-brands like Burberry, Next, GAP and Zara, there is little evidence that today's crop of range brands, such as per una, Linea, Tu and Universal, have much more meaning or staying power than their 1980s' equivalents – Prova, Keynote, Just-In, Top Notch, Lifestyle, Expressions and the rest. Possibly George (ASDA), Trader (Debenhams) and a handful of others will prove to be exceptions, given sufficient investment on the part of their owners.

As the sections which follow show, the last twenty-five years have seen a number of significant trends in fashion retailing. Overall, the number of retail outlets continues to decline as independents and unprofitable branches of chain stores close. In UK retailing overall, around 25,000 shops close each year, but some 20,000 new ones open. This 'churn' continues to produce a healthy influx of new home-grown fashion retail entrepreneurs, as well as an increasing number of foreign businesses. The 2005 *Sunday Times* 'Rich List' shows 20 individuals who have accumulated fortunes of £90 million or more from the fashion industry. The list is headed by Philip Green (Arcadia/Bhs) but includes other notables such as Tom Singh (New Look), Stephen Marks (French Connection), Peter Simon (Monsoon), and Sir Paul Smith and John Robinson (Jigsaw). However, overall concentration is increasing, with a higher share of sales in the hands of a smaller number of firms. The market is polarising between price-driven brands and stores and those offering some added-value benefit. Many of the 1980s' and 1990s' brands have struggled to resonate with a new generation and have closed, been sold or at least lost market share and profitability. Examples include Laura Ashley, Benetton, Richards, Fosters, Horne Bros, Wrygges, Pilot and Etam. Consolidation has been especially pronounced in the department-store sector, with major chains such as Lewis's, Owen Owen and Allders being broken up and House of Fraser being forced to close Dickins and Jones and Barkers, as well as some smaller unprofitable stores. Many famous independent stores such as Goldbergs (Glasgow), Jenners (Edinburgh), David Morgan (Cardiff), Clements (Watford), Keddies (Southend) and Hanningtons (Brighton) have also been sold or closed.

Where fashion is sold

It is apparent that clothing and footwear is sold from a large and growing selection of store formats. A format describes a type of store with a common set of operating characteristics, or 'retail mix'. Hasty and Reardon (1997) identify these as:

- store size and location;
- exterior design;
- interior design and layout;
- visual merchandising;
- merchandise assortment;
- price positioning;
- personal or other method of selling;
- shopper services; and
- advertising and promotion.

Surprisingly, there are no internationally agreed definitions of these store types, although trade organisations like the International Association of Department Stores and Nielsen have developed their own, which are in common usage. The main retail formats relevant to the fashion sector are described in Table 6.1.

Table 6.1 Retail formats for clothing and footwear

Format	Description	Example
Department store	Large store, on more than one floor, selling at least four product groups, including clothing	Selfridges
Variety store	Smaller version, possibly on one floor	Bhs
Hypermarket	Low-priced food-based store with at least 25,000 sq.ft.[a] of selling space and parking	Tesco Extra
Retail warehouse	Large out-of-town 'box' store	Mothercare World
Specialty store	High-street or shopping centre unit specialising in one product sector	Dorothy Perkins
Lifestyle store	As above, with several product sectors	Urban Outfitters
Boutique	Eclectic fashion store, usually an 'independent' with intimate atmosphere and high service	The Cross
Concession	Leased selling area within a larger store	Alexon
Low-price store	Store selling continuous ranges at permanently low prices	Peacocks
Off-price store	Store selling opportunist lines of branded products at discount prices	TK Maxx
Factory outlet	Manufacturer's stores selling at lower prices	Bicester Village
Membership club	Store reserved to cardholders	Matalan
Catalogue showroom	Store where products are selected from a catalogue and retrieved from a stockroom	Argos
Duty/tax free	Selling at discount prices at travel termini	Duty Free Shoppers
Charity shop	Store run on behalf of a charity, usually selling second-hand clothes	OXFAM Originals
Market stall	Stall in a street or indoor market	Portobello Road
Car boot fair	Stand in a temporary fair for new and used merchandise	Blackbushe Sunday Market
Party plan	Means of selling in customers' homes using agents	Ann Summers
Mail order	Selling from catalogues or smaller 'specialogues'	Cotton Traders
Direct selling	Selling via agents at an office or hotel, selling 'off the page' or by inserts	Oxendales
Internet	Selling via websites	www.figleaves.com
DRTV	Selling via interactive TV	QVC

Note

a MK stores of 25,000–50,000 sq.ft. are classed as 'superstores'.

Although not strictly a separate format, the trend towards selling clothing at leisure and health venues such as sports grounds, fitness clubs, theme parks, art galleries, railway stations, historic buildings, hospitals, outdoor events and pop concerts should also be noted.

The market share accounted for by each format has altered rapidly over the years as innovation has led to new types of retailer with advantages of added consumer appeal or operating-cost productivity. Changing consumer demographics and lifestyles and a constantly changing trading environment in terms of government regulation, available finance, competition, infrastructure development and other factors has fuelled, and speeded up, this process of change. Independent specialist stores, which still dominate much of Southern Europe, accounted for 60 per cent of the UK clothing and footwear market in 1960, but by 1977 this had fallen to 29 per cent to only 10.5 per cent in 2004. According to Verdict (Anon 2, 2004) the share of total UK retail space accounted for by the high street has fallen from 74 per cent in 1980 to 55 per cent in 2004. Table 6.2 highlights change in recent years.

Table 6.2 Share (% value) of UK clothing and footwear market

Format	1985	1996	2000	2004
Multiples	22.7	30.8	29.0	30.3
Independents	19.0	13.1	11.8	10.5
Variety stores	21.5	19.6	17.1	15.1
Department stores	9.7	8.6	8.9	8.2
Mail order	10.1	9.4	8.5	6.5
Discount	3.1	3.9	7.4	9.8
Supermarkets	3.0	2.7	3.6	5.5
Sports ⎫		5.8	9.2	10.4
Other ⎭	10.9	6.1	4.7	3.7

Sources: Textile Market Studies; TNS Fashion Trak.

The evolution of fashion retailing

As can be seen, the retailing sector is in a constant state of flux. Much research and investigation has been dedicated over the years to exploring the patterns and causes of retail change, in an attempt to explain the forces at work. One of the first to explore this was Malcolm McNair who, in 1958 produced his 'Wheel of Retailing' model. This essentially argued that new retail format innovations depended on a superior business model to offer consumers better value, but over time they inevitably become more sophisticated until their additional cost base makes them uncompetitive and they become vulnerable to a new innovative format. In 1966, Stanley Hollander showed how these movements follow a cyclical pattern and produced his 'Accordion Theory' of retail fluctuation. Ten years later, in a seminal article in the *Harvard Business Review*, Bill Davidson and his colleagues described how retail-store formats actually follow a 'lifecycle curve' similar to that of the new product lifecycle, from 'introduction', through 'rapid growth', 'steady growth' and 'maturity' to eventual 'decline'. He further proposed that profitability would decline before sales, and market share would fall as a result of competitive pressure on pricing and increased advertising costs, and also that all concepts would eventually disappear, just as the counter-service shop and most catalogue showrooms have done (see Figure 6.1). He later modified this by suggesting that businesses could engineer a 'lifecycle extension' by creating new retail propositions and design concepts within the retail format – as, for example, Selfridges has done over the period 1994–2004.

These theories have been criticised for being more relevant to the mass-merchandise sector than for the fashion industry. Yet examination of the swings in market share and the demise in the UK of thousands of independent retailers and businesses like C&A and Allders, or the 1960s' boutiques like Biba, Bus Stop and Snob, suggests that there are strategic and structural forces at work dictating the shape of the fashion retail sector. Retail specialist Management Horizons has suggested that it is perhaps not the format alone which counts but the best-practice management competence of each firm. It believes that formats do decline but that a residual number of the very best firms can continue to exist, serving a specialised market, and this explains the growing diversity of global fashion retailing.

The notion of retail core competence surfaces again in the attempts by certain experts to adapt Porter's notions of competitive advantage to the retail sector. Ander and Stern (2004) put forward the 'Est' model (Figure 6.2), which suggests that retailers with limited resources must focus on being the 'best' at some dimension of

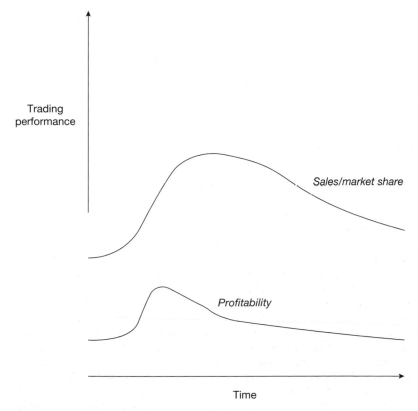

Figure 6.1 The retail format lifecycle

Source: Davidson, Bates and Bass (1976).

consumer demand – and that this falls into four main areas: price; assortment choice; excitement and experience; and convenience (which has several dimensions). Retailers not following this strategy are doomed to fall into the black hole and disappear – a fate not unfamiliar to historical fashion brands on both sides of the Atlantic.

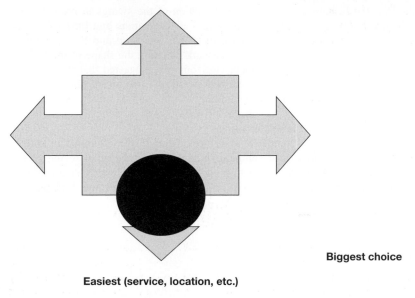

Biggest choice

Easiest (service, location, etc.)

Figure 6.2 The retail 'Est' model
Source: Ander and Stern (2004).

The UK retail fashion market today

There are many estimates of the size and structure of the UK retail fashion market. In some areas, such as the second hand and vintage market, and e-commerce, the statistics are, to say the least, not very robust. Those interested should be careful to triangulate figures from various sources, always checking definitions carefully. Possible sources include various government data from the CSO and VAT authorities, survey data from the industry specialists TNS Fashion Trak, market research data from Mintel, Verdict and others, and company data from the organisations themselves or from Companies' House. Areas of potential pitfall include:

- Geographical coverage: e.g., Fashion Trak excludes Northern Ireland (2–3%).
- Age coverage: Fashion Trak excludes those aged 75 and above.
- Residence: are we talking about UK citizens or UK retail? It is hard to estimate inward and outward international spend, especially on the internet. Tourists are important for some markets, such as cashmere knitwear.
- Does the data refer to retail shops only or total sales including direct marketing?
- What products are included? The inclusion of sports, accessories, beauty products, home 'fashion', etc. can distort some data.
- Selling value – VAT: inclusive or exclusive?

- Timing: estimates based on production and trade data ignore periods of stock holding. Company financial-year ends seldom match the calendar year.
- Mark-downs: some survey data record full prices.
- 'Halo' effect: some survey data over-estimates the sales of well-known brands and inflates the price actually paid.

Table 6.3 shows trends in the value of the UK clothing and footwear market by sector drawn from customer shopping research.

Table 6.3 Value trends (£ millions) in UK clothing and footwear market

Sector	1970	1985	2000	2004
Womenswear	1,249	6,061	12,008	13,839
Menswear	912	4,450	6,644	7,328
Childrenswear	247	1,481	3,232	3,635
Footwear	454	2,573	4,432	5,154
Total	2,862	14,565	26,316	29,956

Sources: Textile Market Studies (1970, 1985) and TNS Fashion Trak (2000, 2004).

Clothing is a product group that lends itself quite well to purchasing on behalf of someone else, so that the customer and the consumer are not always the same. Most childrenswear is bought by adults, but 10 per cent of womenswear is purchased by men and 25 per cent of menswear by women – very much more in some product categories (Fashion Trak 2004). Another factor to note is the seasonality of purchasing, with the peak month of December accounting for some 17 per cent of annual sales whereas February and March average only 6–7 per cent of monthly sales.

It is interesting to examine the impact that demographic and lifestyle changes have had on the structure of the UK fashion market. Table 6.4 shows an analysis of spending by age category over the past twenty years. The growth of the older, so-called 'grey' market represented by the ageing baby boom generation is clearly evident, as is the decline of the teenage market resulting from lower birth-rates and competing spending priorities.

Table 6.4 Age trends (% value) in the UK clothing and footwear market

Age cohort	Womenswear	Womenswear	Menswear	Menswear
	1985	2004	1985	2004
15–19	13.8	8.2	17.1	6.9
20–24	14.5	8.8	16.5	10.0
25–34	18.4	13.7	22.5	19.1
35–44	17.6	19.8	16.8	20.7
45–54	15.2	20.1	12.5	21.2
55–74	20.6	29.4	14.6	22.1
Total	100.1	100.0	100.0	100.0

Sources: Textile Market Studies (1985) and TNS Fashion Trak (2004).

Table 6.5 shows how the sector format trends have evolved over the past twenty years by major product category.

Table 6.5 Distribution trends (% value) in the UK clothing market

Format	Womenswear		Menswear		Childrenswear	
	1985	2004	1985	2004	1985	2004
Variety stores	22.6	18.8	19.1	14.4	24.3	12.7
Multiples	19.7	32.8	27.4	24.2	21.5	25.9
Department stores	12.0	9.1	7.7	10.0	5.6	4.8
Independents	17.9	9.2	22.5	14.3	13.8	6.3
Mail order	12.3	7.9	7.5	4.9	8.5	4.3
Supermarkets	3.1	5.2	2.1	4.6	5.3	14.4
Discount stores	2.5	10.3	3.8	10.8	3.5	13.9
Markets	5.4	0.9	4.8	1.4	10.0	1.2
Sports/other	4.5	5.8	5.1	15.4	7.5	16.5
Total	100.0	100.0	100.0	100.0	100.0	100.0

Sources: Textile Market Studies (1985); TNS Fashion Trak (2004).

While most market analysis is traditionally made in terms of market value, it is sometimes useful to look at the units sold. It was widely reported in 2004 that ASDA had overtaken M&S to become the UK's biggest clothing seller. What was not always made clear was that this was in terms of total garments sold, of whatever type, over a rather short period. Nonetheless, each unit transaction represents a shopper 'vote' for that retailer or format, and Table 6.6 shows just how many 'votes' the discount and supermarket sector is getting compared with traditional methods of clothing distribution. Approximately 40 per cent of garments are purchased in price-focused retail formats – discount/low-priced stores of various types and super/hypermarkets. Additionally, about a quarter of all garments sold are bought at reduced or sale prices, representing over 30 per cent of the value of the market. With price being a key factor in around two-thirds of transactions in the UK, clothing and footwear can be considered a commodity for most consumers.

Table 6.6 Volume distribution in the UK clothing and footwear market 2004

Format	Womenswear	Menswear	Childrenswear	Footwear
Variety stores	18.4	15.0	14.2	7.2
Multiples	19.8	13.3	18.8	37.1
Department stores	5.2	5.6	2.8	3.4
Independents	4.3	6.0	3.1	10.1
Mail order	5.3	3.5	2.6	5.8
Supermarkets	17.4	15.2	25.4	7.0
Discount stores	21.8	24.3	23.8	7.9
Sports shops	2.0	10.3	5.8	17.5
Markets	2.0	4.6	1.3	1.9
Other	3.8	2.2	2.2	2.1
Total	100.0	100.0	100.0	100.0

Source: TNS Fashion Trak.

Fashion retail organisations

Organisation selling fashion can be examined according to their corporate structure, which is, in turn, a major factor contributing to their business strategies and operational tactics. Some types of store tend to be operated by some types of organisation, but the two approaches to retail classification do not entirely overlap. The alternative forms of legal and commercial organisation are shown in Table 6.7.

Table 6.7 Types of retail organisation

Organisation type	Description	Examples
Public limited company	Company with a stockmarket listing, giving it access to funds, better credit rating and market valuation	Tesco Next French Connection
Limited company	Business where the owners'/managers' liability for debts does not extend to their personal assets	Harrods Arcadia
Subsidiary company	Company belonging to a larger parent company, sometimes overseas	Top Shop Zara (UK)
Sole trader	Independent company privately owned by an individual	Many independents
Partnership	Business owned by two or more owners or 'partners'	John Lewis Partnership
Cooperative	Business owned by its customers	Co-op
Franchise	Independent business operating a trading formula 'leased' from a parent company	Benetton Kookai
Buying group	Organisation carrying out wholesale and brand building functions for member retailers	Associated independent stores

Recent times have seen significant changes in the market share of different types of organisation. The 1980s and 1990s saw a large number of retailers seek share listings as their owners tried to fund expansion or establish valuations to assist their exit strategies. However, since 1999 some 40 per cent of the UK fashion retail sector has been taken private; the businesses involved include Arcadia, Rubicon, Bhs, New Look, Selfridges, Debenhams, Bentalls, Oasis and Harvey Nichols. The city stands accused of not being sympathetic to the special cyclical nature of the fashion business. Retailers have generally felt that the stockmarket has valued their businesses too low, considering their property assets the only secure basis and making insufficient allowance for trading profits. This has made them vulnerable to acquisition and distracted management attention. Furthermore management has found the new transparency and the frequent detailed reporting expectations for public companies both onerous and unhelpful to the strategic management of a cyclical and volatile business.

A second trend is the gradual increase in franchising in the UK fashion sector, largely thanks to the growth of foreign-owned brands from Southern Europe where franchising is much more prevalent. Benetton and Stefanel from Italy were early pioneers, but they have now been joined by many others, including Kookai, Morgan and Mango. This is gradually building up a pool of franchise expertise in the UK. Research by Doherty (2000) has suggested that franchising is actually the most effective form of retail fashion internationalisation.

On the other hand, the number of independent fashion stores continues to decline. From nearly 60,000 in 1971 (the date of the last official Census of Distribution) the number has fallen to little more than 30,000 today. Precise figures are hard to obtain, the most useful being those from the VAT authorities. Increasingly, big brands are reluctant to supply the independent sector as order quantities are often uneconomic and brand values are not always maintained at the point of sale. The stores themselves find it hard to compete with corporate business for expensive shop rentals and staff, and to acquire state-of-the-art technology and management skills. Yet the independent sector has recently gained market share in menswear and is increasingly valued for its creativity and originality. New generations of fashion entrepreneurs, many from the immigrant community, are injecting fresh energy into fashion retailing and can be expected to flourish as more consumers seek customised and individualised apparel.

Fashion retail operation

Operating an independent retail shop requires the owner to perform all the management tasks of a larger business, or to use family and staff to do so. These will include planning, buying, merchandising, running the finances and promoting the business, as well as the more shop-based tasks of property management, sales management and staff management. However, for most corporate retailers these functions are carried out centrally, leaving the shop management with responsibility only for local issues. The extent of this responsibility depends on the nature of the shop's relationship with head office – a franchisee, for example, has much more responsibility than a branch store manager – and the management culture of each specific organisation. Zara, for example, allows its shop management much more influence on staff recruitment and tailoring ranges to match local demand than do most UK companies, which give more importance to brand integrity and centralised control. Larger fashion chains will usually have an operations director on their board, who is in effect the 'Sales Director' responsible for generating the maximum turnover and branch operating profit margin. Sometimes he or she will have responsibility for training, although this can fall within the remit of, or be shared with, the human resources department. Similarly, his or her department will be responsible for the maintenance of good standards in all the company's outlet, but the actual selection and negotiation of new sites will usually be carried out by the company's property department, which may also handle shop-fitting, and thus impact the brand design concept. More often, store design will fall within the remit of the head of marketing, or even the chief executive, and marketing will certainly have a say in window display promotions to tie in with other brand communications. In practice, many of these tasks will be steered by meetings or committees with members drawn from different skill disciplines.

For the independent fashion retailer, deciding where to open a new store is perhaps the most important decision he or she will make. There are two distinct aspects to this process. First, the retailer must select the preferred location. This refers to the shopper catchment market, and can be an area (the Peak District), a town (Bromley) or a district within an urban agglomeration (Covent Garden). The next step is for the retailer to find an appropriate and affordable site of suitable size, which can be in a high-street shop (26 Floral Street) or shopping centre (Unit 17, The Glades Centre, Bromley), or even an out-of-town retail park (The Fort, Birmingham). The optimum store size for any retailer will depend on many factors, including the product range and market positioning, and the local market size and strength of competition. Historically, retailers trusted to site visits, observation and 'counting chimney pots' to identify sites for new stores. These days there is a wealth of affordable and easily accessible data from government census websites and commercial organisations like Experian or CACI which enable retailers to base these decisions on detailed analyses of local resident and shopping populations, competitors and infrastructure. Collectively, these data sources are termed geographic information systems (GIS) and their use enables retailers to employ techniques such as multiple regression analysis and gravity modelling to perfect siting decisions – although few companies in the fashion sector are as yet making full use of these skills. It is fair to say that siting a new fashion store is a less precise skill than is siting a new supermarket, as the ebb and flow of consumer fashion destination preference dictates that statistical data must always be combined with judgement based on specific shopping behaviour research, site visits and audits. It has been said that the most important technique for the head office manager of a fashion company is MBWA – Management By Walking About!

Once a suitable site has been found the retailer must be prepared to negotiate hard and knowledgeably for a lease. This means commissioning a professional survey, checking planning consents, calculating the amount of window frontage and prime ('Zone A') retail space available, measuring shopper footfall on different days and times, identifying the amount and basis of rent, business rates and services charges, and negotiating the maximum rent-free period and contribution to fitting-out costs, where appropriate. It is also advisable to check on why the previous tenant left the property and on any new retail developments planned for the market which may have an impact on future shopping patterns. Each retailer will have his or her own trading model which will suggest the turnover potential of a site, likely achieved gross margins, service levels and staff costs, and other operating costs. From this he or she will be able to estimate what level of occupancy and 'fit-out' cost are affordable and will still make the target ROI.

Once a new site has been secured the retailer, of whichever trading format, will need to apply his or her own design concept to the store. This will consist of, first, the aesthetic concept which will give the store a unique identity, atmosphere and personality created by the choice of colours, graphics, lighting, finishes, music and design 'handwriting'. Second, there will be the operational design, consisting of decisions about layout principles, space use and allocation to product categories, shopper circulation – sometimes on more than one floor – sight lines and visual access, window display and visual merchandising, payment processes, the provision of fitting rooms and other services, and security measures to prevent theft (Varley 2001).

Having a distinctive positioning in the market is key to success. Keeping a finger on the pulse of local markets and competitors throughout the country is one of the tasks of a retailer's operations team. Larger chains will have an organisational structure consisting of 3–6 regional managers covering the main regions of the UK

(Scotland, the north, the south east etc.), who will be largely head office-based and act as a conduit between the board and the network of area managers, each of whom typically has responsibility for 10–15 stores. Area managers are continually on the road visiting their outlets to ensure that targets are met, the staffing levels and performance maintained, the stock levels appropriate, the housekeeping standards high, day-to-day problems dealt with, and feedback regularly provided to head office.

The store itself will almost always be headed up by a manager, although at any one time a chain can expect to have several stores without a manager due to vacancies, maternity leave, holidays, etc. This means that there will also be one or more deputy manager whose role it is to stand in for the manager when necessary – if only on his or her lunch break! One of the important tasks of the manager is to agree with the area manager the best level of staffing to reflect fluctuations in shopper footfall according to time of day, day of week and season. Optimising costs in this way can make or break the profitability of a store. So the staff team is usually (in the UK, where legislation permits it) made up of a varied mix of full-timers, part-timers and Saturday staff. Additionally, key employees may be given a 'second-skill' accreditation in such tasks as visual merchandising or cash handling. Together, this gives an opportunity for new staff joining a fashion retail business to follow a career progression in terms of responsibility and remuneration.

Fashion retail performance measurement

It is customary to assess a retail shop's sales against measures such as the annual or seasonal budget, last year's sales or the sales of other stores in the company. However, these offer only a limited evaluation of how the shop is actually performing. Table 6.8 shows some of the other measurements data that fashion retailers find useful. Some are relatively easy to gather, while others require specialist measuring equipment or market research. In practice, resources for running a fashion store are always limited, so it will not be possible to maximise performance across all criteria. Each retailer will need to focus on those benchmarks which best support its positioning and business model, and accept that there will be a negative 'trade-off' impact elsewhere. For example, George at ASDA can buy volume market share at the expense of lower margins; Primark can reduce staff costs at the expense of inferior customer service; Zara can increase stock turnover at the expense of failing to satisfy every customer in terms of colour or size; and Matalan can cut back on occupancy costs at the expense of reduced footfall and impulse purchases.

Fashion retail performance on any of these criteria varies considerably. Next and Monsoon, for example, achieve sales per square foot of around or above £700 per year whereas Etam's and Peacock's is nearer to £200 – with the other main high street names somewhere in between. Many ratios can be calculated from published accounts, although information is not always in the public domain. Definitions also vary – do sales include or exclude VAT, does the selling area include or exclude space given to window displays, cash points, fitting rooms and stairways? It is especially important to be critical of published so-called 'like-for-like' trading data where retailers purport to give comparable financial information. In fact, stores in the same town may have changed site or been enlarged; stores may have been opened only for part of the trading period, and that period may have had a different number of trading days from other periods. A number of respected research groups publish annual analyses of UK retail performance, notably Mintel's *UK Retail Rankings*, to which the reader is directed.

Table 6.8 Measuring fashion shop performance

Type of measurement	Measurement	Definition
Financial measures	Turnover	Sales, including or excluding VAT for any given period
	Gross margin	Net sales less cost of sales, after reductions for markdowns, theft, discounts and stock loss
	Store contribution	Gross margin less store operating costs
	Return on capital employed	Contribution as a percentage of investment in stock and equipment
	Return on increased investment (ROII)	Additional contribution resulting from extra investment in store refit, etc.
	Cash flow	Statement of net excess of periodic income over outgoings
Customer measures	Market share	Share of local market spending, by customer group, product category, period, etc.
	Awareness	Percentage of target customers aware of the shop
	Footfall	Number of customers entering the store
	Conversion rate	Percentage of visitors who purchase
	Walk-out rate	Percentage who leave with nothing
	Average transaction value	Average value of each sale made
	Multiple purchasing	Percentage of shoppers buying linked items
	Visit frequency	Elapsed time between visits to shop
	Loyalty	Your share of periodic fashion shop visits
	Advocacy rate	Customer recommendation measure
Productivity measures	Sales/profit per sq.ft. or sq. mt.	Performance related to floor space
	Sales/profit per linear foot or metre	Performance related to display space
	Sales/profit per employee	Performance related to staff level, usually expressed as FTE full-time equivalent)
	Stock turnover	How many times average stock is sold in a financial year
	Sell-down rate	Speed at which a given line sells in store
	Take-up rate	Percent of customers purchasing a promotion

Major UK fashion retailers

Details of retailers of clothing and footwear in the UK can be easily obtained from any one of a number of published annual surveys, online research or the companies' own annual reports or websites. Companies' House, or online resources such as Fame or ukbusinesspark will provide information on private businesses. This section identifies the main companies, together with recent sales and number of stores, and highlights the main changes taking place. Many general and lifestyle retailers do not break down their clothing and footwear sales from overall turnover, so that it is necessary to make estimates based on survey or other information.

Table 6.9 Top 10 UK clothing and footwear retailers

	1988	1995[a]	2005[a]
1	M&S	M&S	M&S
2	Littlewoods	Arcadia	Arcadia/Bhs
3	Sears	Debenhams	Next
4	Burton Group	C&A	ASDA
5	Storehouse Group	Next	Debenhams
6	GUS	Sears	Matalan
7	Next	Bhs	New Look
8	C&A	Littlewoods	Primark
9	Laura Ashley	John Lewis	JJB
10	River Island	House of Fraser	TK Maxx

Note
a Store-based retailers only – GUS would otherwise appear in 1995 and Littlewoods in 2005.

Source: Deutsche Bank and the author.

Many of the names remain constant although market shares have often changed radically. In 1998 M&S accounted for a market share of over 13 per cent and made profits of £1.2 billion. By 2004 profits had halved and market share fallen to 10.7 per cent. Next on the other hand saw its market share grow from 3.1 per cent to 5.9 per cent over the same period. Other big winners in recent years have been in the low-price sector – ASDA, Matalan, Primark and TK Maxx. Market share in the middle-market has declined, but there have been winners and losers as restructuring has taken place among many of the businesses – GUS, Littlewoods, C&A and Sears/Burton/Arcadia/Storehouse in their various manifestations.

Restructuring has also taken place among the more fashion-forward chains in the second tier, with the Iceland-controlled Mosaic putting together a group with annual sales in excess of £0.5 billion. Many businesses with high-profile brands, such as French Connection, Ted Baker, Hobbs, L. K. Bennett and Monsoon, are influential in terms of the innovation they bring to UK fashion shopping but relatively unimportant in terms of volume sales or market share.

Table 6.10 identifies the major UK fashion retail brands by sector.

Table 6.10 UK fashion retailers by number of outlets 2004

Womenswear	Menswear	Mixed	Department stores and childrenswear	Concessions	Accessories
Dorothy Perkins (541)	Burton (386)	Peacocks (405)	Woolworth (788)	Planet (221)	Claires (409)
New Look (522)	Top Man (156)	Next (335)	Adams (490)	Windsmoor (219)	Accessorize (190)
Bon Marché (304)	Officers Club (150)	Edinburgh Woollen (285)	M&S (270)	Precis Petit (205)	Tie Rack (124)
Evans (319)	Greenwoods (101)	Matalan (185)	Mothercare (235)	Principles (205)	Ann Summers (93)
Ethel Austin (251)	Jaeger Man (92)	Bevise (184)	Bhs (161)	Country Casuals (199)	La Senza (78)
Mackays (245)	Moss Bros (84)	River Island (184)	Debenhams (102)	Warehouse (179)	Sock Shop (71)
Select (219)	Suits You (58)	QS (182)	T. J. Hughes (37)	Viyella (170)	
Etam (198)	Envy (53)	Mk One (164)	John Lewis (21)	Alexon (152)	
Oasis (168)	Ciro Cittero (51)	TK Maxx (132)	House of Fraser (57)	Jumper (141)	
Monsoon (161)		GAP (123)		Dash (139)	
Laura Ashley (102)		Primark (80)		Ann Harvey (126)	
		French Connection (73)		Miss Selfridge (126)	

Source: *The Marketing Pocket Book* (2005).

Internationalisation

Although home-grown brands continue to dominate the UK fashion market, there are an increasing number of foreign clothing and footwear retailers in evidence. Research from the property experts Jones Lang LaSalle (O'Roarty 2003) suggest that nearly 40 per cent of all cross-border retail initiatives are by fashion companies, and that the UK has long been *the* desired destination. In terms of outbound investment, the UK, France, Italy and Germany each account for around 15 per cent of initiatives, with the latest figures showing German brands (where the home market is suffering a long-term retail recession) in first place, just ahead of British brands.

Exporting fashion retail brands to new markets is not a new phenomenon. Burberry opened a shop in Paris as long ago as 1909, and many UK brands had launched international operations before the Second World War. Another big wave of overseas endeavour took place in the mid-1970s to mid-1980s with brands like M&S, Jaeger, Mothercare, Dorothy Perkins, Principles, Laura Ashley, Austin Reed and the Sears Group being prominent.

At the same time it was possible to find Benetton, Stefanel, Galeries Lafayette, Jacardi, Fogal, Lindex, and many others, operating in the UK. Most of these ventures, both in-bound and out-bound, have now ceased, as fashion retailers have found it more difficult than they anticipated to operate their formats in new markets. This is a subject of extensive research, but it is generally agreed that retailers face a more difficult challenge than do manufacturers in exporting their businesses. Among the key reasons are:

- The retail proposition is more complex than a product proposition.
- International fashion markets can be distinctly different in terms of consumer demand, competition and market infrastructure.
- Brand positionings may not be appropriate to new markets, and dimensions of competitive advantage at home may not accrue abroad.
- Additional costs of operating abroad may disrupt companies' business models.
- Profit may accrue only in the long term, with short-term earnings' dilution, antagonised owners and a detrimental impact on home businesses.

M&S's recent withdrawal from its international operations has been well documented. Next, the UK's largest and most profitable specialist retail brand, has entered the world's major markets – the USA, Japan, Germany and France – with a conspicuous lack of success and, together with Arcadia's brands, now has a very limited international presence, mainly with franchise partners. There are of course exceptions. Burberry and Paul Smith perform well in international markets on the back of their contemporary British provenance. Signet is the market leader in jewellery in the USA, C&J Clark has significant international footwear sales, and both Debenhams and Harvey Nichols are opening department stores with international partners.

Yet times are changing. Newer companies with more flexible cultures and systems, and a willingness to invest serious resources, are finding ways to create global fashion retail brands. Stand in Oxford Circus – London's premier retail site – and you will hardly see a UK name. With the exception of Top Shop, the key retailers within 50 metres include H&M, Nike Town, Zara, Mango, Benetton, GAP, Esprit and Borders – mostly recently joined by Berska, Zara's highly successful teenage cousin. Table 6.11 shows the progress of four of the best known foreign entrants to the UK.

Table 6.11 Overseas fashion retailers in the UK

Company	Shops 1995	Shops 2000	Shops 2004	Sales 2004	Market share
GAP	52	129	142	293	1.1
H&M	15	47	88	499	1.8
Inditex (Zara)	0	7	41	159	0.6
Mango	0	7	19	33	0.1
Totals	67	190	290	984	3.6

Source: Deutsche Bank (2005).

Apart from direct operations, a growing number of UK fashion retailers have become acquisition targets for international businesses. Examples include Selfridges, Harvey Nichols, Aquascutum, Laura Ashley, the Mosaic Group and Brown & Jackson.

Direct marketing

As much as 10 per cent of the UK fashion clothing and footwear market has been in the hands of businesses not operating retail stores for most of the twentieth century. Traditionally this share was taken by so-called 'agency' mail-order catalogues such as Littlewoods or Grattans. The system operated through an extensive network of agents who were sent large seasonal catalogues of up to 1,000 pages and then sold from them to their workplace colleagues and networks of colleagues, friends and family. Orders were consolidated and returned to the catalogue company, which then delivered the items to the agent for onward distribution to the purchasers. The agent earned a commission for this work. Nearly all agents were women, and in the days when fewer women worked and those who did were often paid minimal wages, this income was a welcome supplement for the family. However, during the last twenty years several forces have worked against the agency mail-order operation: more women acquired better and higher paid jobs; changing employment and social patterns fragmented friends and family networks; agency catalogues became too large, expensive and inflexible for a fast and focused fashion world; and direct marketing technology made giant leaps forward.

The first result of this has been consolidation in the industry. Mail-order giants from Europe, La Redoute (Redcats) and Otto Versand, acquired Grattans, Empire Stores and Freemans and most recently Littlewoods has taken on the GUS businesses. J. D. Williams has taken over a number of smaller firms. Second, there as been a growth in more focused and frequent 'specialogues' which use computerised customer databases to target market segments, product categories and seasons. Internationally the most successful has been the US firm Lands End, which has a large UK operation, but there are hundreds of others including such names as Boden, Cotton Traders and Kaleidoscope. Many mainstream retailers such as French Connection derive extra sales from catalogues, as do organisations as diverse as charities (National Trust), newspapers (*The Times* and *Telegraph*), and museums and galleries.

Other forms of direct marketing which continue to take small shares are selling directly from newspapers and magazines, via at-home parties such as those held by Weekender or Ann Summers, and via interactive television (dominated by QVC in the UK). Recently, Arcadia has launched 'Top Shop To Go': a team of agents take a selection of clothing samples to busy customers' homes and offices where orders can be placed, a move which has won them the prestigious *Retail Week* 'Customer Service Initiative' award for 2005.

The third recent innovation, however, has had the most far-reaching impact on the distribution of retail goods and services, and that is the invention and, during the past ten years, the development of the internet. It is said that when President Clinton came to power, there were only eight websites in existence – now some 50,000 new sites are created each day. So this form of commerce has achieved in a decade what it took agency mail order a century to achieve, giving some credence to Bill Davidson's contention of ever-faster and shorter retail format lifecycles. The history of the internet to date has been well documented. In the first period (1995–98) it promised so much – the virtual elimination of those two great retail millstones, property and labour cost, precise customer targeting and research feedback, and speed and flexibility of operation. Speculative money poured into this new channel of distribution, and both traditional retailers and new 'pureplay' start-ups launched e-commerce sites on the internet. Although computer hardware and software, books and music, and financial and travel services led the way, clothing saw significant investment. In the UK two especially high-profile brands were Boo.com and Zoom.co.uk (the latter operated by Arcadia). The second period (1999–2001) was a different story. The problematic experience has been well recorded by Ernst Malmsten, founder of Boo.com in his book *Boo Hoo*:

- companies lacked the required management skills and resources, especially in customer service and order fulfilment;
- new customers proved much harder and more expensive to obtain than predicted;
- expenses ran out of control;
- brands lacked visibility and impact without a physical presence;
- customers were slow to purchase what they could not touch or try on, with consequent high rates of returns (up to 40 per cent is common); and
- there were doubts about insecure payment and fraud.

Even large global brands like GAP and Levi's pulled back from their intentions to operate UK transactional websites for fear of channel conflict and sales, cannibalisation, and the breakdown of 'Chinese walls' between international pricing strategies.

In summary, the internet proved to be neither the miraculous panacea for companies suffering from increasing competition in the physical marketplace nor the Eldorado that young visionaries and their rich but gullible financial backers had talked it up to be. However, neither was it a blind alley in terms of retail development. The best operators went through a rapid learning curve, embracing appropriate technology and marketing, judicious investment and hard work, and perseverance. At the same time UK computer household penetration has reached 50 per cent (20 per cent having broadband), with over 30 per cent of individuals having had online access for five years or more. Nearly 30 per cent of the population now shop regularly online. Familiarity in this case breeds acceptance, and shoppers have learned how to use the better designed sites available today; they trust the leading brands and use secure payment systems. According to e-commerce research experts IMRG, total UK e-commerce retail sales in 2004 reached £16 billion, an increase of 46 per cent over 2003. The key trading period of Christmas 2004 saw e-commerce sales rise by 23 per cent whereas store-based retail sales fell by more than 1 per cent in comparison with 2003. The Office of National Statistics (ONS) gives a figure of £39.6 billion for e-commerce sales in 2003, but this includes an unknown element of business-to-business sales. With e-commerce sales of over £0.5 billion, Tesco.com is recognised as a world leader in online retailing where shoppers can find its full clothing range, as well as groceries and housewares.

Estimates of clothing and footwear retail sales vary widely. Fashion Trak still does not pick up sufficient purchases to record them separately. Many sales have an international dimension, either of site or of shopper, and quite a few are for second-hand merchandise, especially from e-bay, by far the world's largest internet retailer; Zendor, the fulfilment arm of N. Brown, estimated them at £525 million in 2003, whereas IMRG put the 2004 figure at over £1 billion. ComScore gives a 2004 figure of £860 million. NOP estimates (June 2004) that 21 per cent of online purchases are of clothes, with an average transaction value of £98. Hitwise, which measures UK website 'hits', give Next a big lead in the fashion sector in 2004 with 25 per cent of all hits, followed by the mail-order company La Redoute with 13 per cent and River Island with 6 per cent.

Few of the larger firms release their e-commerce sales' figures. The major mail-order companies all achieve significant online sales now, as does Next where they are combined with its catalogues sales in its reporting. In the year ending January 2005 Next reported 'Directory' sales of £602 million, but the accompanying statement gave expectations of e-commerce sales in 'excess of £200 million' for 2005. Of the specialists, Boden achieves 25 per cent of its sales online, while ASOS, a fast-growing site which offers replicas of celebrity outfits, Bravissimo (larger sized lingerie), Figleaves (lingerie), Yoox (Italian luxury goods site) and Net-à-Porter (luxury brands) have all reported UK sales of £12–15 million each in 2003–4. Bravissimo has been in the *Sunday Times* 'Fast Track 100' for three consecutive years and has won three Drapers' awards for 'Best Lingerie Retailer'. Figleaves has also won an award for 'Best Lingerie Retailer' and now sells to 66 countries, including taking 3,500 orders in a single day in April 2004. Net-à-Porter has won overall 'Shop of the Year' at the 2004 British Fashion Awards, and, along with the other sites mentioned, has declared that it is now trading profitably in the UK.

This progress has been made as a result of internet retailers learning how to manage this new distribution channel more specifically and more effectively. Key issues which have been addressed include:

• integrating brand identity between online and other distribution channels and marketing;
• the professional management of customer databases and the effective use of targeted electronic marketing;
• improving site functionality and flexibility; Figleaves.com, for example, reveals ends of ranges only to those customers searching its site by size, thus reducing both mark-downs and shopper disappointment; Lands End and others are offering virtual changing rooms, 'shop with a friend' facilities, order tracking and other features;
• more dynamic sites which encourage repeated visits through the inclusion of editorial fashion comment, tie-ups with famous designers or brands, or support for charitable causes – Net-à-Porter is a recognised leader here;

- many sites such as shoetailor, Ic3D, eshirt and NikeID offer products customised to shoppers' own size or style preference;
- improved fulfilment, customer service and returns' provision. Direct-marketing businesses like Boden and Bravissimo are now opening stores to widen their customer base, improve brand visibility and facilitate customer service and returns.

Technological developments are expected to support the continued growth of e-commerce in the fashion sector. The extension of broadband to more homes speeds up the entire shopping process. Actually, IMRG believes that a quarter of all e-commerce in the UK will be executed using hand-held devices by 2009.

The fourth, and final, point to make about the implications of direct-marketing developments is the recognition of a new distribution strategy based on multiple channels. In the early days of the internet commentators feared for the future of physical stores, believing that e-commerce would erode their profit model. However, annual growth so far in the UK has been more or less accommodated within the overall growth of the market, and research by BizRate and others suggest that the internet has actually helped the customer become a more efficient shopper in terms of value for time, value for money and value for energy. In the US, something like a third of shoppers use at least two of the three mains methods of distribution – shops, catalogues and websites – to complete a purchase (Okamura 2001). Typically the process of researching information, short-listing and trying out products, paying and taking delivery is increasingly disaggregated and spread across more than one channel. Brands like GAP (in the US), Lands End, Next and Boden have actively developed a multi-channel strategy to increase their overall customer reach and market share. Thus, recently the internet has been seen as a means of supporting physical stores rather than replacing them. This author is of the view that the divergence of channel-performance fortunes in 2004, on both sides of the Atlantic, suggests that this view is too optimistic, and the continued rapid growth in e-commerce could indeed contribute to a reduction in the provision of physical stores by 2000.

Sector expectations

Fashion retailing is at a crossroads. Traditional business cultures, strategies and skills are being challenged by new enabling technologies, the empowerment of today's shopper and the proliferation of new and more exciting avenues of consumer expenditure. At the top end, an elite of luxury brands continues to serve the wealthy and discriminating customer (see Chapter 4), but even these have largely failed to extend their business model profitability beyond their core brand. In the mass market, the share of consumer expenditure is leaking away, and only a very few brands have re-engineered their businesses to achieve a powerful and charismatic resonance with the psychological and lifestyles' desires of twenty-first-century humanity. Zara, Top Shop, H&M, Abercrombie & Fitch, Victoria's Secret, Diesel, FCUK, Selfridges . . . maybe a few more, but the list is quite short. The only safe prediction is that the next five years will see further disruption and change in fashion retailing which will impact not only distribution channels and formats but the major companies operating them.

This concluding section summarises trends, challenges and prospects, identified by the author, that face the sector in the UK as it enters the second half of the first decade of the new century.

The gulf between IT and HR will finally be bridged

The development and integration of IT functions throughout the organisation will accelerate, supported by innovations like radio-frequency identification (RFID). This will notably embrace:

- supply-chain and product distribution;
- merchandise and price optimisation;
- store location, planning and micro-merchandising;
- space allocation and visual merchandising; and
- customer loyalty and database marketing metrics.

The increased IT literacy of both managers and customers, more user-friendly IT and a focus on individual relationships should at least have the effects of achieving a more intelligent application of IT and of humanising relationships between customer and brand.

The lunatics will take over the asylum . . .

. . . Or so it will seem if you are a product/brand manager. In the same way that the 1970s and 1980s saw manufacturers cede brand ownership reluctantly to retailers, so the next twenty years will see the baton pass to the consumer. Organisations will realise that a brand has no value other than that credited to it by its purchasers, and that consumers of fashion (or any 'added-value' product) are becoming more demanding, more individualistic and more enabled, almost by the day. Wherever the ego is involved in the purchase- and consumption-process, we can expect the consumer to orchestrate what, how, where and when a product is purchased and consumed. Even in the fashion sector it will become increasingly challenging to dictate, or even lead, the shape of consumer demand. So-called 'brand terrorists', such as 'chavs' wearing the Burberry plaid, can effectively undermine the brand manager's good positioning work. Many businesses will choose to 'go with the flow' and essentially become contractors engaged by consumers to satisfy their needs and desires. The fashion buyer's role as selector and editor may change to one of customiser. Those with insight will embrace the contribution of consumers to the positioning of brands and the development of products, and find new processes and business models to allow this to happen peacefully. The evolving lexicography of retailing is already beginning to reflect these changes, as 'conversations' are the new 'messages', 'customers' become 'visitors' or 'guests' and 'colleagues', and 'associates' take over from 'staff'.

Retailers themselves need to respond to consumers as multi-dimensional opportunities, rather than segmenting them in traditional ways. As Hyde (2003: 12–13) states, when people go fashion shopping they could be looking for a speedy and efficient replacement for a garment; they could be on a mission to find a solution to a specific need; they could be trying to express their personality, mood or ambition; or they could simply be out there on a 'voyage of discovery', open to impulse-buying as a leisure activity. The nature of the relationship – and the commercial opportunity – will be different in each case. As Hyde (*ibid.*) says, 'the desire for self-expression may resonate so strongly with some customers as to make other store choice factors almost irrelevant'. Similarly, Tyrell and Feenan (2000: 10–14) have identified four similar shopping situations:

- household and personal shopping;
- morale-boosting shopping;
- top-up shopping; and
- leisure shopping.

They conclude that whereas in the past who you were dictated how you spent your money, now your spending and consumption behaviour define who you are. This new focus on customer moods and situations will mean that retail formats will increasingly be positioned against this segmentation model rather than a product group specialism. As a result, there will be ever-increasing inter-type competition, with many types of store selling clothing and footwear to meet specific needs. Who would have thought that ASDA, Tschibo, Argos, Manchester United and the National Trust would all be gaining a share of the UK 'fashion' market? True fashion will increasingly come together with art and design, and will diverge from commodity clothing. Brands espousing an aesthetic lifestyle, such as Apple, Nokia, Alessi, Swatch and Mini will join the 'fashion' high ground. In the US so-called lifestyle centres developed around brands like Pottery Barn, Restoration Hardware, Crate & Barrel and Bed, Bath & Beyond are already the fastest growing sector of retailing, as shoppers desert conventional malls in their droves.

Differentiation by standing for something

In a retail world of increasing homogeneity and performance parity, what will enable one business to differentiate itself from another? This author believes that retail marketing and branding will no longer be seen as a tool for the sales division to generate turnover and market share, but rather as a cultural underpinning for the values and beliefs of the organisation which will allow and encourage customers with similar beliefs to coalesce with it. Here the benchmark best practice comes from the leisure sector – whether it is Manchester United Supporters' Club, or Friends of Tate Britain. Co-branding with celebrities or charities and good causes is already imparting a new dimension of meaning to many retail brands. Others, such as Muji, Diesel or FCUK are simply recognised as 'brands with attitude'.

With this new emphasis, there will need to be a focus on compliance with ethical standards, and transparency of operation and reporting, if brands are to receive consumer trust and confidence. An increasing number of businesses are already publishing Ethical Codes of Conduct and appointing Compliance Officers. In the age of authenticity, unfocused persuasive marketing is dead. Press reports in March 2005 confirm that Arcadia has abandoned all plans for television advertising (Benady 2005) and we can expect to see further reductions in overt advertising expenditure in the sector (Zyman 2000).

The core competence for achieving brand differentiation will be in the recruitment, motivation, support and reward of staff at all levels. The culture of an organisation, consisting of human beliefs, attitudes, relationships and behaviour, is unique and cannot be copied. Fashion retailing is still not seen as an attractive career for top talent, and retailers will need to address this seriously and soon. At the time of writing

Philip Green has launched his Retail Academy initiative which has already received the support of Stuart Rose of M&S, so there are encouraging signs.

An ancillary skill, closely linked to people skills, is the creation of unique brand experiences to lift fashion retailing out of the commodity trap. Selfridges had pioneered this in the UK with its annual themed promotions such as Bodycraze, Bollywood and Tokyo Life. Other brands like Levi's, Nike Town, Diesel and Urban Outfitters have focused on store design and activities, supported by their websites. Some customers merely seek an efficient shopping process, but others will visit a store more often and stay longer if it offers a stimulating and appropriate experience. However, such experiences require new skills and are costly to produce and update. As there is as yet no willingness on the part of customers to pay to enter a store, the real breakthrough in experience retailing is still waiting to happen.

Retail space saturation

The addition of new selling space in the fashion retail sector is already outstripping any growth in demand. According to Verdict (Anon. 2004b), total UK retail selling space rose by 50 per cent from 380 to 567 million square feet between 1980 and 2004. M&S is considered 'overspaced' since its acquisition of 19 stores from Littlewoods. The dispersal of Allders mixed-use stores among retailers such as Debenhams and Primark in 2005 will further add to the supply of space. ASDA, TK Maxx and Matalan are all adding mezzanine floors to increase stock-holding capacity. Next, New Look, River Island and others are seeking to increase store sizes. In 2003–4 alone Next added 900,000 square feet of new space, mostly from re-sites, and has recently confirmed the continuation of this strategy. As a result, most fashion retailers are seeing declining annual sales per square foot of productivity. Research by the International Council of Shopping Centres in the USA shows that retail sales per square foot have declined from $260 in 1970 to $196 in 2002. Similar patterns are now appearing in the UK. Deutsche Bank (2005) estimates that fashion retail selling space has been growing at more than 5 per cent annually since 2000, and that over 3 million square feet will be added to the stock of retail clothing and footwear selling space in 2005. They calculate a theoretical excess supply capacity equivalent to almost £1 billion of sales in the UK market in 2005.

Couple this with the reluctance of landlords to compromise on upward-only rent reviews, increases in the minimum wage and staff costs generally, and rising energy costs, and it becomes apparent that sustaining current levels of profitability will become increasingly difficult.

New roles for shops

Fashion stores for this new millennium will need to use 'brand personality' and shopping experience instead of identikit 'shop design' as a basis for competitive advantage and differentiation. As Hankinson and Cowking (1993) have described, the old idea of market positioning defines a brand by its competitive context whereas brand personality consists of a 'unique combination of attributes and symbolic values'. Paul Smith is selling from a domestic environment; Ted Baker, Diesel and Red or Dead believe that each outlet should be individual and customers can recognise a brand by its 'handwriting' and are bored by cloned shop designs. Jigsaw, Calvin Klein, Selfridges, Prada and others are now commissioning well-known architects to create distinctive three-dimensional iconic retail spaces to amuse, delight and inspire their customers. As works of art, possibly they will also turn out to be valuable appreciating assets. Some believe that we are slowly moving from the notion of the store as a profit centre in its own right to that of the store as a flagship brand advertisement, as manufacturers and e-commerce operators already perceive stores to be. Some brands like Levi's, Umbro and Vacant have been opening temporary 'pop-up' fashion stores to promote the scarcity and opportunistic value of their wares – much as luxury brands like Hermes and Chanel have been accustomed to doing. As Tesco has put it, the emphasis has shifted from profitable stores to lifetime profitable customers. If all customers are profitable, then shops become just a part of the total supporting mechanism geared to achieve this. But the corollary of this is that just as manufacturers have disenfranchised unprofitable wholesale customers in the past, so retailers will identify and disbar unprofitable consumers – or seek to make them profitable by differential pricing strategies. We may see the growth of a consumer 'underclass' who do not have access to the internet or to a major part of the retail market's brands and best-value offers. This is likely to boost the share of the market accounted for by charity shops, markets, boot fairs and barter – which this author believes is already substantially under-recorded. Conversely, for the more privileged, the days of the 'closed shop' are surely over, as brands are increasingly available to shop '24/7'.

Changing economic environment

Historically retailers have been able to cover growing operating costs by selectively increasing prices. Consumers had become habituated to a level of annual price inflation. For example, between 1985 and 1989 the retail price of clothing in the UK rose by 12 per cent. However, there has been no significant retail price inflation since 1992 and, apart from one very short period in 2003, UK retail prices of clothing have been falling since 1998. This results from the convergence of three factors:

- lower cost sourcing – the entry of China into the WTO in 2005 will further sustain this;
- customers switching from the middle-market to the value sector (see Table 6.2);
- customers increasingly deferring purchases until the next promotion or sale period, and buying at a reduced price

This tendency will put added pressure on like-for-like performance and retail stock management. The incentive to hold stock as opposed to liquidating it as quickly as possible at whatever price will be further eroded. Generating positive cash flow and an 'open to buy' will become increasingly important and challenging for fashion retailers.

A second factor is growing reluctance on the part of both consumers and government to support further increases in consumer expenditure financed by credit. Consumer debt doubled from £442 billion to £883 billion between 1994 and 2003, during which period the savings ratio fell from 9.3 per cent to 5.5 per cent. This was greatly encouraged by the credit schemes aggressively marketed by retailers, often on the back of so-called 'loyalty schemes'. However, falling house prices and an uncertain political environment will reduce consumer confidence and new retail credit. Clothing is an ideal product category for consumers to indulge in 'sacrificial consumption' – trading down in one area to free up funds for consumption elsewhere.

Ownership

The demise of Allders early in 2005 suggests that the private equity houses which have financed so much of the 'privatisation' of the UK retail sector may themselves turn out to be as uncomfortable as bedfellows as were the shareholders they have often replaced. It has become apparent that these firms have not entered the sector to support the spectrum of stakeholders, including customers, staff, suppliers and local community, that surrounds a typical fashion brand. They are in it strictly to make money and earn a return on their investment – in double-quick time. Coupled with the overcapacity identified above, a process of rationalisation, divestment of assets and closure of favourite brands can be anticipated. Whether this is justified in terms of the wider social value of fashion retailing is open to debate. Owners as disparate as Linda Bennett and Giorgio Armani have postponed selling their businesses for fear of the eventual outcome, and others, like M&S with its 'Your M&S' campaign, have opened the debate about a broader social value of retail activity.

Today's fashion retailer is faced with a fragmented market of individual discerning customers who want a great shopping experience, personalised offers, better service, permanent brand access through multiple distribution channels *and* low prices. UK retailers have to compete with the best in the world in the challenging environment that is today's global marketplace, delivering an attractive career path for their workforce and a solid return to their investors. Whoever said retailing was easy!

7 Fashion buying and merchandising

David Shaw

This chapter gives an overview of one of the more important functions in the UK fashion business. Getting the right product at the right price, at the right time, to the right place might sound easy, but is in fact the most mission-critical aspect at every level of the fashion business. The roles of the buyer and the merchandiser are explained, showing how both processes rely on good teamwork and the intelligent use of IT. Buying and merchandising (B&M) is in fact the most important functional element of getting the correct Marketing Mix. The problems of global rather than local supply are investigated, as well as the likely future trends. Although pivotal to fashion success, B&M relies heavily on functional support across the business. The apparently glamorous world of buying is explained in pragmatic terms.

Introduction

To many entrants to the UK fashion industry, the term 'fashion buyer' conjures up an executive lifestyle, which involves jetting off to Milan or Paris, sitting on a gilded chair at the front of a sumptuous catwalk show, mixing with famous designers, possibly sipping the odd glass of champagne to keep yourself refreshed, before jetting back home. Unfortunately, this is a fantasy; the reality is much different. The modern fashion buyer does travel abroad and attend fashion exhibitions, however he/she will be working in a tough, fast-changing, professional and demanding environment. This chapter sets out to look at the reality of modern fashion buying and merchandising across a wide range of different business types. Fashion buying and merchandising are at the heart of successful mainstream UK fashion businesses.

Fashion buying: THE REALITY

No matter how large or small the business, whether it is an individual shop or part of a large chain, in some part of the organisation will be found an individual responsible for buying the merchandise that it retails to the public. With small, privately owned shops, the buyer and arbiter of the ranges stocked will often be the owner or entrepreneur who started the business. In the case of large chains like Top Shop or New Look, there are large, centrally managed B&M departments, often containing a hundred plus staff, all with B&M responsibilities for part of the total product offer. These departments are usually open plan, divided up into product groups and/or garment types. Specialist B&M teams of buyer and merchandiser, their assistants and sometimes distribution staff generally sit at an island formation of 6–8 desks. These small teams are tight knit and their members work in proximity to one another, so that they are able to keep each other fully informed about everything to do with the department's ranges. Buying offices are exciting places to work, strewn with sample garments, computers and the mass of paperwork used to support the merchandise planning process. All around are cabinets and rails of samples, with walls covered with mood boards and fabric swatches relating to future seasons' ranges.

B&M roles and responsibilities vary according to the type and size of the fashion retail organisation. Whether large or small, the role of a single independent store buyer is fundamentally the same as that of a chain store buyer, i.e. they both buy merchandise that their customers need or want to purchase.

The need to understand what your customer wants is fundamental to all fashion buying. So many entrants to the fashion business initially believe that buying for a large organisation is simply an extension of their own personal Saturday shopping trips; for which they will be handsomely paid! However, many experienced and successful fashion buyers will tell you that they never personally wear the clothes that they buy professionally.

Fashion is probably the fastest changing and most unpredictable of consumer goods' categories. Trends, styles or brands are often extolled by the fashion media, which then champion and promote them to death. Some of these trends, styles or brands explode on to the marketplace and become the look of the season, which lasts only for four to six weeks, before being over taken by the next trend. Other fashion looks have greater longevity and become a fashion evergreen, i.e. one seen year after year, although usually in a new format or designed with a new twist, e.g. blue jeans have been available as fashion item since the 1950s, but can still be found regularly in most designer-wear ranges.

As people become wealthier, clothing is seen less as a basic necessity and more as a way of self expression. Clothes are now seen as transient and disposable, especially as a majority of fashion items fall into the category of casual rather than formal. The modern UK consumer has never enjoyed such choice as is now available. The best luxury designer jeans can cost anywhere between £200 and £300, while at the other end of the scale it is possible for the canny shopper to find a more basic pair in a supermarket or discount chain for under £5. Between these two extremes, jeans can be found at every intervening price point, being offered for sale in luxurious and opulent stores such as Harrods, as well as more basic retailers like Primark. The customer's first impression of a store's surroundings and environment indicate almost automatically the level of product pricing likely to be offered.

In previous times, when incomes were lower, mass fashion was not always available to the majority. Although being fashionable has long been a human pursuit (originally more by men than by women), it has only really been in the last twenty years that fashion can be said to have been fully democratised. The wide retail offering available in almost every high street in the land, combined with the growth of fashion magazines and media, now allow those on low incomes to be fashionable.

There are now over 40,000 clothing and footwear outlets in the UK, although a majority of these form parts of larger chains, with independent stores still declining. Large-scale retailing developed in the UK as result of the expansion in the number of variety stores or chain stores at the start of the twentieth century, such as M&S and Bhs. From its early origins as a market stall in Leeds, M&S is still the largest clothing retailer in the UK with around a 12 per cent market share by value. Another large multiple clothing-retailer is the famous Arcadia Group of stores (previously known as the Burton Group). Arcadia comprises many famous fashion names, including Top Shop, Top Man, Burton Menswear, Dorothy Perkins, Wallis, Miss Selfridge, etc., which with approximately 3,000 stores is the second largest retail group in the UK in terms of its market share of around 10 per cent by value. One thing that M&S and Arcadia have in common is their need to buy fashion merchandise on a scale sufficient to stock large numbers of shops, albeit that the level of fashionability varies in accordance to the retail fascia involved. The approach of buyers at different levels of the market varies in accordance with the following key variables:

- the level of fashionability of the business;
- the type(s) of customer being targeted;
- the overall price-competitive stance, i.e. high-end or low-end prices.

Later on in this chapter the buying approaches taken by the various types of fashion retailer are discussed and explained. Whilst there are generic similarities, e.g. between chain store and department store fashion buying processes, every business has its own approach. To illustrate, a typical day in the life of a Selfridge's buyer is outlined.

A day-in-the-life of Selfridges buyer David Walker-Smith

As buying manager for Men's Contemporary in Selfridges David Walker-Smith has a busy and demanding schedule. His role is primarily to buy the right menswear brands for Selfridges, striking a balance between supplying what customers are asking for now and what he thinks the future hot names will be. As with many buying jobs, the working day is frantic and very diverse. Although there is rarely a typical day in any fashion business, there are common elements concerned with the role (such as meetings with suppliers and brands). Displayed is an itinerary that might be considered a typical Monday for David in Selfridges.

Typical Monday itinerary

0900   *Review sales figures* from previous week by department and brand.

1000   *Floor-walk* around the relevant departments to review stock and previous week with sales staff.

1100   Four *internal appointments* with existing brands to discuss new joint-marketing ideas for forthcoming season – lasting until lunchtime.

1300   Lunch.

1400   *Meeting with the architects* responsible for the Men's floors in new Birmingham store.

> 1500   *Second meeting with prospective European Brand* – negotiations over stocking brand in-store.
>
> 1600   *Review performance* of two existing contemporary concession brands with merchandiser.
>
> 1645   Catch up with *paper work* and review day with assistant.
>
> 1800   Attend *private party* to celebrate birthday of the managing director of a leading brand stocked by Men's Contemporary in Selfridges.

Although not a definitive list, some of the specific brands either currently or historically stocked in the Men's Contemporary section of Selfridges include Diesel, Boss, Gant, Duffer of St George, Stone Island, Ted Baker, Paul Smith, Hackett and Firetrap.

Important elements of David Walker-Smith's role at Selfridges

- *Reviewing sales figures*: this is an important part of the job of any buyer because it enables the retailer to react quickly to any emerging trends. In a store that stocks brands there is a need to assess the performance both of product departments, such as trousers or jackets, and of the brands that are stocked. The importance of sales and stock analysis is covered later in the chapter.

- *Walking the sales floor*: unlike a buyer for a multiple retailer whose product may be stocked in excess of 100 stores, the Selfridges buyer can literally walk out of his or her office onto the shop floor to keep in touch with the customers and sales staff. Remaining close to both the shop floor and the customers means that buyers can gain crucial insights into the reactions of customers to the shop's products, brands and selling environment. All too often in fashion, mistakes are made by managers being geographically removed from their customers. Detailed feedback from staff about the views, preferences and attitudes of customers can be valuable to maintaining a relevant product offer.

- *Internal management of brands*: constant dialogue with the brands is a vital aspect of the buyer's role in a department store. The buyer has to ensure that the brands continue to be relevant to the spirit and market positioning of the store. Ideas are shared between the buyer and the brands over product innovation, packaging, concession presentation and window stories. The windows of a store such as Selfridges offer valuable advertising opportunities, equivalent to, if not better than, a billboard at the same location.

- *Meeting with the architects*: as retailing has become more competitive, so stores have focused more on the shopping experience as both a means of differentiation and of encouraging customers to enter the store and spend money. Customers will spend more time and money in a store that is exciting, so getting the right balance of theatre, ergonomics and selling space is critical. When the new Birmingham Selfridges store opened in 2003, the buyers had to have a view of the environment that would house their future collections. Lighting, use of space, and the textures of materials to be used were some of the important issues discussed with architects many months before the products arrived.

- *Continual meeting and review of potential new brands*: newness is the lifeblood of a store such as Selfridges, which has positioned itself as 'the house of brands'.

Buyers are always interested in a developing fashion brand with the right profile. The market positioning of any new brand in-store is a key factor for Selfridges as it continues to develop its distinctive place in the market. Brands need to be compatible in terms of fashion direction, exclusivity, innovations and price points.

The work pattern of any Selfridge's buyer will almost certainly be different from that of one working in a faster moving high-street multiple, although many parts of the job will be similar. Needless to say, those considering a career in buying should note the widening management and marketing role of the modern fashion buyer.

How fashion-buying roles vary in different types of fashion business

Buying for an own-label retailer

Most of the UK's main high-street mid-market clothing chains sell their own products, sometimes alongside other well-known brands. This type of buying is probably the most complex and demanding genre of buying, as here the buyer usually works on original design development, in conjunction with an internal or external design team. Increasingly, fashion retailers at all levels in the market are developing their own in-house design skills. Even with the lower-end products, the consumer requires that they are reasonably fashionable, and not simply a cheap commodity. It is interesting to note how Top Shop has moved in the last decade from being solely a supplier of young high-street fashion towards also being a more design-orientated business. The modern consumer wants to wear what the stars are wearing, but, just as importantly, as quickly afterwards as possible. The term 'fast fashion' is now part of the fashion vocabulary, thanks to the fast-moving ranges of businesses like Zara and Top Shop.

Own-label buyers are responsible for sourcing products from a wide range of international manufacturers, and their selection may start with an idea, which is then transferred into a two-dimensional sketch, finally to be made up as a sample garment, which may or may not get through the rigorous product development process. Planning a range from scratch is a far more demanding task than it is to simply select from an international brand's existing range. Own-label buyers feel that their department store equivalents sometimes have a much easier existence.

Own-label buyers tend to be less involved with the selling environment, although they carry the major responsibility for the general range direction. Their focus is squarely on achieving the planned sales and profit targets, which means they need to work closely with their merchandisers to keep the right quantities of stock flowing at the right times. (N.B. The role and responsibilities of the merchandiser are fully explained later on in this chapter.) Originating garments from scratch often requires a high level of technical advice, which is normally available from in-house garment technologists. This essential role ensures that garments selected are fit for the purpose intended. The buyer and garment technologist are essential parts of the product development process, but sometimes they enjoy a love–hate relationship over issues such as fabric suitability. The own-label buyer also has to be conversant over many general supply-chain issues, resulting from the high dependence in Europe on imported products.

Own-label buyers, like department store buyers, undertake international sourcing and competitive shopping trips as part of their work calendar. At set times during the year they will attend fabric exhibitions such as Première Vision, the leading European fabric show, as well as many different ready-made garment exhibitions which occur bi-annually, mainly in Germany, France, Italy and the USA, most having huge international attendances. These shows and exhibitions are normally aimed at the trade, not the general public. Although the British press gives over many pages each season to the international designer and couture catwalk shows, chain store buyers are rarely among those invited, although fashion buyers at any level in the market need to pay attention to such shows. Fashion-trend forecasting services such as WGSN provide immediate online reporting of the looks that emerge from virtually all types and levels of international garment and fabric shows.

Buying for department stores

Usually buyers will select certain elements of their ranges from fashion brands or manufacturers brands. In this instance the buyer is not creating the original style and colour of that range, but is generally selecting an edited version of that brand's total offer. It is important that the brands selected are positioned in the market for the store's customer profile, as well as their ability to display well within the context of the store. Department store buyers generally have a much higher involvement with how the product will appear in-store than buyers working in own-label retailers. Often department stores will run themes throughout the store, e.g. the famous Bollywood promotion run by Selfridges, which encompassed all things Indian. There are, however, some department stores that buy existing brands as well as creating their own in-house labels, e.g. Debenhams' 'Maine' range and House of Fraser's Linea range.

Department store-buyers have to keep abreast of new brands and designers, which involve them in the more glamorous side of fashion buying, i.e. attending fashion and product shows, as well as extensive international travel to undertake competitive shopping. The UK has some of the best department stores in the world, such as Harrods, Selfridges and Harvey Nichols, therefore making it essential for their buyers to keep an eye on what is happening in international stores. The excitement of department-store windows and their general in-store visual merchandising is an essential part of overall marketing and promotion. A buyer can be pivotal in ensuring that product excitement keeps them ahead of competitors.

Buying for independent stores and luxury stores

Although independent stores have been on the decline in Europe over the past few years, there are still many very successful small independent businesses trading through one or more shops. The buyers for small businesses have the advantage over those buying for large groups, in that they are usually more knowledgeable about the needs and wants of their customers. Often a buyer for an individual store will also have direct shop-floor selling responsibilities, therefore keeping them in direct contact with their customer base. Understanding exactly what your customer wants is the key ingredient of all successful marketing. The small fashion retailer is unlikely to afford a fully developed merchandising function, and therefore the onus of stock control falls onto the buyer. The independent buying model is similar to that of the early department stores which had no specialist merchandising function, relying instead on the merchanting skills of the buyer, supported by a buyer's clerk.

The changing structure of UK fashion retailing

Table 7.1 gives a breakdown of the recent turnover and market share of the major UK fashion retailer by type and also a view of their importance in terms of older and younger age groups. This information is reproduced by permission of Fashion Trak, a division of TNS, the UK's leading marketing research company working in the field of consumer fashion.

Table 7.1 Key market share information on retail outlet type and consumer age groups for women's clothing and accessories, September 2004

a) Type of retail outlet

	Retail share by % volume (units)	Retail share by % expenditure
Clothing multiples	19.7	32.3
General stores	18.9	19.2
Supermarkets	16.8	5.2
Department stores	5.2	9.2

b) Top 5 retailer shares by age

Under 20	% expenditure	55–74 yrs	% expenditure
Top Shop	11.3	MS	21.1
New Look	8.7	Bhs	4.2
River Island	5.3	Debenhams	3.8
Dorothy Perkins	4.7	Littlewoods	3.5
Next	2.9	Bon Marché	3.2

Source: *Fashion Trak* (2004).

This snapshot of the UK women's clothing and accessory market in September 2004, shows the clear overall dominance of the clothing multiples e.g. Top Shop, Etam, Dorothy Perkins, New Look *et al*. It also highlights the older age profile of general and department stores, compared to the clothing multiples. The UK has and ageing population, where soon a majority of the population will be over 50. In fashion retailing, as Table 7.1 reveals, there is a very evident age divide in terms of fashion shoppers and where they shop. Over the past five years, there has been strong growth in clothing and accessory sales by the supermarket sector. Once considered unsuitable as clothing outlets, we now see Florence & Fred at Tesco, George at ASDA and more recently TU at Sainsbury. While their ranges may not be right at the leading edge of fashion, they offer inexpensive modern clothing for the masses. Parts of all of the supermarket clothing ranges are quite basic, although other elements are becoming increasingly fashionable. The potential power of supermarkets in UK fashion clothing should not be underestimated and their market penetration is likely to increase dramatically over the next few years. At the time of publication (2006) it is estimated that nearly one garment in every five is purchased in a supermarket. This presents a critical and increasing competition problem for middle range high street retailers.

Fashion merchandising: THE REALITY

The words 'merchandiser' and 'merchandising' are used extensively by various sectors of the consumer goods industries. However, in the context of fashion buying and merchandising, the role played by merchandising is very specific and often is misunderstood by those outside of the industry. Fashion merchandising is about the management of stock flows into and around a fashion business. It is a highly numerate profession, requiring excellent arithmetical skills, which are used to plan bulk stock deliveries into the organisations' distribution centres, and then to logically distribute the right amount to their retail outlets. The huge number of styles, colours and sizes, added to the huge regular variation in fashion demand, make this job highly complex and vitally important for all fashion retailers. Getting the right product at the right price to the right place at the right time in the right quantities is what fashion merchandising is all about.

The term 'merchandiser' is used in other contexts in the fashion industry, e.g. visual merchandiser and store merchandiser. The term 'visual merchandising' has superseded the older term 'store display'. Display teams would consist of window dressers, whose job was mainly concerned with the creativity of store windows. Generally, windows are no longer as elaborate as they once were, with a more open aspect being preferred in most middle-market stores. However, middle-market retailers use visual display throughout the store at the point of sale (POS) to encourage positive consumer reaction to their products. Many of the larger prestige department stores still undertake highly complex window displays, to differentiate themselves from the lower mass market. The term 'store merchandiser' is applied to staff who simply lay out stock and replenish the rails and shelves, again adding to the confusion over the term 'merchandiser'. It is important to understand the fundamentally different responsibilities of all three types. In this chapter's references to merchandisers/ merchandising, the context relates solely to the role of merchandise management, unless otherwise specified.

Although fundamentally a numbers-driven job, the merchandiser will work very closely with a buyer, normally on one or more associated garment areas. The ability to look at sales and product-demand patterns both historically and currently enables the merchandiser to plan ahead and help the buyer decide on the right quantities and the best delivery times. Although the merchandiser assists the buyer in the numbers planning element of buying, it is always the buyer who has the final say as to what products are actually purchased by the business. A good merchandiser will always ensure that the business is well stocked with best-selling lines but is also aware of any slow selling merchandise that may require a mark down in price to speed up its rate of sale.

The modern merchandiser needs to be very creative and at ease with high levels of detailed line sales and stock information in order to be able to spot emerging trends in demand for, say, specific fabrics or colours. Often trends emerge gradually and are sometimes not spotted by the less experienced merchandiser. Despite this 'accountant-like' description of the fashion merchandiser's role, the merchandiser needs to be very fashion savvy about the latest looks and fashion trends, as well as possessing a commercial approach. Merchandisers will, in a buyer's absence, e.g. during a foreign buying trip, make repeat buying decisions to ensure that the business is stocked effectively. Merchandisers also play an important day-to-day role in communicating with suppliers and the rest of the business over a wide range of commercial issues. In Chapter 10, there are descriptions of the typical key elements of both the buyer's and the merchandiser's job content, as well as the preferred candidate qualities needed for those wishing to enter either buying or merchandising.

The creative and logical management of numbers undertaken by the fashion merchandiser is an example of a close conjunction of mathematics and art. Applied well, it can fundamentally improve the sales and profit performance of a fashion business, hence the high salaries currently being offered to good merchandisers. Unfortunately, simply due to a lack of understanding of the 'fashioness' of the merchandising role, it is often an option disregarded by many potential entrants to the fashion industry, who perceive the role as being dull compared to the glamour of buying. This is a mistake.

As the UK fashion business has become faster moving and more competitive, the rate at which fashion fads come and go has created new challenges for the fashion merchandiser. Luckily, as a result of the personal computer revolution of the late 1980s, much of the numerical management of fashion has now migrated from its original pencil-and-paper approach to being full computerised. Stand-alone office PCs networked to even more powerful mainframe computers have enabled the development of increasingly sophisticated types of merchandise-management software that now help merchandisers quickly and in greater detail than previously understand the sales dynamics of their ranges. Many younger readers will find it hard to realise that the use of PCs in fashion buying offices was unusual until the late 1980s, before which time planning was done largely on paper and then fed into large mainframe computers which processed the detail. Some famous UK fashion retailers were still counting their stock manually and not really relying on computing until well into the early 1990s!

Early merchandising-management systems and software were expensive and complex to develop, so that many were created by in-house IT and business teams, although now there are many proprietary systems and applications that are being used across international fashion retailing. Some of the more widely found applications to assist merchandising management are *Merchandise Planner* (previously known as *Makoro*), now owned and marketed by i2, and JDA's *Merchandise Planning* by Arthur™.

Often these large software and systems companies provide more than merchandise-management software, sometimes offering a 'right through' IT solution, enabling the software of the cash tills to feed seamlessly through into back office and finance systems, and, more importantly, directly into the buying and merchandising support systems and, ultimately, into distribution and logistics. At one time these large-scale IT systems were available only to the larger retailers, but are now coming down in price, with 'lite' versions of the more complex, larger systems available to small-scale and

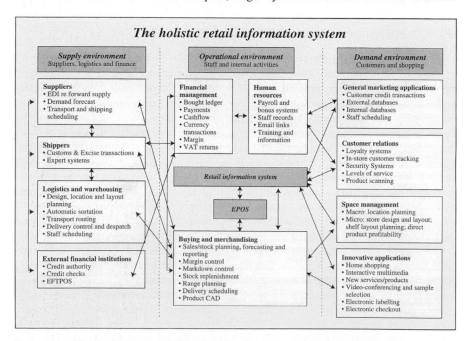

Figure 7.1 The holistic retail information system

Source: Leeming and Shaw 1996.

independent businesses. This trend has largely removed the competitive advantage that IT once bestowed on the wealthier and larger fashion companies. Retail and all other types of fashion business that need to control their stock all now have the potential to buy into IT solutions. The need for information in great detail is a norm at all levels of the fashion trade. Being unaware of what is and what is not selling is a certain recipe for failure in the medium to long term. The huge advances within retail IT have now integrated all of the business functions involved in fashion retailing. The holistic way in which IT is being employed by the leading fashion businesses is shown in Figure 7.1. This diagram shows the huge interlinking potential of IT into all fashion business function.

Figure 7.2 shows a typical screen that a merchandiser would face on day-to-day basis in the average modern buying office. This screen clip, provided by JDA, is an *Arthur*™ screen, which shows a visual representation of the product involved, together with all other relevant product information relating to the line, e.g. margin, supplier number, code etc. The tabs in real time use would reveal a host of other data to help

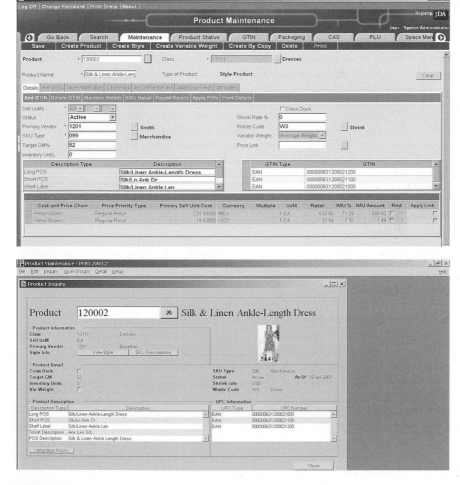

Figure 7.2 Two typical screenshots from JDA's *Merchandise Planning* by Arthur™

the business know everything about the line, which helps all personnel with access to the system to familiarise themselves with the product in question. It is becoming increasingly the norm for all merchandising management systems to have a pictorial representation of the product readily available. Planning and managing fashion merchandise using only numbers without pictorial representation, can be an abstraction that does not give reality to what is essentially a product-led business.

The complexity of planning range requirements for huge businesses such as Top Shop or Selfridges would be almost impossible without the considerable advances being delivered by the makers and designers of merchandise-management software.

Some key performance indicators (KPIs) for merchandising

There are several important key performance indicators that are used by almost every buying and merchandising department. The list and brief explanation of each, given below, are not exhaustive, but those included are important for any fashion business, where being left with poor selling lines can be a very expensive and profit-destroying proposition. It is during the annual/bi-annual planning process that buyers and merchandisers become deeply involved with these key performance indicators. The method by which individual companies undertake the planning process varies immensely, although good planning is now essential, as a result of the UK's high dependence on longer lead-time imported merchandise. The complexity and level of detail required in fashion planning have increased exponentially over the past ten years, driven mainly by the huge advances in computing power. The risk is that planning can become too detailed and complex, leading to 'analysis paralysis', a dangerous situation of information overload where the likelihood of the plan succeeding is statistically minimal because of the huge numbers of variables and imponderables involved. Generally, the best merchandise planning is simple and well grounded in historical data. Ahead of each buying season, buying and merchandising teams will plan using most of the KPIs listed below. Many large fashion retailers create valuable incentive schemes, using a combination of KPIs, to encourage each buying team to manage its operation as effectively as possible. In some businesses, the bonus schemes can nearly double basic salaries.

Key performance indicators of merchandising

- *Sales (Retail Sales Plans)*

  Most critical is for a buying and merchandising team to achieve its weekly/ monthly/period/season/annual sales targets. These are planned down to line level by shop. This is the first and most important of all KPIs to be checked each week.

- *Gross buying margin (GM)*

  This is sometimes also referred to as profit, in its most basic form it is simply the difference between the cost price paid to the manufacturer and the retail selling price (RSP) at which it is offered for sale, expressed as a percentage.

  $$RSP - Cost\ Price\ (CP) = Gross\ Margin\ (GM)$$

  Therefore if a ladies' coat cost £30 and the retailer sells it at £100 the following margin is achieved:

  $$£100 - £30\ (cost\ price\ tax\ exclusive) = £70\ (margin\ or\ profit)$$

  Therefore the gross margin expressed as a percentage is

  $$\therefore\quad GM = \frac{£70}{£100} \times \frac{100}{1} = 70\%\ margin\ (or\ sometimes\ called\ the\ \%\ profit)$$

An overall planned gross margin would be set at the start of each buying season for each product type to ensure that buying and merchandising teams were buying and selling their ranges at levels that would generate a profit in line with their business's overall profit plan. Each product type is likely to have a slightly different percentage plan, although these do not vary by very much more than 1 or 2 per cent either way. What is termed the net achieved margin after discount (NAMAD) is also planned, but is simply a derivation of the GM, less the cost of any mark downs, commonly called price reductions. The NAMAD is a true reflection of the profit that an individual product has actually made for the business. The level of margin varies dramatically by type of fashion retailer, with high-end design-driven businesses generally having margins around 70 per cent with lower-end businesses anywhere down to around 40 per cent.

- *Mark down (MD) and mark up (MU)*

There has never been a fashion organisation in history that has sold every garment at full price. Some lines always sell out in a matter of days, while others will stay on the shelf forever, unless of course they are made more attractive to the consumer by reducing the price. Sometimes, possibly as the result of increasing raw materials prices, a basic line of underwear might have to be sold at an increased price, in order that the company's planned profit can be achieved. This will result in a price mark-up of existing stocks, in order not to confuse or annoy the customer by having merchandise on offer at two differing prices. All fashion businesses realise that they will have to reduce the price of certain lines in their ranges, so in order to preserve their overall planned profitability they plan a mark-down per cent at the start of the season, usually based on past levels. Mark-down percentages are normally planned as a percentage of the overall planned sales. Less adventurous and classical fashion businesses will generally plan lower mark-down levels than younger, more fashionable, businesses, where the riskier high-fashion products are more likely to fail. The planning and managing of the mark-up/down for a season is a key merchandising role and KPI.

- *Stock turn and weeks' stock cover*

The life-blood of all fashion is newness. At whatever level in the market a business trades, it is essential to keep customers coming back to that company in search of new products. Fresh-food shops often have to sell their produce in a matter of days, as otherwise stock is likely to go off and become inedible. Fashion is very similar to food, with many businesses targeting the young, and stocking merchandise that can go out of fashion in matter of weeks. It is important to keep renewing the offer and changing the look of the business regularly. Essentially, no fashion business wants to hold more than a few weeks' stock. If the entire season's stock were delivered on day one of the season, regular customers would return only to be disappointed to see no change. The secret of successful fashion retailing is to turn over your stock several times a season, thus allowing fresh merchandise to pep-up remaining stock throughout the season. Stock turn is defined as the number of times a business turns over its stock per year. If a business changed its stock every 4 weeks it would have a stock turn of 13. The calculation for stock turn is as follows:

$$\frac{52 \text{ weeks (total year)}}{4 \text{ weeks of stock cover}} = 13 \text{ stock turns}$$

Most really fashionable business want to keep as few weeks' stock cover as possible, thus allowing them to introduce new lines. More conventional businesses do not mind a higher number of weeks'stock cover and consequently achieve a lower stock turnover. For more classical and less risky lines of merchandise, more weeks' cover and lower stock turnover are not an issue, as the merchandise is less likely to go out of fashion. Fast-fashion businesses such as Zara and Top Shop will probably try to keep very few weeks of stock, whereas that would be less important to department stores. At the start of every season, the buyer and merchandiser will agree the number of weeks' cover (or number of stock turns), as an essential part of their planning process and, more importantly for them, the basis for their bonus calculation! A business whose merchandise fails to sell starts to see stock build-up; high mark-downs, and ultimately lower than planned profitability ensues – hence the importance of measuring, monitoring and controlling the level of stock against sales, i.e. the business's stockturn.

There are many other less important KPIs relating specifically to buying and merchandising, but generally the four listed above are the ones essential for a majority of UK fashion businesses.

Merchandising and the importance of stock distribution/ allocation

Another major element of the merchandiser's work, apart from the reliable delivering in of stock to the fashion business's own distribution centres (DCs), is the need to accurately plan and manage the complex distribution of stock deliveries in the right sizes and colours and in the right amounts to each outlet. The detailed planning and distribution of these deliveries to individual branches can also be referred to as 'stock allocation'. Sometimes buying offices have separate distribution or allocation teams, although in most the distribution team will be an integral part of each buying team. By having distribution integrated into the buying and merchandising teams, there is the obvious capacity to manage the product right from conception until its arrival in-store, ready for sale to the consumer.

One of the major problems specific to UK fashion retailing is the variable size of retail outlets. In such a densely crowded island, many of the cities and towns have grown up over thousands of years, with whatever space was readily available. Often the shape and layout of our conurbations were the result of accident, meaning that current retail outlet sizes bear little relationship to the size of the population and hence to the demand level in the local area. Very often retailers have either too much or too little space inside individual stores, which makes it vitally important that the distributors send just the right number of lines of stock to fit the space available. Using sophisticated software that remembers available selling space, locally preferred brands, colours, sizes or other product attributes, allocation or distribution plans are created for groups and individual outlets. Too many lines can lead to an untidy look which can alienate or confuse the customer. Too few lines can lead to a range or an outlet simply lacking interest and/or credibility. Customers usually react by walking away and going to the competition. Recent developments in merchandise-management systems enable visual merchandising planners to use virtual reality software to recreate the actual layout of each store and then to lay out or hang virtual stock onto the fixtures. Senior management can actually see how the merchandise will look once allocated in-store, ahead of the final despatch instruction being given. These spatio-visual merchandise-planning systems are developing rapidly and will soon become commonplace among the burgeoning suites of fashion merchandise-planning software and systems now on offer. Merchandise planning becomes so much more realistic and valid when the merchandise and its associated numbers can be turned into a picture. Visual store planning, as a central function, also enables head office to electronically transmit ideal shop layouts, rather than relying on variable local display initiatives. In today's hyper-competitive fashion-trading environment, the consistency and quality of visual merchandising effort have to be of the highest level to ensure that all marketing activities are both effective and efficient.

Logistics and distribution in the fashion industries

In the UK, fashion is sold predominantly through chains of stores, which as matter of course require large amounts of hanging and boxed garments to be delivered to central DCs. Depending on the geographical concentration of the store group in question, centres are generally centrally located, often around the Midlands region for national UK store groups.

Most DCs are becoming automated, so that both hanging garments and boxes are moved by conveyor systems around the centres to temporary storage positions, ahead of them being split into sizes and colours and then 'picked' in the right small quantity for each retail outlet.

Large lorries, or wagons as they are known, arrive loaded with merchandise in either a hanging or boxed format. Garments are moved automatically on overhead tracking systems on a small hanging truck, or dolly. The merchandise dolly moves slowly and quietly towards a predetermined position or bay in the DC to await random quality checking, before being released to be picked and despatched to stores. Boxed goods are moved on conveyor belts in a similar way. In general the most efficient DCs make little use of workers to move merchandise around. From a central control room, reminiscent of a railway-signal box, full of track layouts and lights, etc., the DC controller is able to automatically guide merchandise to designated holding areas. Centres have to be run with military precision, with as little double handling of merchandise as possible. Increasing labour costs have made most large retailers install as much automation as possible for handling merchandise.

The flow of stock into and out of DCs requires exacting management, as handling huge stock build-ups during the pre-Christmas period often stretches the overall handling capacity available. There is always a total finite handling capacity, which means that available staff and equipment have to be used either on goods inwards or goods outwards, or a combination of the two. This ensures that the retail outlets are fully stocked at this peak trading time. Distribution executives and managers plan and monitor the work in progress hour by hour, often using flexible warehousing manpower resources to work through the night and over weekends to fulfil the stock demands of the business. The effort and skill required to get the right amount of the right merchandise to shops exactly when customers demand them is one element of the UK fashion trade that is never seen by the public. The hidden army of workers responsible for distribution and logistics in the UK fashion industry is critical for business success.

Once merchandise has been delivered in bulk and then allocated to an individual outlet, IT applications again ensure that each group of garments is loaded onto the delivery vehicle in the right order, with the last shop to be delivered having to be loaded first. Cleverly the most drive-time-effective delivery routes are worked out automatically, ensuring that drivers go by the fastest and most direct route to a designated number of stores. The wasteful use of delivery vehicles is minimised, with many travelling through the night to avoid traffic congestion. Many companies deliver throughout the night, giving trusted drivers keys to the shops, so that they can open the doors at night to leave the required stock. Next day, the retail staff will arrive early to sort out the stock and to replenish the stock floor. High turnover shops in city centres may need to receive up to three or four deliveries a week, while other small outlets may receive only the norm of two a week. Satellite tracking technology is used to monitor the progress of delivery vehicles, to ensure that the drivers are making good progress and that adequate resources are being applied to meet the product demand at branch level. The effective and efficient control of stock deliveries is again fundamentally important for the fast-moving world of fashion. Delivery vehicles travelling along key trunk roads and motorways can also act as effective mobile advertising, hence the high number of fashion delivery vehicles seen with logos promoting businesses.

Importing and shipping fashion

As less and less home-produced fashion is being manufactured and sold in the UK, the fashion business is becoming ever-more reliant on imported products. Fashion fabrics, finished garments and accessories arrive from all over the world by sea, air, road or rail, the larger orders being despatched in metal freight containers. The containers are sealed, thus increasing security as well as protecting the contents from the elements. Inside the containers, fashion products are either packed in individual boxes or, with more formal and structured garments (that may be prone to creasing and damage), transported hanging from rails.

Road delivery

Merchandise from anywhere in Europe, and even from as far away as Turkey and Syria, is often transported by road to the UK in large container-carrying trailers. The general improvement of road networks throughout Europe and the Near East makes it possible to move freight by road in a matter of 2–3 days from the extreme fringes of Europe across the channel and into the UK. The Eurotunnel has vastly speeded up the movement of lorries from the Continent. Within the UK, most national fashion retail DCs are located in the central region of the UK, meaning that their vehicles, once arrived from the Continent, are able to deliver their loads within a matter of hours.

Sea freight

Increasing amounts of fashion merchandise are now being imported from China and India with many other Asian and Pacific Rim economies also quickly developing their textiles and clothing industries. These more distant supply sources naturally use sea freight as their main method of shipping merchandise to Europe. As with road transport, sea-freighted merchandise is packed into sealed containers, which are then automatically stacked on specially built freighters which can carry many hundreds and even thousands of containers at a time. Ships arrive at specialist container ports, such as Felixstowe and Tilbury, where the containers are automatically unloaded and put directly onto vehicles for road delivery onwards. In general ships from the Far East take 4–5 weeks to arrive in the UK, some vessels stopping en route to deliver at other ports. Sea freight is relatively slow, but cheaper than by air, and generally is pretty reliable.

Air freight

Air freight is the most expensive way of moving fashion around the globe, although it is of course the fastest. A plane taking off from China can land at a UK airport in under half a day, a saving of several weeks over conventional sea freight. Only certain businesses can justify using air as their major mode of freighting, as it can easily add 30 per cent to the factory cost price. In general air is used for high-value luxury products which have a high profit margin which allows the freight costs to be easily absorbed, e.g. formal tailored products. Other high-value, low-volume, fashion items such as fashion watches can similarly absorb air freighting costs. It does not make economic sense to send low-value, high-volume, items such as sweatshirts by air. Air freighters can carry both boxed and hanging fashion products, although there is a tendency to tightly pack some products, even though they might crease in transit, necessitating the use of reprocessing companies that specialise in unpacking and ironing or steaming creased garments before the product is sent to the DC. Air freight may also be considered for more mid-priced garments if demand is exceptionally high or if the fashionability of the line is likely to be extremely short lived.

The import or shipping department

Large fashion retailers normally employ their own import and export experts in a specialist department to ensure the smooth receipt of internationally sourced fashion merchandise. Smaller companies without their own import department will normally appoint an external shipping agent to undertake a similar role. Fashion buyers and merchandisers work closely with the import office to keep their delivery schedules accurately updated and thus ensure that the business is receiving the stock it ordered exactly when it is needed. One of the major issues facing any UK fashion-buying office is dealing with late import deliveries. Merchandise being transported from certain countries, despite their improving transportation infrastructure, still tends to be delivered late. Often, local culture and tradition does not allow urgency to interrupt its slow and steady pace! Most organisations importing fashion from abroad impose financial fines on suppliers who deliver late. These fines are levied to compensate a business for loss of sales as a result of the late delivery. A supplier who is at fault can expect to be asked for a substantial price and/or order quantity reduction. Retail customers will not wait for merchandise to be delivered late, but will simply go next door to a competitor. Late delivery invariably always equals lost sales that are never truly recoverable. Although there has been a general global improvement in the efficiency of international shipping, being so reliant on imported merchandise makes the UK more vulnerable than countries that retain a substantial home-produced element in their fashion ranges. An efficient import department, one that works well with the buyers and merchandisers, is an essential resource for all fashion retailers. Large organisations that deal on a large scale with one country, e.g. Monsoon with

India, will often have their own buying/export offices set up and operating there, in many cases staffed by indigenous bilingual staff, who have the advantage of being on the spot and culturally better able to manage the exportation process than would be staff sent out from the UK. Foreign buying or shipping offices can be expensive and difficult to run and manage, although when done properly they can yield huge dividends in terms of good supplier liaison, high quality standards, good prices and efficient delivery services.

For a UK business which is not large enough to sustain and support its own foreign office, there are many specialist buying management services that will act on its behalf for a fee. Such third-party services will more often than not also supply technical expertise to ensure that factories are checked and that merchandise quality is being monitored during the manufacturing process.

The garment technologist's supporting role

Today's consumers have high expectations of all the products they purchase, especially fashion items that are worn on a daily basis. Consumer groups and consumer rights continue to demand more for less, and therefore garment and fabric quality and performance have become a critical differentiator for many consumers. To assist the buyer in ensuring that the product being selected is fit for the purpose intended, most large fashion groups will have product technologists employed to:

- assist in the selection and monitoring of manufacturing sources and the setting of minimum factory production standards;
- advise on getting garment samples to fit correctly;
- visit factories to monitor products going into full-scale production;
- undertake physical and scientific testing of garments and fabrics for their overall quality and suitability;
- help with the acceptance and control of sealed samples;
- create and develop minimum garment specifications that must be adhered to by all approved suppliers (specifications are normally available to all suppliers in the form of a suppliers' manual);
- manage and supervise random product testing as garments are received by the DC, to ensure that no faulty product arrives on the shop floor.

The average technology department resembles a scientific laboratory, full of testing machinery that exactly measures the different physical aspects of fashion product performance. Among the tests carried out are:

- *Tensile strength*: this test ensures that when performance sports fabrics are sewn together, the garment will not tear under strain.
- *Colourfastness*: to ensure that when exposed to extremes of ultra-violet light or while being washed, garments do not fade or release dye onto other clothes. Especially important for swimwear.
- *Rubbing*: fabrics are tested to ensure that they do not wear out too quickly, or lose their physical strength or general appearance. This is important for trouser

fabrics, where the wearer may be sitting down all day creating extreme wear on the trouser seat.

*   *Pilling and snagging*: this test ensures that knitted or other loose-weave fabrics do not easily catch and pull stitches, or that some flat-faced fabrics do not produce what appear to be small balls of fluff (pilling).

These are just some of the tests used, but for a fashion business selling accessories, cosmetics, jewellery, etc., many other forms of testing are required.

Garment technology and the control of the overall quality level involve complex and technical processes, so most buyers work very closely with a relevant technologist to ensure that the proposed purchase gets to the customer in a perfect condition. Faulty lines delivered to a fashion business have several fundamental downsides, as they can:

*   dissatisfy customers, who usually tell their friends;
*   waste retail management time in refunding money to customers;
*   irretrievably lose sales if a line gets through to the shop floor and then has to be recalled;
*   incur loss of time, and therefore money, for all business functions in getting the problem resolved.

The modern buyer and technologist aim to prevent faulty or low-quality goods getting out of the factory in the first instance. If faulty merchandise gets to the shop floor, the overall cost to the business in terms of lost customer loyalty and bad word of mouth are immense.

B&M and its relationship to marketing

The B&M functions are, in many respects, key to the overall marketing efficiency of any fashion retailing operation. B&M are fundamentally responsible for ensuring that the product is right, and that the price is correctly positioned in the market, as well as ensuring that it is sent to the right place. In the context of the classic 4Ps model of the marketing mix, it has a major responsibility in getting the right mix, which is a fundamental of good marketing practice. Often the B&M functions will also become involved with the *promotional* elements of trading, such as price and product-related promotions. Although larger retailers often have marketing departments, their role in overall marketing management varies between companies. Often marketing departments involved with higher-end products will take a lead role in promotional activity, especially when high-quality advertising is required. For some of the more mainstream fashion retailers, marketing departments tend to be more involved with day-to-day visual display aspects of marketing, whereas in other organisations, the marketing department simply fulfils a general marketing research role, the results of which are then fed to other business functions to help their decision-making processes. Because of the profound significance of B&M on the overall marketing effort, the notion of a separate marketing function in the normal FMCG sense is often absent from the fashion business.

Design-led fashion retailers are becoming increasingly interested in the power and value of their brand names. Top Shop is a good example of a fashion retailer that has emerged from being simply a high-street fashion retailer to become an internationally recognised fashion brand. Its involvement with young and established fashion designers is now an important part of its unique offer, which in part may have led to the introduction of brand managers, a title borrowed from the FMCG sector. Brand management is now an established part of many other large and more design-led fashion retailers' approach to managing their marketing effort.

Keeping in step with the highly competitive UK marketplace is a continual battle for fashion buyers and merchandisers working at all levels of the trade. One element of the B&M role is to continually monitor competitors' ranges and promotional activity. Competitors' ranges and marketing approaches change rapidly, often creating problems and issues throughout the trade. The full-scale attack on the clothing market by the UK supermarket giants over the past few years appears to have been largely ignored by many mid-market retailers, who have made minimal responses to the price challenge facing them. There has never been a greater need for detailed on-going research on the competition. Large profitable organisations that once appeared to have enjoyed an invulnerable market position can now be easily toppled in the fast-moving world of fashion.

To assist the B&M and retail operations' functions understand what is happening in their own businesses, longitudinal field studies of the competitors can be undertaken by marketing research agencies which employ their own researchers to provide regular and detailed competitor updates. Such services do not come cheap, but they can often provide invaluable help to fashion retailers by keeping them informed of both major and minor competitive changes. Mystery-shopping services are another form of field research that retailers use to ensure that their own outlets are providing a consistent approach to customer service. Mystery shoppers undertake shopping missions to specified outlets, objectively measuring all aspects of the customer experience: issues such as staff helpfulness, knowledge and stock availability are key, although they are often asked to measure other elements relating to customer service and satisfaction. Fashion retailers with many hundreds of outlets, have great difficulty in ensuring the consistency of their customer service. The use of mystery shopping by marketing research agencies can help businesses fully understand their real positioning in relation to their competition. Field research can help ensure that service standards are not allowed to slip over time. Good buyers and merchandisers need to be instinctive marketers.

Key issues now facing UK B&M

Private ownership of fashion retailers

The UK has recently come under competitive pressure from foreign retailers wanting both to operate here and also to acquire UK fashion retailing businesses for themselves. The market is seen as high value, well developed and cash generative. Over the past few years several large public companies have been taken over by private companies and individuals, which have realised the intrinsic value and logic of direct ownership, without the interference of the City and private shareholders. At present, fashion retailers representing nearly 40 per cent of all the UK fashion clothing market by value are owned by private individuals and their families or private investment groups. Whether this move will be in the long-term interest of both customers and employees remains to be seen. Under public ownership, shareholders could hold the directors of such businesses accountable for their actions; under private ownership this no longer possible. The direct impact of the private ownership of large fashion retailers on the integrity of the decision-making and professionalism of both buyers and merchandisers is as yet unclear.

Fundamental shifts in sourcing and supply-chain policies and strategies

It is estimated that by 2005 nearly 90 per cent of all clothing and fashion accessories sold in the UK will be sourced from abroad. It was just a few decades ago that M&S proudly pronounced that over 90 per cent of its merchandise was made in the UK. In common with most of their competitors, M&S's strong relationship with the UK textiles and garment manufacturing sectors is waning fast. Cheaper priced products from the Far East, the Middle East, Eastern Europe, the Pacific Rim, China and India have fundamentally changed the way in which UK buyers now work. When the UK manufactured most of its own fashion requirements, foreign travel and international communications were limited, but the average buyer is now expected to spend long periods of the year working abroad with their manufacturing base, developing new ranges and of course continually looking for new product opportunities. International travel in a buying role is often seen as a glamorous perk of the trade, though the author's own experience is that foreign buying trips should never be confused with foreign holiday travel!

Foreign sourcing requires a great deal of forward and contingency planning to ensure that any fashion business is adequately provisioned with the right product, in the right quantity at the right time. Among the problems of buying foreign-produced merchandise are:

- generally longer lead times;
- currency fluctuations – mainly of the US dollar – which can cause profit management issues;
- lack of physical control of the merchandise;
- cultural and communication barriers – delivery urgency is not always a global norm.

While it may sound very exotic to travel to China to discuss ranges and products, in reality travelling to Leicester to do the same, although less glamorous, used to be much easier and more practicable. Despite improved internet communications, some buying offices now use high-definition dedicated video links to talk with factories and to see actual samples in progress. There is no substitute for personal presence and input when dealing with such a variable product as fashion.

As India and China develop their huge manufacturing capacities for both textiles and garments, it becomes evident that what used to be producers of low-cost merchandise such as Turkey and Eastern Europe start to look expensive against the product prices on offer. Although lower product prices are becoming increasingly important to UK consumers, fashion's limited shelf-life makes it important for UK and other

European buyers to try wherever possible to keep some level of home-produced, or close-to-home-produced, manufacturing sources, in an endeavour to keep lead times short. Once the north and east of London had a strong 'rag-trade' manufacturing base, where factories would be able to quickly produce simple cut-and-sewn garments. These small factories were dubbed 'sweatshops', where mainly immigrant workers were paid a pittance for long and arduous days of repetitive work; a few still survive in most European capital cities, but even these are finding it almost impossible to make a profit. Sweatshops have been part of European culture for many years; although now deemed illegal and politically incorrect, they often provided a first step on the economic ladder for both legal and illegal immigrants to the developed world. The less expensive fringes of Eastern Europe and the Near East are now some of the closest and cheapest manufacturing sources for UK fashion buyers to consider. Philip Green, the famous billionaire owner of Arcadia, announced on television in 2004 that his company had moved an element of its production requirements closer to home, undoubtedly driven by the need to keep its supply chain as short as possible. Long lead times can make decision-making difficult for high fashion businesses.

As product procurement has become more difficult as result of the general manufacturing shift away from Europe, most large retailers have developed specialised supply-chain departments and expertise, to help and support the B&M functions. The role of the supply-chain manager varies with the type of retailer involved, but essentially he or she will be looking at every aspect of how the organisation reacts and works with its product and service providers to ensure that every last action and operation works effectively and efficiently. By doing this, the business can be certain that it is bringing its products to market without wasting effort or resource. The most economic route to market ensures that the retailer optimises its profit returns and also gains an edge over the competition. The huge complexity of sourcing and shipping from abroad has been one the main driving forces of supply-chain management development in the fashion business. Most UK fashion retailers have now developed highly professional product import specialists and departments.

The changing roles of fashion buyer and merchandisers

The world of fashion buying is normally portrayed by the media as both glamorous and exciting, and that tends to be the perception of potential new entrants. Although there are other careers that are less demanding and more mundane, many elements of fashion buying are very unglamorous, repetitive and demanding. The seasonal changes in fashion dictate an annual rhythm of work. At Christmas when the shops are busy selling, the buying office will be quieter, with the buyer preparing for or just returning from a foreign buying trip in preparation for a future season. Internal meetings reviewing range and sales performance occur on a cyclical basis throughout the year, with key seasonal meetings taking place ahead of the finalisation of the season's look. At times buyers and merchandisers can be dealing with up to four seasons at a time: the season that has just passed may be presenting them with residues and the promotional activity associated with slow stock; new seasons' deliveries need to be managed into and around the business; the next season's planning and sampling may already be starting; and the buyer may be looking two seasons ahead for colour, for style and fabric inspiration. Fashion B&M is about past, present and future seasons, not simply about the now.

As the competition gets more aggressive and tougher, the speed and skills required to match and better it become ever more important. In less competitive times, the market was more forgiving of average B&M performance. Poor or below-average performance leads to sales and profit failure, making increased professionalism more necessary than ever. As a result of the increasing enthusiasm to enter B&M, competition has become more intense, with large fashion retailers usually being many times oversubscribed with applicants for both first and established posts. Even for first buying positions, it is normally expected that a graduate-level applicant, preferably with a fashion/business-related degree, will be put through a series of aptitude tests, involving numeracy, verbal reasoning, negotiation skills and a mock range selection. Most recruitment agencies in the sector will also require some form of testing prior to introductions to fashion organisations and interviews. These skills being demanded by employers (see Chapter 10) give some insight to the competitive and demanding nature of B&M.

Future trends in B&M

The challenging competition now coming from outside of the UK from foreign retailers is unlikely to diminish and therefore the buyer and merchandiser of tomorrow will have to be continually improving their skills set by a combination of self-directed learning and, it is hoped, internal organisational training. New fabric and manufacturing technologies are developing at an increasing rate, as well as the continuing sea changes to the trading and business environment. New and emerging countries and manufacturers are continually challenging the old order. Nothing can be assumed to remain constant.

The merchandiser's role is likely to change out of all recognition, as merchandise-management systems achieve higher levels of artificial intelligence that are aimed at improving the rate and quality of decision-making. The historical reliance on numbers-driven planning is likely to give way to hybrid visual–numerical planning that will help buyers and merchandisers plan the way a range will actually appear in-store at a point in the future. Planning using numbers alone, without paying regard to the look of the range, is an unwise approach.

The best buyers and merchandisers will require interchangeable skill sets, with merchandisers having a well-honed sense of fashion and buyers being comfortable with the disciplines of visual and numerical planning. The continual drive of cost reduction throughout the whole of UK retailing will ensure that the B&M team of the future will be lean, mean and efficient.

The ethos of a modern buying office can be electric: it is fast moving, unforgiving and, most importantly, continually challenging. The rewards are high, but it is certainly not easy, nor a place for anyone without a thirst for lifelong learning. For more detailed information readers should refer to Jackson and Shaw (2001), *Mastering Fashion Buying and Merchandising Management*.

8 Fashion journalism

Brenda Polan

Fashion gets more coverage in the media than any comparable area of human interest or endeavour. It may not fill more column inches than news, scandal, politics or show business, but it exceeds space devoted to many worthier topics like art, education, architecture, theatre, literature, the environment or technology. If you count in all the areas fashion has co-opted for its purposes – from cosmetics to celebrity, from music to food, from furnishings and interiors to social events and charity initiatives of all kinds – it's astonishing just how wide the fashion journalist's remit now runs.

This is explained partly by the growth of the communications media. Whether printed, broadcast or online, these form a vast industry that consumes huge amounts of material, little of it totally fresh. Yet the media need to maintain at least an illusion that the information they disseminate is new and original. Within the industry everyone is competing – for space, airtime, hits and sales – so what one offers has to be newer and more original than what their rivals have to offer. The journalist's job is to provide copy that falls into that category. Since fashion is above all about change and novelty, even the most puritanical of editors has learned to love it – and his fashion editor.

Sometimes she can deliver by breaking a story that is genuinely news (even if merely the new look from Paris); more often it is a matter of coming up with a clever or amusing angle on an old story. Or, as is the case from the mid-1980s onwards, expanding the territory. Fashion's territory has proved a natural for expansion simply because, with very few exceptions, the bottom-line competition in the media is for advertising revenue, and the extended fashion industry has a lot of money to spend on judicious advertising. So, since 1980, in a chicken-and-egg great leap forward, the populations of the developed world have become aware of the extent to which fashion permeates most aspects of their lives and defines what is now called their 'lifestyle' and the media have developed coverage of every one of those aspects – and have elbowed their way into some that were not obvious. Consequently, at the start of the twenty-first century, the fashion-obsessed media stand accused of trivialising serious issues and even undermining the standards of probity practised by those in public life.

Take the case of the Oscar frocks. In the days of the great Hollywood studios, movie stars were dressed for Academy Awards night in gowns designed by the great costume designers like Edith Head and Travis Banton (Head even designed Grace

Kelly's wedding dress when she married Prince Rainier of Monaco). With the demise of the studio system actresses were left to dress themselves in shop-bought frocks. Two things resulted. The women who got it wrong were ridiculed in the newspapers, and the first question asked by red-carpet television interviewers became: 'Who made your dress?' In a world that had come to define itself by the labels it bought into, they knew what their viewers/readers really wanted to know. Soon the PR departments of the high-end international designer labels were scrambling to offer loans, gifts and, eventually and inevitably, bribes – not only a free frock but also US$100,000 to wear it. Movie folk grumble but the coverage of the frocks and rocks now hugely exceeds that of the awards, who won them and what for.

The same beady editorial eye can also make premieres, society parties, race meetings and fashion-shop openings a panic-ridden hell for celebrities. Women's anxiety to avoid a media pillorying for their dress sense has spawned the new profession of 'personal stylist'. The individuals taking up this career vary enormously in talent, experience, contacts and corruptibility.

The realisation that women (and men) would more happily buy into labels if they were photographed being worn by actresses, singers and footballers' wives than they did when they saw pictures of models wearing them was a turning point in the coverage of fashion. A fashion editor's endorsement of a brand might still count for something, but not nearly as much.

But if fashion-directed media have spread a little corruption elsewhere, they are themselves not immune. Goodie-bags and extravagant Christmas presents aside, the competition for advertising revenue may often compromise editorial judgement. In the often too-cosy relationship between media and advertisers, the latter long ago usurped the upper hand. PR executives, initially a conduit for information and access, have become the enforcers of the industry, doling out threats along with the champagne breakfasts. There are some honourable exceptions among the ranks of newspapers and broadcasters but most of the media have succumbed to the power of the paymaster. Editorial criticism will provoke an offended designer to withdraw both his advertising and access to his fashion shows. Some discerning fashion editors have been known actively to court a lifetime ban from certain tedious designers and bullying PR executives.

The cosmetics companies play toughest, orchestrating two-pronged advertising and PR deals on new products whereby the biggest story comes with the biggest ads. Magazine publishers tend to impose a three-line whip when an advertiser sponsors an event or invites a beauty editor to breakfast. The 'cover credits' are an institutionalised form of payback – allocated to the cosmetics company with the biggest ad 'presence' in the issue or simply to a favourite PR executive. The make-up artists who do the faces of the models in the photographs chosen for the covers of magazines use a selection of products of varying provenance, often blended promiscuously together. Yet the photograph is sent off to the PR executive of one selected brand who attributes every last molecule of the model's 'slap' to one of her products and the 'credit' is then run on the contents page.

Another problematical area is the make-over, a fashion staple since the 1950s. Although the genre has always been subject to a little spin – a scrubbed face, flattened, pinned-back hair, unflattering clothes and harsh lighting in the 'before' shot, the full battery of soft-lit fashion photography on the 'after' – it developed in the late 1990s and early 2000s into something resembling witch-burning. Trinny Woodall and Susannah Constantine, the partnership that developed the *What Not To Wear* franchise, introduced the practice of humiliating their subject before remaking her/him. This approach was fairly restrained while the patronising pair worked in print for the *Telegraph* newspaper, but it had to be sharpened up for television.

Reality TV was always a genre destined to get boring very quickly. Watching the untalented and fatuous display their flaws has limited appeal. Its practitioners responded by making ever-more shocking/revelatory/disgusting programmes. This became known as car-crash TV. In order to hold their own in this world, Trinny and Susannah developed a *de-haut-en-bas*, jolly-hockey-sticks, upper-class boarding-school mode of address, invading their subject's physical space and her/his psychological privacy boundaries. Constantine in particular had an elephantine earthiness that disconcerted many subjects. She would grab their breasts and remove their knickers on camera – without so much as a by-your-leave.

Why, you may ask, did the victims permit these humiliations to be broadcast? Because they had been bought off with the prospect of a transformative haircut, a miracle make-up and £2,000 to spend on new clothes. It probably sounded like a good deal to a provincial mum with a part-time job and a bit of a style bypass. Trinny and Susannah, however, were banking millions. This, of course, is not the fate of many fashion editors. Stylists can do very well from work in advertising, in fashion show styling, design consultancy and private wardrobe engineering, but it's a rare writing journalist who gets rich.

In fact, television has always had a problem addressing fashion in an intelligent or reflective way. Fashion coverage on French television is, of course, uncritically obsequious and Elsa Klensh's US *Style* programme may have better production values, but it's a PRs' paddling pool. Any attempts at a serious approach such as C4's *The Look* have played to tiny minority audiences and, on video, to generations of fashion students exploring their college's archive. While *Woman's Hour* on BBC Radio 4 has for half a century managed to discuss fashion intelligently without the benefit of visuals, British television's first successful fashion programme was not launched until the mid-1980s. It was a cheerful magazine called *The Clothes Show* which, while covering fashion stories in an editorial way, discovered early on that make-overs were what the viewers liked most. (Clothes Show Live, an annual weekend event held at the National Exhibition Centre outside Birmingham, is all that remains of this long-lived programme. Essentially it sells merchandise and provides a happy hunting ground for model scouts.) The make-over formula was hijacked to make several stand-alone programmes during the 1980s and 1990s – notably *Style Challenge* which benefited from the excitable and knowledgeable presence of the *Daily Telegraph*'s fashion editor, Hilary Alexander.

Make-over programmes came and went, supplanted by make-overs of your garden, your kitchen or your neighbour's front room. As they became steadily more banal and less miraculous, the genre appeared to be fading fast – until Trinny and Susannah gave it a poisonous kiss of life. Since then, copycat articles and programmes have discounted even *What Not To Wear*'s modest scruples. Various kinds of extreme make-over involve publicity-hungry plastic surgeons, dentists, fitness trainers, nutritionists, cookery coaches, interior designers, etiquette advisers, psychologists and social engineers as well as the standard hairdresser, make-up artist and fashion stylist. One such programme piles on the humiliation by taking victims out into the street in order to ask 100 passers-by to guess their age. The programme then aims to knock off a decade before repeating the hideous process.

So is the modern fashion journalist a sadistic know-it-all, mistress of a 100 different kinds of artifice for rejuvenating and remaking helpless, tasteless, know-nothings – after having totally humiliated them in the most public way imaginable? Or is she an uncritical chronicler of brands and labels, the corrupted or intimidated mouthpiece of a mighty PR machine that exists to part the punter from her money? Certainly, in some cases. But, exactly because fashion journalism has colonised so much new territory, there are still many areas where good journalism is the norm, where exacting research is done, honest investigations completed and straightforward, truthful opinions delivered. But the make-over mavens and the PR poodles don't do much for the profession's reputation.

Fashion journalists have always had a problem being accepted as equals by their peers covering other areas. Since moral, upright people concerned with running the world have always rather despised fashion and its adherents, it is logical that those who choose to chronicle the despicable should be similarly dismissed. The origins of fashion journalism lie in the ladies' magazines of the nineteenth century – titles such as *The Lady's Magazine, La Belle Assembleé, The World of Fashion, The Ladies' Treasury, The Gentlewoman, Queen* and *Woman at Home*. These magazines were part-entertainment, part-instruction manual, and tended to promote the domestic virtues in the driest of manners, the fashion articles concentrating on technical matters, on fabric and colour, detail and, in the second half of the century, construction. They were, as Cecil Willett Cunnington pointed out in his seminal book *English Women's Clothing in the Nineteenth Century* (1990), 'thinly disguised advertisements of particular dressmakers, while others were obviously supplied broadcast to English papers from a French source' (p. 4).

The illustrations were mostly rather banal drawings, sometimes hand-tinted, which varied enormously in quality and clarity. Photographs were used in the second half of the nineteenth century but they tended to follow the pattern of the drawings and made no effort to convey atmosphere. It was only at the beginning of the twentieth century that fashion drawing developed into something capable of communicating the mood and spirit of the clothes (photography took longer to find its fashion vocabulary). The genre's most significant artist was Paul Iribe, who was initially commissioned not by a magazine editor but by the couturier Paul Poiret. He wanted idealised images that rooted his designs firmly in the romantic Art Nouveau culture that produced them. Not only did the style of drawing place them firmly in their art-historical moment but within them his models also lived in Art Nouveau interiors and landscapes.

In 1908 Iribe produced a beautifully coloured album entitled *Les Robes de Paul Poiret racontée par Paul Iribe*. It made his name and changed the course of fashion illustration. Poiret went on to work with the equally creative Georges Barbiers, Georges Lepape and Erté, probably the greatest of fashion illustrators. This was the nom de plume (from his initials) of the Russian-born Romain de Tirtoff who, at twenty and trained in both art and ballet, left St Petersburg for Paris, where Poiret immediately employed him. He moved on to work exclusively for *Harper's Bazaar* and produced every cover for the next twenty-five years.

Although Erté remained faithful to his attenuated lyrical style, illustration followed fashion and fashionable art movements like expressionism into more naturalistic styles. André-Edouard Marty set his clean, easy stamp on *La Gazette de Bon Ton, Femina* and *Vogue*. Etienne Drian's strong line was in the tradition of Sargent, Toulouse Lautrec and Boldini, and brought a sense of movement and immediacy to his drawings for *Gazette du Bon Ton* and other magazines of the 1920s. Eduardo Garcia Benito, another *Vogue* stalwart in the 1920s and 1930s, favoured strong-lined woodcuts that delineated a lean silhouette on a plain background. The style of Eric (American-born Carl Erickson) was softer, more impressionistic. In the 1930s and into the 1940s he headed *Vogue*'s team of illustrators that included the painter Christian Bérard, as well as René Bouet-Willaumez and René Bouchet.

Cecil Beaton who, starting in the 1920s, worked for *Vogue* for fifty years, was probably the only great fashion illustrator equally at home with brush and camera. His style often had a narrative dimension and a journalistic voice, the former owing much to his habit of creating elaborate settings for his portraits and fashion drawings and the latter deriving from his tendency to verge just far enough towards caricature to express a waspish opinion.

Visually, Beaton's near contemporary René Gruau probably had more impact on the way fashion was perceived through the late 1940s And 1950s. His was a graphic line, sinuous and sweeping. A partiality for flat planes of colour and his talent for imparting subtle character to the men and women in the drawings are reminiscent of Henri de Toulouse Lautrec. Gruau's style was inextricably linked with the work and image of his friend Christian Dior, whose advertisements he illustrated.

Although there are talented illustrators working in fashion today, from the 1930s on, image-making for magazines increasingly became the photographer's province. Initially photographs were, of course, in black and white and the earliest colour was crude. As the technology improved, photographs began to look as glamorous as drawings. By the 1960s the photographer had all but eclipsed the illustrator. This is not surprising since in the twentieth century reality came mediated by the camera lens: we experienced the world through photographs, films and newsreels. If fashion is about novelty and modernity, then it demands to be expressed in the technology invented this morning.

Despite the much larger circulations of newspapers, the most important title in the fashion business is still *Vogue*. In 1909 an ambitious young publisher called Condé Nast bought an ailing American society magazine and transformed it into the style bible it still is, 100 years later. *Vogue* was relaunched on the cusp of a fashion revolution in which its readers would discard their corsets and their passivity and embark on the long journey – its distractions, victories and defeats reflected in their clothes – towards social equality. *Vogue*'s visual vocabulary, the immediacy and accuracy with which it reported fashion's moods, its indulgences and delusions, its conformities and revolts, were the features of the magazine which made it one of the social historian's most treasured documents of record.

In 1914 Nast put a photographer on salary. In the days when the new season's couture clothes were photographed on society ladies rather than models, Baron Adolph de Meyer was appropriately well connected and totally *belle époque* in his sensibilities. His pictures, posy and painterly, baroque and flatteringly soft-focus, also appeared in *Vanity Fair*. In 1921 he defected to *Harper's Bazaar* and Edward Steichen, a First World War aerial photographer, replaced him. Steichen's style had a post-war sense of living in the present, an easy narrative quality that was unposed and immediate. In the pictures Steichen took when working closely with Carmel Snow, a young fashion editor who became the legendary editor of *Harper's Bazaar*, photography began to find a fashion voice.

More than an illustration, a photograph is a team effort. An illustrator could work with a frock and a sketch pad – though a model is always a good idea. But even in these days of Photoshopped images, it takes an art director, a fashion editor/stylist, a hairdresser, a make-up artist, a model and a photographer (plus assistant or entourage of assistants to manage lighting, background, props) to make a photograph. And in the very early days no one was quite sure how to get the most out of the new technology. The first fashion photographs mimicked both the show-me-the-detail fashion drawings of the Victorian age and – as the great Alexander Liberman, art director of *Vogue* through six decades, noticed – the formal portraits of self-important aristocrats, cool, distant, disengaged. Until Edward Steichen, the stiff, well-bred ghost of the society magazine lingered on.

While technology and paper quality still limited newspapers to carrying drawings, magazines were able to exploit photography to the full. In the 1930s George Hoynigen-Huené played with perfect light; Horst P. Horst married a sculptural classicism to the subversively erotic; André Durst lent a surreal frisson to simple clothes; and Toni Frissell pushed Steichen's natural approach to its snapped-running-in-a-rainstorm limit. At *Harper's Bazaar*, in 1932, new editor Carmel Snow directed the Hungarian photographer Martin Munkacsi as he did the first ever on-location action fashion pictures. It was a cold day in late autumn, and the model, in a swimsuit and cape, suffered goose bumps and chattering teeth as she ran along the beach. It is an iconic image – and a terrible precedent. Thanks to the many weeks it took to produce and distribute a magazine, a fashion model's life was from then on to be spent shivering in swimwear in November, sweltering in furs in July.

Condé Nast never forgave Carmel Snow for her defection to *Harper's*, and that intransigence was at the root of the intense rivalry and ruthless competitiveness that inspired such a flowering of talent. In 1934 Mrs Snow hired the great art director Alexey Brodovitch. He exhorted his photographers, 'Surprise! Change! Shock!', and created a 'design factory' which nurtured the talents of Louise Dahl-Wolfe, Richard Avedon, Hiro and Lillian Bassman. Brodovitch also commissioned artwork from Salvador Dali, Raoul Dufy, Marc Chagall, Picasso, Matisse, Braque, Brancusi, Giacometti and Jackson Pollock.

At *Vogue*, from the 1940s on, Alexander Liberman was art director first for the US edition and then for the magazine's international family of *Vogue*s. Under his regime, Diane Arbus, Irving Penn, Helmut Newton, Guy Bourdin, Antony Armstrong-Jones, Erwin Blumenfeld, William Klein, Norman Parkinson, Gordon Parks, John Rawlings, Clifford Coffin, Frances McLaughlin, Lisa Fonssagrives and many other formidable talents helped define the magazine's approach to fashion.

Throughout the decades the illustrator, however original, was very much the conveyor of the editor's vision. The great photographers are retrospective stars, their creative contribution recognised more by modern historians than by contemporary commentators. In the 1960s, however, the clickers became celebrities – a process expedited by a film called *Blow-Up* directed by Michelangelo Antonioni. The lead character in the movie was doubtless based on David Bailey, a photographer who was later to reject the label 'fashion photographer', insisting: 'I photograph women who wear clothes.' This sentiment reflects unchanged that persistent snobbery about fashion, an activity that the serious-minded have long held to be of interest only to the frivolous. It was logical that the higher the opinion late twentieth-century photographers had of themselves, the more they would seek to both redefine their role and rename it.

Steven Meisel, along with Herb Ritts, Peter Lindbergh and Bruce Weber, one of the most successful fashion photographers of the high-gloss, supermodel-dominated 1980s, thought of himself as an 'image-maker' and claimed to be a 'mirror of his era'. Certainly, the neo-realists of the 1990s – Craig McDean, Juergen Teller, Nick Knight, Wolfgang Tillmans, Corinne Day – worked energetically to produce pictures that many perceive as more social commentary than glossy commerce.

Fashion writing, or writing about fashion, on the other hand, has a long history of social commentary. A long line of churchmen, moralists and dress reformers has railed against fashion and its foolishness while the self-regarding wits whose articles, doggerel and cartoons filled the pages of *Punch* over a century or so just never got enough of it. In a search for human foibles to mock, fashion was always the easy option.

But rant as the anoraks and their ancestors might, no amount of mockery or threats from the pulpit could dampen the interest in fashion of nearly anyone living above subsistence level. People have always sought ways to stand out from the common herd and originality in dress is a harmless enough solution to the quest. Initially, fashion was a function of Europe's great power bases, the courts of tyrants and autocrats – be they imperial Rome, Renaissance Florence, the London of Elizabeth I or the Paris of Louis XIV. The fashion word was disseminated by diplomats, travellers, merchants and tradesmen, and by gossipy, excited epistles between friends and acquaintances.

In the nineteenth century publishing found its feet and the cut of a crinoline could travel from Paris to London in a day. Interestingly, the copy in those early fashion reports adopted a jargon that C. Willett Cunnington called 'dressmaker's French' and its authors wrote 'in a spirit of deadly playfulness, ranging from the arch to the inane'. Some of those anonymous authors may have been women but most were men. Surely no woman could have penned the piece from the 1885 archives of the *Manchester Guardian* that begins:

> It is an admitted fact that every woman dresses, not to please herself, but to please her husband, her father, her brothers and their male friends; yet the more any particular fashion is abused and ridiculed by the coat-wearing part of the community the more persistently she clings to it, and the more loath she is to resign it, even after its death-knell has struck.
>
> Thus it will be with the *tournure*, or bustle; it has survived the criticism and mockery which have been showered on it; but the caprice which introduced it and has granted it so long an existence now decrees that *tournures* are to be very much reduced in size preparatory to their being abandoned altogether. In spite of this, *tournure*s will probably endure for some time longer, until all are convinced that the cushion at the waist and a few steels in the dress skirt constitute all that is really required to sustain the heavy draperies of costume and the weighty trimmings on mantles.
>
> If the *tournure* is abandoned, however, greater attention than ever must be paid to the arrangement of the *jupons*, especially under ball and evening dresses . . .

And on and on and on. Given that this pompous melange of detail, advice and patronising comment was pretty much the norm, a change in approach had to be in the offing. That change happened almost inevitably in America where a republican-minded but upwardly mobile middle class was ready for a magazine that could show them how to express their new wealth in ways that were classy, tasteful and, while affordable, just a tad exclusive. The catalyst was an employee of Condé Nast. Edna

Woolman Chase was born in New Jersey in 1877 and was brought up by her Quaker grandparents by whose principles she lived all her life. She joined *Vogue* when she was eighteen, addressing envelopes in the circulation department, and stayed for fifty-seven years. When she retired in 1952 she had been editor-in-chief of the US, UK (founded 1916) and French (1920) editions of *Vogue* for thirty-seven of those years and had created the template for all fashion magazines. She trained artists, photographers and writers, and, together with Nast, made *Vogue* a standard bearer for quality – in fashion and in fashion journalism.

One of her protégées was Carmel White Snow who worked at *Vogue* as fashion editor until she was invited, in 1932, by William Randolph Hearst to become editor of his company's newly acquired *Harper's Bazaar*, a post she held until retirement in 1956. She it was who, according to legend, coined the phrase 'New Look' after seeing Christian Dior's 1947 collection. Like Mrs Chase, she was a nurturer of new talent and championed it even when no one else would – the Spanish-by-birth couturier Cristobal Balenciaga was one such project of hers. She was, however, more rigorously didactic in her approach than was Mrs Chase, instructing the women of America in most aspects of their material lives.

In her turn, Mrs Snow recruited the next great doyenne of fashion journalism, Diana Vreeland. Born in Paris but raised in New York, Mrs Vreeland brought an international sophistication and wit to the magazine she joined in 1937. She made her name with her 'Why don't you . . .?' column, a series of amusing, sometimes outrageous, suggestions that met with mixed if usually passionate responses. She got away with suggesting her readers turned their ermine coats into bathrobes or had furry elk-skin trunks on the backs of their cars, but her advice that they should use leftover 'dead' champagne for washing their blonde children's hair earned her parody from S. J. Perelman in the *New Yorker*. In her biography, *DV* (1984), she confessed that she simply loved the attention.

In the early 1960s Vreeland moved to *Vogue*, editing it until she was summarily fired in 1971. Some accounts have it that she took to her bed for a year, others that she barely took notice. She became adviser to the Costume Institute of the Metropolitan Museum of Art in New York and directed many major exhibitions, including a Balenciaga retrospective, *The Glory of Russian Costume*, and *Manchu Dragon*. Thus the journalist whose colloquial writing style made literary purists flinch began a process of marrying the ephemeral and trivial with the enduring and significant. Costume historians, rummagers among dusty fragments of cloth and paper, had only just begun to recognise that they had any kinship at all with fashion journalists. Vreeland was doubtless influential in inspiring today's fruitful collaboration between academics in museums and universities and the chroniclers of current change, the men and women who scramble for a good view at the international round of fashion shows. It is the latter who are instrumental in encouraging designers to create tomorrow's archive today by gifting to museums the clothes they might have bought expensively at auction some time in the future.

The intellectual weight that an academic-influenced approach might add to fashion coverage was, however, a long time coming. Fashion magazines in the mid-twentieth century might include great writing on themes literary or cultural, but for their fashion coverage they still employed a vocabulary that relied heavily on drawings and photographs to express the essence of the clothes, supported by words that were, for the most part, banal, exhortatory, gushingly descriptive and tediously detailed.

Newspapers, on the other hand, were limited by hot-metal technology in what they could convey visually. The bylined fashion editor, reporting from the couture shows and commenting on trends, was a post-war development. Through the 1940s and 1950s, however, hers was a mature voice of authority addressing a mature middle-class, readership. The most influential of these were probably Alison Settle of the *Observer*, Winefride Jackson of the *Daily Telegraph*, Ailsa Garland of the *Daily Mirror*, Iris Ashley of the *Daily Mail*, Alison Adburgham of the *Guardian*, latterly a distinguished historian of shops and shopping, and Ernestine Carter, Woman's Page editor of *The Sunday Times* from 1955 until 1972.

Mrs Carter, a southern belle and curator of architecture and industrial art at the Museum of Modern Art in New York before her marriage brought her to wartime London and British *Harper's*, was adamant in her opinion that fashion was a serious subject. Marilyn de Keyser, for several decades the PR of the milliner Graham Smith, was one of the many young women who went to work for her at *The Sunday Times*. She remembers that among the grand dame's strictures were a ban on the use of first names and an insistence on the wearing of white cotton gloves and hats at all times. Mrs Carter made neat little pillbox hats her signature headgear.

Ernestine Carter was the first fashion writer on *The Sunday Times* to use her own name. In a practice common to many newspapers and magazines (one that prevailed on the general interest women's weeklies into the 1970s), her predecessors had all written under a pseudonym, a 'house' byline that ensured continuity – in this case the suitably brisk and nannyish 'Mary Dunbar'. This fictional character had traditionally reported in what Mrs Carter described, in her autobiography *With Tongue in Chic* (1974), as diary form – more or less chronicling what her pile of invitations had provided. This meant that all clothes were featured six months too early and lacked anything resembling a price or a hint of where they might be bought.

When Mrs Carter introduced themed articles on clothes currently available, the prices were left in her copy but the names of the stockists were deleted by the sub-editors. 'Only advertisers, it seems, could be mentioned,' she discovered. Enlisting the paper's advertising manager, Vernon Stratton, to her cause, Carter went into battle (p. 104):

> My argument was two-fold: one, that if the page pulled (i.e. evoked response), non-advertisers would become advertisers (they did); two, that if the page gained readers, advertisers would continue to advertise even if they did not receive editorial mention (they did). My aim was to be free to establish a standard of quality, not necessarily based on price, but on excellence of design, creative ability and value.

Half a century later it still reads like the most sensible manifesto for a newspaper's fashion coverage. Mrs Carter's pages were, she was able to boast, 'invulnerable to advertising pressures'. While the blurred boundaries between journalism and public relations persist to the present, newspapers in general remain more robust in their efforts to stay the honourable side of the line. But a perception of fashion journalist as PR poodle remains one reason why journalists specialising in the field are often accorded scant respect by colleagues whose work calls for healthy scepticism or a confrontational approach. But while subversion has rarely been a motive for the fashion press, it does have a long and honourable history of accurate reportage alongside all the puffery.

When Mrs Carter joined *The Sunday Times* she was one of the first journalists to make the crossing from magazines to newspapers. When in 1947 Harold Wilson at the Board of Trade had summoned both sorts of fashion journalist in order to instruct them to ignore Dior's New Look in the interests of the economy and fabric rationing, she was on the British version of *Harper's Bazaar*. She noted that 'the glossies found themselves forced into unaccustomed solidarity for we faced the newspaper journalists. Although the latter were distinctly antipathetical to us, I found them impressive in their confidence and professionalism.' (p. 81.)

On *The Sunday Times* she was to prove their equal as they all witnessed a period of huge change in the fashion business. The industry she first covered was dominated by twice-yearly couture showings in Paris, Florence and Rome. Journalists attending the showings could write in their notebooks but not sketch, and certainly no cameras were permitted in the salon. A hand-out sketch or photograph might be available but the same one tended to be issued to all. Editors hated that. The glossies were permitted to borrow clothes to photograph overnight in conditions of strictest secrecy and in the knowledge that they would not (could not, given printers' lead times) be published for several months.

Then, in 1962 two Parisian couturiers, Dior and Balmain, broke their own embargoes by succumbing to the seduction of television. CBS offered to beam their collections around the planet by the newly launched satellite Telstar. Every art student who could hold a pencil was employed by one fashion editor or another, one mass-market manufacturer or another, to do lightning sketches directly from the TV screen. The dread authority of the Chambre Syndicale had been slightly weakened – albeit in a very dramatic way – and a handful of professional sketchers accredited to certain important newspapers were from then on admitted to the shows. (Phalanxes of photographers crammed into the bull pen at the end of the catwalk were still a decade or two in the future.)

The greatest power in this world of fashion was wielded by the Chambre Syndicale de la Couture Française, an organisation founded in 1868 with the aim of supervising the training of couture's essential craftspeople and setting and maintaining standards of quality. In the 1880s, under the leadership of Gaston Worth, it began to develop into a body that could coordinate showings and represent the couturiers as a unified – if not always united – body. It was instrumental in re-establishing Paris as the capital of fashion after the Second World War. Its chief function then was to organise the couture showings, construct the calendar, accredit the press and buyers, and police the release dates for images and information. Only Coco Chanel defied its edicts and did as she chose, revelling in publicity and the flattery of copyists.

A similar Camera Nazionale in Rome did much the same job for Italian Alta Moda and in London, the Incorporated Society of London Fashion Designers, founded during the war to promote British exports, did its best to match schedules. New York had a few couturiers and couture showings, but most European journalists did not cover them. In the 1950s in a challenge reminiscent of Renaissance rivalries, Florence, home of the Marchese Pucci, aristocrat and designer of sexy skiwear and resort clothes, launched a fashion event to show the clothes of a younger, sexier generation of couturiers. The Pitti shows, however, faded in importance to the level of mass-market trade exhibition as, at the beginning of the 1970s, Milan became the focus of the Italian designer-label RTW shows. As RTW replaced couture, designers in Milan, London and New York were to found new organisations, often with some financial support from national governments to promote their increasingly globally selling industries and run the fashion shows. (In the UK the British Fashion Council is partly funded by the Board of Trade but could not function without sponsorship from various mass-market companies and even magazine and newspaper publishers.)

A new generation of consumers, the well-salaried young, was dressed by a new generation of bright young designers the most high-profile of whom were in 'swinging London': Mary Quant, Jean Muir, Biba, John Bates, Foale and Tuffin, Zandra Rhodes, Gina Fratini, Ossie Clarke. But Paris, too, was splitting into the youthful – Saint Laurent, Cardin, Emmanuelle Khanh, Daniel Hechter, Christian Bailly – and the bourgeois, the old guard still dressing its ageing society princesses. Many of journalism's old guard did not understand the youth revolution – Mary Quant's husband, Alexander Plunkett Green, correctly sensed 'whiffs of disapproval' emanating from Ernestine Carter's office. But younger editors like Brigid Keenan, Molly Parkin, Prudence Glyn, Felicity Green, Deirdre McSharry, Meriel McCooey, Barbara Griggs, Jean Rook, Cherry Twiss, Jean Dobson and Serena Sinclair did. Unsurprisingly, American journalists like Bernadine Morris, Mary-Lou Luther and Carrie Donovan were instantly open to the thrill of the new – democracy and the mass market coming much more naturally to them than it did to some of the upper-class British fashion journalists.

In 1964, however, Clare Rendlesham (actually Lady Rendlesham and as upper-class as they came), fashion editor of *Queen* magazine, carried black-bordered pages entitled 'The End' and in a short and histrionic introduction beginning, 'Balenciaga is fallen, fallen, that great designer. The inspiration of the king of couturiers is dead. How are the mighty fallen and the weapons of fashion perished!' went on to declare of the couture collections: 'The mood was fiftyish. The colours were drab. The evening clothes were dreary.' That, of course, got her banned – and was exactly, she said many years later, what she'd intended. However, bans are rarely eternal. In 1966 Rendlesham managed to have William Claxton photograph the collections on Danny La Rue, the female impersonator. That didn't go down well either. Cherry Twiss in *The Sunday Times* Colour Supplement went one better, and created and photographed an entire funeral cortège to bury couture and its elitist pretensions.

Although Paris couture does in fact persist (championed by Suzy Menkes of *The Times* in the early 1980s as a 'crucible' in which the pure fires of creativity could turn inspiration into beauty – and damn the cost), it has been supplanted by RTW there and in every other country that aspires to manufacture well-designed clothes. This has made the journalists' schedule increasingly gruelling. One described his itinerary in early 2005, starting in January at Milan menswear, moving to Paris for the couture shows followed by the Paris menswear shows, then straight to New York for the American RTW shows, back to London for London Fashion Week, out again to Milan for the women's RTW and back directly to Paris for the marathon RTW showings in early March. After a week and half's respite he flew to Singapore for fashion week. He was invited to São Paulo and Beijing, too, but hadn't the strength. Fashion weeks happen everywhere (twice a year) – from Sydney to Hong Kong, from Barcelona to LA, and no one can hope to take in all of them.

Even so, fashion shows remain the fixed dates in a fashion editor's calendar – except that 'fixed' is hardly the word. They are not set in concrete. They have to avoid certain dates like *Yom Kippur* and the anniversary of 9/11. Rivalry has resulted in them changing sequence several times over the years (New York was once last by a month until the slurs that it was leaving itself time to copy Paris got too much for its designers and, after some confusion, the Council of Fashion Designers of

America decided to go first instead) and moving gradually earlier and earlier to accommodate manufacturing schedules and delivery deadlines. Although the international fashion shows are still technically thought of as press showings, at least half the room has, in the last half century, been filled with buyers. In the days of couture, the house's private customers, the European aristocrats and US industrialists' wives, perched thigh-to-thigh with the journalists on plush sofas or little gilt chairs. Sprinkled among them would be selected manufacturers who had paid a large 'caution' to gain access to a fashion show. They could then buy the *toiles* (the paper patterns) of chosen garments for mass manufacture. In Britain Jeffrey Wallis built his company, Wallis, on his 'Pick of Paris' line, pulling off a double coup when he bought not only a Chanel *toile* but the exact same tweed from Linton Tweeds as well.

As RTW supplanted couture at the cutting-edge, the owners of and the buyers for boutiques and designer departments in stores occupied the seats opposite the press. From the beginning the seating plan was of crucial importance. The most important invited guests sat in the front row, the least important stood at the back with the fabric suppliers and seamstresses from the *atelier*. Demotion was – and is – a humiliation too hard to bear. The very best position was at the foot of the catwalk, because you could watch the models walk towards you and did not, as those along the sides did, develop tennis-match neck. These days the foot of the catwalk is usually reserved for the photographers and video and television cameramen – and everyone has the number of a good masseur.

Other things have changed, too. The 'friends of the house', originally the designer's family, friends, supporters and suppliers, have morphed into a designer's celebrity roll call. In the twenty-first century designers like Donatella Versace think nothing of flying in their celebrity 'fans', accommodating them at the best hotels, feasting and plying them with extravagant presents. In some cases even the most august journalists have found themselves bumped to the second row behind Madonna or Jennifer Lopez.

Mounting the collections is hugely expensive (£200,000 is about average) and so is travelling to them. At the pace at which all publications must now work, it is positively dangerous for journalists to spend so much time away from their offices where the culture of 'presenteeism' tends to prevail – i.e. if your editor cannot see you, you're not working. Rivalry and ambition are also encouraged in the interests of keeping everyone sharp – what has been described as 'a productive atmosphere of fear and loathing'. And the saner members of the fashion community regret lost husbands, absconded lovers and alienated kids. Consequently, many pundits have called the passing bell of the fashion-show circuit – who needs it with video and the internet? – but they have yet to be proved right.

For, on the other hand, the collections are an opportunity to network and gossip, to observe one's peers and competitors, to meet the designers and the moneymen behind them, to eyeball the new models and generally soak up colour and detail for your articles. In short, for newspaper journalists, the collections are a source of insider info, background and good stories. In addition, most newspaper journalists file at least one story a day in time to catch the next morning's paper. Once that was a matter of bellowing copy down a bad telephone line to a copytaker back home – and putting up with mis-hearings and some comical mis-spellings. Now laptops and email make it a much easier operation. While magazine journalists doubtless enjoy the buzz, for them attending the collections can be more a matter of business. Advertising revenue may hang on their presence not just in their front-row seats but at breakfasts, cocktails and dinners as well. For the biggest spenders chairmen and chief executives abandon the office, fly in and pay court.

After the 1960s, fashion coverage in the media became polarised into two quite separate categories: the division Ernestine Carter had sensed at the Board of Trade meeting became a chasm. The glossy magazines – of which there were very few – continued to give us the wit and sensuality of fashion. In the UK, as the 1970s segued into the 1980s, Grace Coddington, Mandy Clapperton and Liz Tilberis of Beatrix Miller's *Vogue*, Michael Roberts of *Tatler*, Caroline Baker, ex-*Nova* and important freelance stylist, Ann Boyd of the *Observer* and Hamish Bowles at *Harpers & Queen* made pictures of great beauty and extraordinary narrative impact, images that could remain in the imagination for decades – and have done.

But although Mandy might be seated cosily next to Prudence Glyn of *The Times* at the Saint Laurent show, Liz might share a subversive sense of humour with Serena Sinclair of the *Daily Telegraph* and Michael and I, in my role as fashion editor of the *Guardian*, find plenty to gossip about together, there was an unbridgeable divide. On the newspapers and general-interest magazines – from *Woman's Realm* to *Woman's Journal* – fashion coverage was utilitarian, didactic, analytical, occasionally critical, practical, value-driven. While styling our own pictures as best we knew how, we covered news stories, interviewed and profiled designers, retailers, collectors and archivists. We kept pace with readers' changing lifestyles and tried to advise them on appropriate wardrobes. (The *Daily Telegraph*, under the triumvirate of Serena Sinclair, Ann Chubb and Avril Groome, went into business offering well-chosen clothes by designers like Jean Muir and Roland Klein at excellent prices by mail order.) We all tended to focus on trends, and the miracle make-over was a beloved staple.

The men who ran the newspapers valued the fashion content for its nicely decorative pictures of pretty girls (they are still not very comfortable with pictures of pretty boys). They were certain, however, that the written content should reflect the new consumerism, should be essentially problem-solving and value-oriented. So those of us creating the pages manufactured a hybrid. Almost without exception our pictures were taken by staff photographers, men and women who might be covering a football match one day, a train crash the next and your lingerie shoot after that. The lighting was rudimentary (these were available-daylight men) and they were under pressure from the picture desk to conserve film. They did stalwart duty, particularly at fashion shows, though in newspapers we couldn't do the magical images that so cogently expressed a fashion magazine's point of view. We could, however, use words to conjure up those moods and references.

We all found different ways – ways appropriate for our particular readers – to write about fashion. Reportage remained informative, descriptive and laced with practical advice, but it began to place fashion in its social, demographic and aesthetic context. It began to discuss design ideas and inspiration with designers, to deconstruct trends and assess how market forces within the industry shape its products. Interestingly, when approached thus, the fashion pages managed to attract and hold the attention of both the lover of fashion and her frumpy friend.

Some of the new backbone that was entering fashion journalism was inspired by a strong trade press. In 1960s America John Fairchild had turned *Women's Wear Daily* into a newspaper that kept a mostly impartial, if critical, watch on the international industry while also covering the social and celebrity scenes. It is a breakfast must-scan for every consumer press journalist, and it both reinforced and broadened what the fashion writer was free to consider news or a news peg to a feature. UK titles are less compelling, but the most enduring, *Drapers Record*, has proved not only a useful weekly source of information but an excellent training ground for young journalists, immensely improving the nose for news of any would-be fashionista.

The 1980s also saw an expansion in the magazine world, fuelled by the new inexpensive technology and the economic boom. Once divided into the glossy monthlies (preoccupied with fashion and society) and the general interest women's magazines (some fashion plus beauty, cookery, home, features and fiction), some of which were monthly like *Women's Journal* and *Good Housekeeping*, some weekly like *Woman* and *Woman's Own*, the hobby-based men's magazines, the trade mags and the political mags, the market suddenly blossomed with men's magazines – *GQ*, *Esquire*, *FHM* – and lifestyle magazines – *The Face*, *i-D*. These magazines arrived on the scene flaunting new approaches and techniques and lots of 'attitude'. They were only the precursors of a flood of new titles, some of which made it past issue one, many of which did not. Desktop publishing has made it possible for almost anyone to get a magazine out. Many are highly specialised and, because of that, they are known as 'fanzines'. Some minority-interest fanzines have, however, become fully fledged magazines.

Another factor was, of course, the spread of a new kind of feature writing, defined by Tom Wolfe as 'the new journalism' where features could read like novels or discursive memoirs, where genre boundaries became blurred and opinion could salt reportage and jokes pepper a serious investigative piece. The cool voice of the reporter gave way to the warmly engaged voice of the observer who was open to experience. Undercover reporting, fly-on-the-wall reporting, trying-on-a-lifestyle reporting, stream-of-consciousness reflection on a topic, the comic or furious blow-by-blow account of the interview that went terribly wrong, that didn't happen – and ultimately Hunter S. Thompson's gonzo journalism which reads like a short story with the disaster-prone writer at its solipsistic heart – all are aspects of the new journalism and helped shape fresh approaches to writing about fashion.

Writers like Liz Smith, Suzy Menkes, Michael Roberts, Katherine Samuel, Lesley Ebbetts, Jackie Modlinger, Sally Brampton, Colin McDowell, Sarah Mower, Susannah Frankel, Marion Hume, Judy Rumbold, Dylan Jones, Tamsin Blanchard, Roger Tredre, Lisa Armstrong, Peter Howarth, James Sherwood, Mimi Spencer and Tamasin Doe raised the level of address in many different ways so that fashion in all its complexity, all its functions, was illuminated, explained and made accessible. As a critic's purpose is to deconstruct for us why we respond as we do to a play, a book or a movie, fashion journalists saw their primary role as similarly interpretive. For their readers, they enabled choices that had been instinctive to become conscious and creative. As the essentially practical Lesley Ebbetts, long-term fashion editor of the *Daily Mirror* in the 1970s and 1980s, put it: 'Yes, fashion isn't art – but, unlike art, we all do it. And most of us really want to do it well. That's where our constituency lay. But the readers had to trust you.'

Along with Hilary Alexander of the *Telegraph*, Lesley Ebbetts remains a rarity in that she still styles pictures as well as writing copy. For the 1980s saw the beginning of a further division within the profession. As newspapers switched to more sophisticated technology which permitted colour photography as well as much greater clarity to black and white images, editors began finally to give way to the pleading and bullying of their women's editors and fashion editors on the matter of employing specialist fashion photographers. Some, of course, wouldn't work for a newspaper at any price. (In fact their way of saying so was to indicate that their fee for a day's shoot would be US$50,000 – or more.) Others gave it a go. Their fees may have been more modest but they were not insignificant, and fashion editors whose strength lay in their writing became nervous. They began to hire assistants who were strong stylists or to commission freelances. Without anyone really noticing or commenting, fashion editors began to divide into two separate professions: stylists and writers.

Consequently, some newspapers employ stylists as fashion editors, some employ writers. Although some publications are rich enough to employ both, in most cases when the alternative skill is needed, a freelance is called in. The new fashion writing did, however, have an influence on the world of magazines which, while continually developing on the visual front, had become stale when it came to writing. In the early 1980s *Harpers & Queen* was edited by Willie Landels, an art director by profession. His deputy, however, was a very clever writer, Ann Barr, who had, together with advertising man Peter York, produced the *Sloane Ranger Handbook*, a slender volume of pop-sociology that dissected the lives and preferences of a class of well-bred gels who lived within dashing distance of Peter Jones. (Their timing was impressive: Prince Charles became engaged to one not too long afterwards.) Their anthropological approach was to become a fashion writer's favourite and was perhaps most adroitly practised by one of their own writers, the young Nicholas Coleridge (latterly managing director of Condé Nast, London), destined to take over the editorship in 1986. His book *The Fashion Conspiracy* (1988) was the first of several timely exposés of the more exploitive practices of the fashion industry. In the 1980s, however, *Vogue*'s features content seemed unnaturally preoccupied with literary dynasties in general and the Bloomsbury Group in particular. Some tentative change was apparent during Anna Wintour's short editorship, but it was not until Liz Tilberis took the chair, under the editorial directorship of Mark Boxer, that the post of fashion features editor was created and writing about fashion was given a new status. Sarah Mower, previously of the *Guardian*, was recruited to lend intellectual rigour and some wit.

During the 1980s, the decade of ultimate consumerism, this kind of fashion writing colonised all the areas we learned to call 'lifestyle'. As TV became the chief conduit for news and news analysis, newspapers snatched territory from magazines and magazines had to fight back by broadening their remit. These were great times for journalists who wanted to do thoughtful, witty pieces about all aspects of contemporary living. They were also times that saw a great flowering of different approaches to fashion writing.

Suzy Menkes on the *International Herald Tribune* is generally considered the doyenne of contemporary fashion writers. While certainly capable of flights of lyrical prose, her true drift is business-oriented. She writes for the worldwide industry as much as she does for the reader who wants to know what to wear. Significantly she chairs a hugely successful annual conference on the luxury goods industry, and her advice is much sought and highly regarded.

Then there is the approach of Colin McDowell, author of sixteen books on fashion and senior fashion writer on *The Sunday Times*. He regards himself as a fashion critic and, apart from an authoritative 'Fashion Moments' column, restricts his articles to critiques of the collections and designer interviews/profiles with the odd polemic thrown in. His tone is magisterial, occasionally waspish and impartial; he particularly relishes the 'without fear or favour' aspects of his brief. Like Menkes, he is not content to remain a commentator. In 2004 he founded Fashion Fringe, a competition to discover talented young designers and fund their first collections.

The US newspaperwomen have always seen their function as a reporterly one. They would always attribute any criticism – or indeed praise – of a designer or a fashion show to a buyer, a store president or a passing celebrity or expert. Terri Agins of the *Wall Street Journal* is probably the ideal of the US fashion reporter. Her book *The End of Fashion* (1999) is certainly an ideally independent view of an industry and is illuminating on what she argued was a millennial crisis in fashion (driven by four social mega trends). Similarly Naomi Klein, a reporter on the *Toronto Star*, has made a specialism of branding targeted at the young. Her book *No Logo* (2000) exposes every exploitative aspect of the logo phenomenon. Instant opinion or criticism has, however, been rare in US fashion journalism. In the 1990s Amy Spindler at the *New York Times* initiated a change to a more critical, authoritative stance and her successor, Kathy Horyn, is to some extent following in her footsteps.

A change became apparent in the early 1990s. Fashion writing began to be redirected; reduced and trivialised, it became a means of amusing the non-fashion-aware. The first sign – the runaway success of *Hello!* magazine – was easy to ignore. But then, how could serious fashion writers dream that celebrity fever would eventually distort and impoverish their work? Under the editorship of Jane Procter and the fashion editorship of Kate Reardon *Tatler* started photographing all its fashion content on *real* people, partly because a cash-strapped mob will do anything for a free frock and a new haircut but chiefly because readers were perceived to be more interested in who was wearing the clothes than in who designed them. The celebrity bandwagon was rolling. From a position of deepest ignorance Trinny and Susannah, both minor celebrities, launched themselves as fashion experts in the *Telegraph*, photographing a motley selection of garments on themselves. And the magic make-over lurched out of the crypt to dominate fashion – and eventually beauty, health, interiors, lifestyles and lives – in all media.

What editors wanted was *uninformed* opinion: not the designer's thoughts or the writer's but the wearer's. Increasingly, the second paragraph of every designer profile or interview consisted of a breathless list of 'celebrity' clients. With few exceptions these lists were remarkably similar; indeed I once calculated that the same twenty women were buying up all the top-label frocks on the planet.

Only they were not, as we have already seen, buying them. As soon as the marketing departments of the design houses understood that their exposure and credibility rested on the fame of a handful of socialites and soap actresses, they set about securing it. When some fashion journalism students have revealed (only half in jest) that they're doing it for a lifetime of goodie bags and free frocks, I have suggested they transfer to RADA – lots more free frocks.

Celebrity is only the *most* destructive force in fashion journalism. There are others. One is the Bridget Jones effect. Actually, there was probably a disastrous top-secret attempt to clone Mimi Spencer some time around 1998 and it got horribly out of hand. The original Mimi is a gloriously funny, clever fashion writer with a sharp, pacey, opinionated, colloquial, anecdotal, intimate style. Ever since she was fashion editor of the London *Evening Standard* her imitators have been legion – and all of them thin, shrill, unfunny and not nearly clever enough.

She and her shadows are, however, part of a shift in the nature of journalism in general. For an older generation of journalists brought up on *Manchester Guardian* founder C. P. Scott's dictum 'Opinion is free but facts are sacred' and the well-known rider that I first heard from a journalism lecturer, 'Or, in the case of the *Guardian*, opinion is free but facts are expensive', the current preponderance of columns is easily understood. True news-gathering costs money, time and, sometimes, lives. Better to let a legion of columnists – freelance and uninsured – ponder and pronounce on some scantily detailed topic of interest to the readers. Most newspapers are more than capable of publishing half-a-dozen mutually conflicting opinions on a single topic on one day. So the egocentric urge to have a good, 'look-at-me, listen-to-me' rant is present in most journalists – especially the young. The fact that few of them are capable of constructing a logical argument is irrelevant. This is about visceral reaction to a news story.

On the coat-tails of the ubiquitous column has come the fictional, sometimes only semi-fictional, column which reached its apotheosis in *Bridget Jones's Diary*. Suffice it to say that cult status was achieved along with a very large fortune for its author, Helen Fielding. Other writers have tried copycat projects, attempting to carry us with them through various repulsively detailed traumas – my search for a mate, my divorce, my mastectomy – but none have yet hit pay dirt. However, newspapers and magazines continue to give them and their cosy introspections lots of space. One of the more successful is Rebecca Tyrrell's 'Days Like These' in the *Sunday Telegraph* – but then she does have long-deceased movie star George Sanders waiting in the garden shed to give comfort and counsel.

Young journalists covet just such a starring role and often fail to comprehend the extent to which it is a genre on its own and how very, very difficult it is to do well. The honourable and very readable exception is Hadley Freeman on the *Guardian* who approaches her topics with a professional scepticism and no stridency at all. Certainly, the new journalism embraces reportage in a style appropriated from another genre, but at its heart there must be reportage: there must be a bedrock of good, fact-based journalism, not a froth of self-regarding nonsensical rhetoric.

The third destructive force is the enormously increased effectiveness and therefore power of the PR industry. In the fashion world, journalists and PRs can have a mutually rewarding relationship; they are, after all, often the same people, switching roles sometimes several times in the course of a career. If there were no intermediary between press and manufacturer or retailer, gaining access to merchandise and information would be tough. But it really works well only when boundaries are respected. In the world of glossy magazines, the relationship between advertisers and publications has always been a cosy one. Today in the giving and taking of favours, freebies, facility trips and control over content, it goes way beyond that. It is always possible to operate for a while within the self-imposed constraints of a tit-for-tat system. Eventually, however, the more ruthless and commercially oriented party gains the upper hand. That has happened. Celebrity publicists demand the cover of the magazine in return for a half-hour interview opportunity, stipulate the photographer and the interviewer, insist on copy approval – and free frocks. Designers' PRs ban critically inclined journalists from fashion shows and deny titles they dislike access to their product. This makes for a cowed press, one that automatically grovels, seeking approval, abdicating control and integrity.

Of course, not all is lost. There are many good fashion writers and many publications prepared to run their copy. Not least among these are the new media. While radio and television may find themselves stymied when it comes to finding a way to re-create the best fashion coverage, the internet is proving to be the medium that can best showcase all aspects of fashion journalism. There are legions of bloggers with idiosyncratic, opinionated websites of their own as well as professional operations that range from the business-to-business news and forecasting site WGSN.com, through Vogue.com (UK *Vogue*'s site), Style.com (US *Vogue*'s), strong on gossip and instant fashion-show slide displays, Hintmag.com, an electronic glossy and Net-a-porter.com, for online designer shopping, to Showstudio.com, a true crucible of creativity. Good specialist sites are based all over the world and there are already hundreds. As the internet grows, they will multiply.

Illustrators and photographers do not have to radically change their work to publish it on the internet. Writers, on the other hand, are finding that brevity is best. Most internet users don't like scrolling through long tracts of type. The weakness of much shoestring web journalism is its self-indulgent, unedited quality. Sarah Mower's show reports for Style.com are examples of how to do journalism online: they are tightly written, clearly constructed, authoritative, witty and short.

But while other fashion journalists researching a story may print out her reports, along with the stuff off WGSN and the websites of the major newspapers, lovers both of fashion and of magazines do not thus far consider the sites a substitute for those seductive glossy pages. The likelihood is that they never will – but it won't stop them using all the media they can as sources of information and entertainment. For fashion journalists it's a big world, and it's getting bigger.

9 Fashion PR and styling

Carmen Haid, Tim Jackson and David Shaw

T
he first part of this chapter explains the importance of PR in the context of the UK fashion industry. In comparison to many other consumer items, the ever-changing nature of fashion products, brands and ranges can provide a huge PR opportunity for the endlessly hungry fashion journalists who seek new angles to excite and interest their equally fashion-hungry readers. Public interest in fashion stories both of a business kind and of a fashion nature has never been greater, with the plight of ailing fashion companies finding its way into general editorial items, rather than the normal business of the fashion pages. The UK public appears to have developed an insatiable interest in celebrities and what they wear. The ways in which fashion is communicated to a wide variety of media is discussed in this chapter, mainly from the luxury fashion perspective of the authors. The means of communicating with the press and the tools used are also explained, and the full range of fashion press events is discussed. Most importantly, the criteria by which PR is measured and evaluated are explained, an increasingly important part of the overall marketing management process that can prove pivotal in these very cost-conscious times.

The second part of the chapter explains in detail the role and significance of fashion styling in the overall marketing communication process. A generation of youth-obsessed narcissists, or 'Lookists' appears to be in the ascendant, with a host of magazines and TV make-over programmes advising on the latest looks, what to wear and what not to wear; even our once-stuffy politicians being quizzed more about their style of dress than their political policies and allegiances. Using the creative skills of the fashion stylist, even the most mundane and apparently lifeless garment can be transformed into the latest must-have item. However, to achieve this metamorphosis additional help is needed from models, hair and make-up stylists and fashion photographers. Their roles in this process are explained and some of their trade secrets revealed.

Public relations

PR is one of the most important promotional tools used by the UK fashion industry. At all levels of the fashion trade, PR is seen as the natural promotional tool, and in many situations it is better favoured than advertising. The fun but frivolous image of PR portrayed in the 1990s *Absolutely Fabulous* comedy series on BBC TV, misrepresents the tough and frenetic realities of the industry. PR is both a tactical and a strategic tool of marketing. It is generally either run as function within a fashion brand, sometimes as an adjunct to the marketing function, or – more often than not – is provided by an external PR agency or freelance consultant. There is no single ideal way to manage the fashion PR effort, although at the luxury end of the market there is a greater wish to take complete control of the process, to ensure that brand integrity is maintained at all costs. Some of the larger high-street fashion retailers retain the services of prestigious external PR companies such as Halpern, Lynne Franks, etc. Whichever route is chosen, the function and operation is predominantly similar.

PR also involves the personal relationship that builds between a brand and the media, particularly the press. The fashion press plays an important role in the image- and brand-building process, because it is an integral part of influencing, educating and forming the opinion of the general public. A key role of the internal PR department is to gain coverage for the company's fashion products for a specific season. Therefore a PR manager is employed to build up, develop and sustain relationships with the media, in order to enhance the image of a brand without actively investing in media space (such as advertising). For instance a handbag is photographed for a fashion shoot – the brand does not have to pay for this, but photographs will help to sell the product. The reason why that handbag gets to be photographed is that some special relationship exists between a given publication and the specific brand. The advantage of PR here is that the financial investment is minimal in comparison to the possible achievements. In some cases the cost of a lunch plus a gift is the only financial investment, as the PR proposes an idea to the fashion editor in a restaurant, which in comparison to buying media space is minimal (for instance a single page in *Vogue* costs around £17,000). The IPR estimates that the value of the editorial is four times that of advertising in terms of its effect and influence. Another advantage is the credibility attached to the involvement of the host publication, as readers perceive it to be an independent endorsement in contrast to straight advertising by a brand. The disadvantage of PR is that there is no direct control (the brand cannot decide how that handbag is photographed, the space to be used, on which page it will be shown and on what date).

While the rocketing costs of advertising are often given as the rationale for using PR, the issue of advertising overload is now becoming a general industry problem. The UK population is now reading, watching and listening to the mass media in ever-decreasing numbers, mainly as a result of transient and ever-busier lifestyles. Added to this is the problem that publications are also proliferating and readerships are therefore being stretched. With this as the backdrop, it becomes even more difficult to get people to pay attention to advertising, and the power of fashion PR here is that it can generate interesting editorials for target readers/audiences, as people generally read or pay attention to what interests them. Levels of consumer awareness, recall and enquiries are the objective ways to measure the effectiveness and efficiency of most marketing communications.

Knowledge of media

A fashion PR must have a good understanding of how the media work to be effective. PR exists to take advantage of opportunities for publicity in the media. When meeting up with a media contact to propose an idea it is essential that the PR is well acquainted with the programme or publication, the sections, the messages and the stories. It will help the PR to communicate the idea. Categories of media include: print (magazines, newspapers, flyers), broadcast (television, radio and cinema), banners, posters and the internet. The type of medium to be used depends on a brand's customer target. Once this is defined, the suitable medium can be selected. It is essential for all involved in fashion PR to be fully appraised and aware of each media's target audience, readership, circulation and/or audience. The UK has one of the highest number of fashion magazines and newspapers carrying fashion-interest items anywhere within the developed world. Its national press and TV stations offer opportunities to communicate to the whole nation, making the potential for powerful national fashion PR considerable.

All media in the UK have their key statistics listed in *British Rates and Data* (*BRAD*), the regularly updated media directory, which is used by all involved in marketing communications. In this publication data relating to the circulation, readerships and target audiences of UK media vehicles are to be found to assist in the accurate targeting of PR activity. More detailed information to support PR decision-making can be obtained by requesting a media pack from any relevant or proposed medium. Good fashion PR organisations will automatically be fully appraised of all relevant media.

Press relationships

The development of a media relationship does not happen automatically, but could be described more as an art. Undertaking PR in luxury fashion might be termed, therefore, a fine art. There are different levels of PR; luxury PR for instance is like a luxury service, where nothing is spared to give superlative delivery. It is the extra mile that one needs to go, and is about delivering superlative service to the magazine or programme in question. All fashion PR executives need to be creative, proactive and outgoing. The job is all about one's personal approach, diplomacy, manners and developing a fine-tuned understanding of the person on the other end. Being a good communicator is probably the most important requirement of the job.

Press relationships take a long time to build up – and very little to be destroyed. Most PR relationships begin over the phone or via email, and can continue like this for many years; however, once the two parties meet, you might discover that you have several things in common and the relationship begins to deepen. PR is like most business interactions in that, over time, strictly business relationships can blossom into personal friendships. Business relationships vary from country to country: in the US, for instance, PR-related meetings happen only when a specific business issue needs to be discussed; in Europe, on the other hand, people tend to meet up for a business discussion and to get to know each other better, and this in turn enables the business aspect of the relationship to cement and flow more easily.

Relationship with the store/buyer

For PR to work in a successful way, it is obligatory to know what the store has bought. Only lines that actually go into production and will be stocked should be used for press purposes. So often, poor PR can mislead the media by suggesting that a store will be stocking a particular product, only to learn later from disgruntled and frustrated customers that the line was never even stocked by the store. These are many examples of consumer relationships with retailers being ruined by sloppy PR management.

How to make a deal

In London, it is reckoned that every twenty seconds, a news release lands on a journalist's desk and joins the many hundreds still unread. The offices of some fashion magazines have wastepaper bins overflowing with untouched press packs and unread news releases. It is becoming increasingly difficult to create a news release that stands out from the crowd and immediately grabs the fashion journalist's attention. In an endeavour to make certain that a product is featured, a professional fashion PR uses a variety of tools to attract media attention.

Most media are open to new ideas and interesting novelties because it helps to sell their publication better and increase their circulation numbers. So it is up to the PR to find a suitable approach that works both ways for the brand and the media. This is a process where creativity and compromise are essential. Example: a new product is launched and should ideally appear in a certain publication at the exact time when the product will be in stores. A PR's dream is to have the product featured on its own, photographed in substantial size on one or more pages. In general, the number of pages for feature stories will have been discussed and agreed. In return the publication might want to run the feature exclusively.

Press tools

Sample collection

Key to the success of PR are the reciprocal benefits that exist in the relationship between the press and the fashion PRs. The fashion press needs real products and brands to reference in their editorials and features, while the brands need publicity. Such products obviously come from fashion brands (including retailers) and are administered by PR executives either from agencies or from the internal marketing and PR functions of the brands themselves. Consequently a press office needs a complete and well-managed sample collection for each season in order to send samples to the media for photo shoots and celebrity dressing. Usually the RTW clothes have a press sample size, which is the popular model size (8–10 for women, 38–40 for men), shoes size 5–6 for women, men size 9–10. All items are borrowed for photo-shoots and then returned to the press office of the brand or its agency.

The process normally begins with an initial press-sample request from a particular publication or fashion stylist. In general these requests are made via fax, email or by personal appointment. Depending on the availability of the press samples and the importance of the publication to the fashion house, the press officer allocates a selection and confirms this to the publication/fashion stylist. Agencies and brands have target media (newspapers and magazines) that best reflect their customers and market positioning, so that those media will be prioritised over others when a sample request comes in. Generally only a single sample of a new style or product will be available and so they need to be managed efficiently.

Every press sample leaving the showroom is recorded on a docket along with the date by which it is to be returned. At the end of the season usually a press-sample sale will be organised to make space for the new collection. Some press samples might be given away as gifts to thank selected editors for their support. Keeping track of the whereabouts, availability and condition of press samples can be a PR executive's nightmare. Therefore, meticulous management and sample booking-in and -out systems are essential.

Press kits/packs

It is common for fashion brands to produce a press kit for a new product launch. This necessitates the writing of a press/news release, which describes the product to be promoted and sold, and gives the contact details and company logo; visuals are also included, and much thought is given to the packaging in order that the press pack has some chance of being noticed and looked at by fashion journalists and editors. It is wrongly assumed that just because a press pack has been made available, it will be opened and seen; this is often not the case. Fashion magazines can receive hundreds of press packs a month and will discriminate in favour of the brands they believe to be appropriate to their readers (especially those that advertise), with many other packs going straight in the bin unopened. Again, it is important to decide which media vehicles to inform. Press-kit mailings should be personalised rather than mass mailed. Nowadays, visuals can also be sent via email (as jpeg attachments), on CD-ROM (tiffs), as well as in the more traditional form of slides/transparencies (trannies).

Look books

A look book is a collection of photographs of samples to be retailed during a particular fashion season; a sort of product catalogue for the press, which is a convenient source of visuals for journalists to use when deciding on which products to feature and can also stimulate ideas for fashion stories and features. For the luxury end of the market the books are produced *after* a season's fashion shows. The look books are sent out to all relevant media and remain with them for the duration of the season.

Catalogues

At the luxury end of the market a catalogue of the styles is also produced, shortly after a season's fashion shows, many companies producing separate accessories and fashion catalogues. Catalogues are sent out to all clients and potential customers.

Visuals

Many print media use still-life visuals prepared for their stories, because of time and cost savings. Transparencies or images of the product on CD-ROM are popular and often replace the despatch of the physical samples.

PR events

'Events' play an integral part of fashion marketing communications, and are commonly divided into press and commercial events. For the planning process an annual events calendar needs to be produced.

Press events: fashion shows

Fashion shows are segmented into women's and men's ready-to-wear (WRTW and MRTW) and haute couture.

WRTW

WRTW is shown twice a year in the four international cities of New York, London, Milan and Paris, in the sequence: New York, London, Milan, Paris. Each city has a so-called fashion week where designers show their creations in an on-schedule show. (On-schedule means that there is an official programme of the week and each designer has a specific slot for their show.) In order to be on-schedule a fee needs to be paid to the city's fashion council (e.g. in London: British Fashion Council, in Milan: Camera Nazionale, in Paris: Chambre Syndicale). It is common for up-and-coming designers who lack the funds to be on-schedule to showcase their collections in off-schedule locations in the four cities. Also the fashion council of each city gives out sponsorships to talented designers so that they can show on-schedule. Applications for sponsorship is generally made to a city's fashion council and must be submitted six months before the fashion week.

There are two main seasons in WRTW: autumn–winter (A–W) and spring-summer (S–S). A–W is showcased in February–March to be in the stores from July–August onwards, S–S is showcased in September–October to be in the stores from January–February onwards. As the market is in an ever-faster environment and consumer demand is all year round, there are in addition so called 'pre-collections' and 'cruise', or 'resort', collections to complement the assortment. Usually no official fashion shows are organised for these in-between collections.

MRTW

MRTW is a twice yearly event and is shown only in New York and Milan: S–S is showcased in January and A–W in July.

Haute couture

Haute couture is at the very core of the fashion business. It is the creation and skilful tailoring of personalised one-off pieces that only a handful of clients worldwide can afford. The debate today is about the actual need for haute couture, as the collections are unprofitable, time consuming and very expensive to produce. However, haute couture sets the trends for the rest of the fashion world: it is inspirational, inviting people to dream, and is the essence of fashion.

Haute couture collections are shown in Paris, making that city, as some argue, the home of fashion. The shows are held twice a year, in January to showcase S–S, and July to showcase A–W. Haute couture can be traced back to the mid-nineteenth century English couturier Charles Frederick Worth, who was followed by Paul Poiret, Coco Chanel, Elsa Schiaparelli, Nina Ricci, Madeleine Vionnet, Alix Gres, Jeanne Lanvin, Jean Patou, Karl Lagerfeld, Marcel Rochas, Edward Molyneux, Mainbocher,

Lucien Lelong, Pierre Balmain, Christian Dior, Yves Saint Laurent, Jacques Fath, Pierre Cardin, Guy Laroche, Cristobal Balenciaga, Hubert de Givenchy, Andre Courreges, Emanuel Ungaro, Philipp Venet, and most recently, Giorgio Armani who showcased his first haute couture collection in 2005.

The organisation of a fashion show is the task of the show's press office. The show's *production* is usually handled by a production agency, which is in charge of building a location space, the lighting and the sound. Depending on the individual location, a fashion show can take up to 1,500 people, consisting of international press, buyers, photographers, VIPs and of course the models who showcase the collection. There are several sections at a fashion show: front of house (the front of the location); outside the show space; inside (within the location); photographer area (marked area where all photographers stand); catwalk (where models walk); and backstage (where models, designers, dressers, hair and make-up personnel stay).

The seating plan at a fashion show is absolutely crucial, and can make or break relationships. The seating position depends on title, rank and importance to the fashion house, the first three rows being for the most important individuals. The seating process requires a high level of diplomacy, patience and knowledge, and is very time consuming as changes are likely every minute right up until the show. It is impossible to make everyone happy: priorities must be set by the individual brands, and there is no blueprint pattern to follow.

Press days

After each international fashion show, each house holds a press day to allow journalists and stylists to view the collection in more detail. This takes places usually 2–8 weeks after a show, generally a time when fashion editors think about and brainstorm for their trend stories for the forthcoming season. Fashion publications generally work about 4–6 months in advance, so that S–S collections are displayed and fashion stories are shot and put together from October to December; A–W collections from March to June. For the press day, the collection is displayed on mannequins in a static show, food and beverages are served, and journalists can see the show on video. It is common for journalists to receive a little thank-you gift for attending the press day, which is sometimes referred to as a 'goody-bag'.

Commercial events: trunk shows

The trunk show has emerged only recently, starting in the USA. It is similar to a press day, but for clients only: customers are invited to an exclusive preview of the new collection way before it hits the stores. This is an opportunity to place personal orders to be sure to be among the first to have items from the new collection. Trunk shows can be done in the form of a small fashion show or by appointment only.

The fashion calendar

The fashion world follows an annual schedule that has evolved over the years and is built around fashion weeks, publication lead times and seasonal selling periods. Within the calendar are regular events that provide important opportunities for fashion brands to achieve publicity.

Fashion events calendar

January	MRTW shows, haute couture shows, pre-collection
February	WRTW fashion weeks (New York, London, Milan, Paris), A–W advertising campaign shoot, A–W look book shoot, BAFTAS, Golden Globes, Oscars
March	WRTW fashion weeks (New York, London, Milan, Paris), A–W advertising campaign shoot, A–W look book shoot, A–W press days, A–W look book send out
April	A–W press days, A–W trunk shows
May	Cruise collections, Cannes Film Festival, A–W trunk shows
June	Pre-collections
July	Christmas press days, Valentine's press days, MRTW shows, haute couture shows
September	WRTW fashion weeks (New York, London, Milan, Paris), S–S advertising campaign shoot, S–S look book send out
October	WRTW fashion weeks (New York, London, Milan, Paris), S–S press days, S–S trunk shows
November	S–S press and Easter press days, S–S trunk shows
December	Christmas events, despatch of Christmas cards

Celebrities

Celebrities are the icons of the early twenty-first century. Film stars, artists, models and singers play an important role in contemporary life: what they wear, how they live and what they do are promoted all over the world in all forms of media. Gossip magazines and talk shows are highly popular and have millions of readers and viewers. So relationships with celebrities are an especially valued form of promoting a brand. However this is not a new phenomenon, as the couturiers Worth and Poiret used popular and influential figures of their day to promote their clothes. Later, following the evolution of cinema, leading designers such as Chanel, Yves Saint Laurent and Christian Dior dressed and had friendships with the emerging and influential film stars with whom they had friendships throughout the 1930s–50s. So there is nothing new in the use of celebrities to cement a designer's reputation.

The modern cult of celebrity, which has dominated the Western media for a number of years and is now a global phenomenon, presents many more and varied opportunities for designers and brands to gain public exposure. Awards ceremonies, such as the Golden Globes and the Academy Awards (Oscars), and film previews provide opportunities for designers to dress the attending celebrities and so achieve significant publicity in the media covering the events. Sometimes the celebrity will attract more publicity because of the outfit, as in the case of Elizabeth Hurley and the Versace dress, commonly referred to as 'that dress', because of the rather flimsy safety-pin fastening. Some celebrities are naturally loyal customers of designers, whereas others are persuaded to wear a designer's outfit. The significance of celebrities wearing designers' frocks at the Oscars is so great that some banking analysts report on who wore what after each Oscar ceremony. The investment bank

Bear Sterns provides a review each year and noted the following combinations at the 2005 Academy Awards:

- Annette Bening – Armani Privé;
- Halle Berry – Versace;
- Cate Blanchett – Valentino;
- Gwyneth Paltrow – Stella McCartney;
- Natalie Portman – Lanvin;
- Julia Roberts – Dolce & Gabbana.

Bear Sterns also reported on the accessories that each star was wearing, including the estimated value of any jewellery worn; for example, Natalie Portman wore a matching tiara estimated to be worth US$75,000.

Every celebrity has an agent or publicist, and most of them have a personal stylist and a personal assistant. Very rarely is it possible for a PR to work directly with a star. Celebrities can be very demanding and there is no control over what they wear and how they wear it – unless they are bound into an exclusive contract with a fashion brand (one Kylie Minogue tour was sponsored by Dolce & Gabbana and she wore exclusively D&G clothing for a certain period of time. Giorgio Armani is another big sponsor of celebrities.). They normally have a busy social calendar and need to be dressed for events regularly. Some of them use stylists to buy their clothes, but most of the time they either borrow a press sample or are given the product as a present, or even have it specially made – depending on their status and popularity. It is a great endorsement for a fashion brand if a well-known personality wears its products, because celebrities belong to the elite of opinion-formers and have a considerable following. The cost to the brand is still minimal relative to the potential exposure.

Measuring successful PR

A PR department's effectiveness can be measured in different ways. In general it is about the extent of editorial coverage it secures and the number of credits and covers per season. Each credit is measured by the page-space it occupies – full-page, half- and quarter-page – meaning that a credit is worth what it would cost to purchase the same space for an advertisement per product, in comparison to their direct competitors (each fashion house determines their individual direct competitors on a map).

Advertising

Advertising complements PR. The hugely successful FCUK campaigns of the late 1990s illustrate how advertising can generate substantial press coverage. It is important because it is a means of sending out a controlled message. The brand invests in a media space, which can be very costly, depending on the media type and on the position of the advert. In print media usually the first 15 per cent of the publication, the inside and outside back cover, right-hand locations and particular dates/times of year are the most popular and expensive ones. For motion pictures, TV and radio, it is about prime time, though the length of the programme/film and the particular day it airs are also important.

Advertising campaign

When a company invests in advertising a campaign is produced showcasing its own personal message, mostly in combination with its product for the season. Often, well-known models and photographers are used for advert campaigns to demonstrate the company's spirit and enhance the promotion. The campaign shoot usually takes place about three weeks after a fashion show.

Media plan

The base of a successful media campaign is the media plan. This is segmented in the first two semesters of the year with a set budget. The art is to place the right insertions at the right time within the right medium or media. This is a time-consuming process requiring close acquaintance with the individual media and good negotiation skills.

Advertising agency

Many brands therefore use an advertising agency to handle the negotiation of the rates, the location of advertising space and the supply of the artwork on their behalf. The criteria for selection of an agency should be based on their knowledge, efficiency and relationship with the media deemed important for the brand. Publications have general prices for their pages, called 'rate card' prices. The advert agency's main role is to negotiate a price that hopefully is better than the rate card, though this will depend on the relationship of the publication with the agency and on the position and the page on which the advert is to appear. Each fashion publication is divided into sections: front, fashion well, back. The fashion well is the main body of the publication, the purely editorial fashion pages – and they cannot be interrupted with advertisements. Consequently the advertising happens before and after the fashion well. Prices for positions before the fashion well are higher, because more desirable, than those after, except for the outside and the inside back cover. The best positions are the outside covers, inside back cover, the first 15 per cent of the publication and right side pages (there is evidence to indicate that readers look first of all at the right hand pages of all books, magazines and newspapers). Brands which book their pages regularly at certain times and positions will be entitled to an 'anniversary page', meaning that those brands always have first preference for that position, and a special deal may be done over the price.

Role of the fashion stylist

Almost every picture, fashion story, still life shoot, product, person and celebrity we see in publications is styled – even though the images can look very natural. Stylists are central to photo shoots. Their visual ability, creativity and attention to detail ensure that the presentation of the product increase its desirability.

To work as a stylist it is important to gain 'on-the-job' experience. Normally this involves working as an assistant to a senior stylist to 'get the eye', understand the procedures and learn the protocol. After each fashion shoot, the stylist should keep the best visual (called a 'tear sheet') for his or her own portfolio. It is important also to get involved in as many photo shoots and stories as possible to build up the portfolio (these are called testing or test shoots). A stylist's portfolio changes constantly.

It reflects the ability, creativity and mood of the stylist and it grows over time. Many stylists work either freelance with an agency or independently. There are agencies that specialise in styling, photography, hair and make-up although there is no guarantee that having gained experience of styling one qualifies to be on the books of an agency. Finding a suitable agency is like finding a business partner. It depends on the style and needs of both the stylist and the agency as to whether such a relationship can be formed. Alternatively, a stylist can work exclusively in-house for a publication. The usual career path of a stylist runs from fashion assistant to fashion editor, fashion director, style director, shopping or market editor. Some publications regularly commission freelance stylists, who are called contributing fashion editors.

Some stylists work best with a particular photographer (for instance Annie Liebovitz of *Vanity Fair*). It is a matter of creative teamwork, and there is no formula for matching stylist and photographer. Experience, a creative eye and reputation are, however, essential and necessary.

Briefing

Once the agency, publication or photographer, have selected the stylist for the job, the theme can be discussed. Research must be done in great detail for everything. For instance if the theme is 'Victorian Melodies', the stylist might research Victorian-style dresses, shoes, facial expressions, poise, interiors, music, food – frankly anything to do with the theme – and it is here also that the creativity comes in: there are no rules, just views. Often ideas can be put together into a 'mood board' – this is a display of editorial cut-outs, fabric samples and any research put together in order to create the right feeling, story or message.

Budget

For most fashion publications there is normally a detailed and carefully pre-planned production budget, although some more trendy and cutting edge magazines take a more relaxed approach to budgeting and costs. Fashion productions for glossy magazines, advertising campaigns, music videos, theatre plays, etc., all have a budget. Sometimes, the budget can determine the degree of creativity possible.

Preparation for a fashion shoot

Once the theme has been researched and the budget is set, the stylist is responsible for the selection of clothes, models, shoes, accessories, hair and make-up, and sometimes also for the location.

Clothes

A good fashion stylist will have a great diversity of contacts in different fashion houses, which is a help in acquiring clothes for a fashion shoot. The timing of the shoots, its duration and the location can determine what clothes one can get. If the stylist needs the yellow dress or a pair of shoes from a certain brand's collection, acquiring them can depend on the stylist's relationship with the brand's PR executives. A PR will always give priority to the publications which offer the brand the greatest benefit. For example, *Vogue* will have priority over a newspaper in covering a shoot because it is one of the most influential and widely read fashion publications.

Models

In order to get models, the stylist will contact model agencies and specify the ideal attributes; for example, red hair, blue eyes, skinny, tall, certain shoe-size, for catwalk only – needs to be able to walk well, etc.). Once these have been established the agency or agent will send the stylist a selection of set cards or composites (a visual business card of the model, which gives measurements of height, bust, waist, hips and shoe-size, as well as eye and hair colour, consisting usually of 3–5 pictures). There are several sections in model agencies: new faces, main board (men, women and children), special features. New faces deals with newly acquired models, normally beginners, who may have little experience of correct posture or cat-walking, and who therefore might be shy; she will have a lower fee than the rest. Models from the main board are those who work successfully on a regular basis and have a certain level of fee. Special features are models with a certain feature like a scar, bald, wrinkly, extremely tall, albino characteristics, etc.

From the set cards the stylist will organise a casting, a time slot where models attend for a 'go-and-see' appointment. They will turn up with their model portfolio (a book containing the best visuals of their career) and they may be asked to try on an item of clothing, and shoes, and may be required to do a short catwalk. It is essential to do a casting because in many cases the models rarely appear in the flesh the way they do on their set cards. It is important to get a feeling for an individual model's personality, shape, poise, etc. Once a model is selected, the stylist calls the agency and can either book the model straight away or put an option on her or him. An option is like a reservation: a first option means that there is only a single reservation on that model for a defined period of time; a second option means that someone else has priority, and so on. If the stylist books the model straight away, the date and time, the venue and the fee are negotiated, up to 30 per cent of the fee going to the model agency. If a shoot exceeds the agreed duration, an overtime rate can be applicable. All such details are put into writing in a contract that has to be agreed and signed prior the shoot. Models usually turn up to the fashion shoot with freshly washed hair, no make-up and clean finger- and toe-nails, though such requirements will be specified separately (especially if a model will be coming from another fashion show/shoot). The models may be required to go to a fitting prior to the shoot in which case the clothes or a 'look' are made-to-measure for that model. At the fitting a polaroid photograph is usually taken in order to record the look, the styling, etc.

The photographer

Usually photographers work freelance. They might, as do stylists, work with a specialised photographic agency, which may categorise them into different sections, such as new/up-and-coming photographers, Photographers' specialisms include still life, landscape, portrait, fashion, music, personalities, etc. Just like stylists, they always keep an up-to-date portfolio available for viewing. When working with a photographer teamwork is essential, in order that everyone keeps to the same idea, sees with the same eye and is on the same wavelength. It is similarly important for a fashion photographer to understand how clothes work. The format needs to be discussed, e.g. should it be black and white or colour, a 35mm film (gives rectangular shape), or 6 x 6 or 6 x 7 (usually used for cover shoots), or now increasingly the digital image specification. Prior to the actual shoot a picture is taken using a digital camera. This preliminary image gives an indication of whether a set up, the lighting and position are right, and helps to prevent waste of film rolls. Usually only the photographer, the stylist and the model discuss this picture. The photographer typically works with one or more assistant (if more than one assistant is used, the first assistant is responsible for carrying, installing and organising the equipment, and the second assistant prepares the light set-up and sheet).

Hair

Hair stylists, too, usually work freelance and are specialists in every aspect of hair care, though some do make-up as well. Hair stylists are normally booked through special agencies. Like models, they will keep a portfolio available for viewing. Some hair stylists work exclusively for a hair or beauty brand, for example Aveda or KMS, in which case they will be sponsored by that brand and so will be required to use only the brand's products for a fashion shoot/show. It is common for fashion shows to require a hair and make-up stylist, to establish the exact look which needs to be achieved. Again, this is digitally photographed prior to the shoot, and needs to be approved by the fashion stylist, the photographer, sometimes the model (if a celebrity is involved) and also the publication or the creative director.

Make-up

Make-up artists work in a way similar to hair stylists – usually freelance through a make-up agency or for a beauty brand, e.g. MAC make-up artists use only MAC products. Hair and make-up artists ideally need to know which models are booked and the colours of the clothes, and will use different techniques for either black and white or colour photographic work. Knowing the type of shoot is also important for their preparation – for example, is it for a fashion show, a photo shoot or a close-up cover photograph?

Location

The location is critical to the styling process. Often the scenery of the location will assist in communicating the whole image as intended. The photographer together with the stylist will decide whether the photo shoot is to take place indoors or outdoors. Depending on the type of shoot, it could be in a photographer's studio for still-life visual, or outdoors for a swimming-pool story. Sometimes, the creative direction might require building a background set design for a photo shoot, which would then require a set designer (usually contacted via photographic and styling agencies). The set designer is contracted to create an entire world specially for the photo shoot (the theme might be elves in the woods, or velvet red).

Sometimes, a special location is required, e.g. a castle on a cliff with an eighteenth-century interior in green. In such cases agencies are used to find the perfect location for the photo shoot. If shooting outdoors on the street or in front of a private house, it is important that the owner's permission is obtained, and a user fee might be applicable.

Editorial fashion shoot

Editorial styling refers to the styling involved in a shoot to be published in print media (magazine or newspaper). Such work is good for building up the stylist's portfolio, but usually is rather poorly paid. In general, the stylist's and the photographer's name will be credited in the publication. Depending on the publication, each individual product used for the fashion shoot is also credited (either with or without retail price). It is the stylist's responsibility to check all product descriptions and prices (credits or captions) with the fashion PR. When shooting for a publication, the stylist might work direct from the publication office and all clothes/products to be used will be sent to the publication for the stylist's attention. They are also responsible for the return of all items in perfect condition, nicely wrapped in tissue paper and (if appropriate) on hangers to the fashion house or the PR executive.

Commercial fashion shoot

Look books
These are a type of seasonal catalogue that show each individual look, from head to toe, of the fashion show, individually, each of them numbered. Some fashion houses also provide a separate look book for accessories only, numbered the same way. The styling for a look book is commercial in the sense that the styling is done in order to show all products in the best possible way. It is creatively restricted and more formal. Look books are sent out each season to fashion press and stylists in order for them to source clothes for fashion shoots. In the last few years online look books have emerged (such as on vogue.com and style.com), so that approximately two hours after a fashion show the entire collection is available for viewing. These images are taken by the photographer at the fashion show and are not styled separately.

Advertising campaigns
Each season those fashion brands with an advertising budget will produce advertising visual(s). These visuals usually reflect the fashion show and its essential message. Some fashion houses like their visuals to have more of a cutting-edge and an arty approach than others – e.g. Levi's and Gucci – while others prefer a more commercial look for their image – e.g. Louis Vuitton, Céline, Escada and Burberry. To style an ad campaign, the stylist needs to really understand the brand's essence, translating it with a creativity that will communicate to the public. Hopefully, the ad should be able to attract new customers and should also reflect an image, so that targeted customer groups can associate themselves with it. Levi's has a cool, cutting-edge image, Versace a sexy body-conscious image, Sisley controversially sexual image and so on.

At the start of a shoot a budget has to be negotiated and allocated. The photographer, stylist, model, assistants, hair and make-up, tailor, wardrobe, jewellery, etc. all have to be paid at the going rate. Usually the photographer is the link with the stylist to be used. It is also better to work with a renowned stylist from a fashion publication such as *Vogue* or some other leading title. This benefits both parties by keeping a good relationship between the magazine and the advertising fashion house.

The idea/message behind an advert has to be brainstormed and researched in depth before any photographs can be taken. If, for example, vintage glamour is to be portrayed in a Prada campaign, the stylist will research several vintage shops, markets and areas, before creating a mood board of the proposed concept, so that it can be approved by the fashion house before the shoot goes ahead. In most cases additional items are needed for the photo shoot that the fashion brand cannot provide (for example De Beers' jewellery is shot on a model whose clothes have to be purchased – a wardrobe budget needs to be allocated for that).

In some cases, the budget does not stretch to the purchasing of additional items, therefore a press sample or shop stock may have to be borrowed. Several luxury brands do not loan their products out for other brands' advertising campaigns. However, the large luxury goods groups usually have policies to loan items only to brands within their own group (for example, a pair of Céline black gloves can be used for a Tag Heuer advert campaign, as long as they are not recognised as Céline gloves). It is the rule that no logo and blazons can be used for other ad campaigns. You must not use a Louis Vuitton bag in a Marks & Spencer or a Rimmel advert (because it will be recognised as LV). For a big ad campaign shoot the stylist may have several assistants. On average, an ad campaign is shot within a 2–4 day period.

Catalogues
Shooting a catalogue is very similar to shooting an advertising campaign, though all products for the former are supplied by the fashion brand – for the Victoria's Secret catalogue all products are supplied by Victoria Secret.

Advertorials
An advertorial is an advertisement that looks like an editorial fashion shoot, except that the model(s) normally wears products from one brand, e.g. tying in GAP with the cast of *Sex in the City*, which would be credited: SJP wearing GAP; or Cindy Crawford wearing Omega. The advertorial approach is popular for fashion brands that like to change their image by introducing their message in a more subtle way to the reader. The stylist's duties are the same as for an editorial and an ad campaign shoot.

Still lifes
Still life photo shoots are creatively very restricted because they are purely for product placement in a magazine or newspaper. If the theme is the ten best trench coats of the season, the stylist either photographs individually ten different trench coats in a photo studio or asks the PR for a still-life visual to be supplied for editing; they are usually called 'shopping pages' or similar.

Fashion shows
First, the designer relays the theme – e.g. 'An American in Paris' – to the stylist. The stylist researches the theme and the collection is designed and put together by the design team, and prototypes are produced. Approximately ten days prior to the fashion show the stylist works on-site with the designer and the design team on the creative realisation of the final idea. A stylist is a creative consultant and submits new ideas, which can be put into production; e.g. the stylist finds a vintage brooch, and the designer and team like it so much that they produce a similar brooch which then will be styled for the catwalk and ultimately goes into production for selling. Often a casting director is contracted to find new faces and the best hair and make-up stylists. Fashion houses fight over the hottest models of the season. The casting director works together with all the agencies and bookers to negotiate and get the right deal. Once the models are selected, the stylist and designer start the fitting (the outfit is put together on each model, tailored individually for that model) and hair and make-up tests. When the designer/stylist approves the outfit, a

polaroid is taken to record the exact look. After this the stylist puts together a running order and prepares a rail for each look. On the rail everything will be readied, with the model's name and a polaroid picture, and the accessories prepared, clothes steamed, etc. To make sure the show runs smoothly, the dressers are fully briefed (a dresser helps to dress the model during the fashion show, making sure that the model has a quick and smooth change, opening zips and buttons beforehand, and scratching the soles of shoes to prevent the model slipping on the runway.

Trunk shows

Trunk shows originated in the USA in the late twentieth century and are a small reconstruction of the runway show for commercial purposes (a mini-fashion show for customers to view the new seasonal collection and then be able to make personal orders before the new collection hits the stores). The stylist's duties are exactly the same as for other events, except that the collection is already designed. However, it is essential that the message is followed, i.e. same looks, similar models, hair and make-up, same music, etc.

Personality styling for celebrities

Celebrity dressing has become a powerful promotion opportunity in the fashion industry. 'Oscar night itself is one big and long runway,' says Patrick Mackie, fashion stylist in New York. The stylist meets with the celebrity and sources a large variety of clothes (like a personal shopper). Depending on a celebrity's status, it can be very easy or not so easy to get all the clothes (many times clothes are sent as gifts to the celebrity or else are custom made). The shoot can be either an individual photo shoot for a publication or a press junket. This is similar to a visual press conference for the celebrity. Pictures are taken, and only these pictures are used and sold to several diverse publications. After the photo shoot the celebrity needs to sign a picture release (most will sign only after seeing and agreeing to the visuals) in order for that picture to appear in print media. It is sometimes the case that the stylist develops a close relationship with the personality and continues to style him or her for occasions beyond the photo shoot.

Whatever the type of styling required, the best stylists are those who are both creative and meticulous. Fashion styling looks so easy, but in reality it takes effort, planning and the support of many other specialists to achieve the right effect.

10 Careers in fashion retailing

Tim Jackson and David Shaw

Introduction

The UK fashion industry is very diverse and comprises a wide range of commercial activities, including design, manufacturing, retailing, trend prediction, journalism, PR, photography, styling, modelling and many other specialised industries. There is a perception among some in non-fashion businesses that fashion is lightweight, a bit flaky and not a serious career. This is very far from the truth as each area is highly competitive and contributes to consumer spending on clothing, which amounted to £35.5 billion in 2003 (Mintel 2004b).

The fashion industry is seen by many as offering glamorous careers involving travel, fashion shows and opportunities to design and buy clothes for a living. While there is a certain element of truth to such perceptions, the facts often present a rather different view of the realities involved. This chapter does not deal with all careers in fashion (to do so would take a book in itself) but aims to provide factual insights to the types of job and career available in fashion retailing. Many of those jobs, such as marketing and PR, are directly connected with other fashion roles. For example a marketing or PR manager working for a fashion retailer will have regular contact with fashion journalists, PR agency staff (normally account managers), photographers, stylists, fashion show and event organisers and marketing services businesses, including advertising agencies and design businesses. Many of the individuals working in fashion journalism, photography and styling are freelance, making it difficult to present a structured view of careers in these areas.

Fashion retailing and associated jobs

This chapter focuses on fashion retailing, which represents the largest sector for careers within the UK fashion industry. In addition to the obvious retail opportunities in shops, which most people are familiar with, there are many and varied careers among the head office functions of fashion retailer brands. These include design, garment technology, buying, merchandising, distribution, supply chain, marketing, visual merchandising, finance and human resources. Fashion retailers are also significant in the UK fashion industry due to their support of UK fashion designers. This is most commonly demonstrated through commercial relationships between retailer brands and individual designers.

The relationships vary according to retailer brand and the status of the designer. An established designer may distribute exclusive diffusion products through a retailer or operate a licence agreement, as in the case of Jasper Conran's J range at Debenhams. Over the years retailers such as M&S have worked with Matthew Williamson and Betty Jackson. Such relationships are not simply based on the philanthropy or goodwill of retailers; there must be good commercial reasons and a strong market positioning argument for the 'co-branding' arrangement from both sides. At the other end of the scale Top Shop has helped nurture new fashion design talent through its sponsorship of Graduate Fashion Week and ongoing sponsorship of 'New Gen', the new generation of design talent; New Gen is also supported by the British Fashion Council (BFC). In 2004 Top Shop sponsored the following 'New Generation' designers: Miki Fukai, Jonathon Saunders, Jens Laugesn, Bora Aksu, Mawi, Vevers, Camila Staerk, Roksanda Ilincic, Jason Ansell, La Petite Salope, Ann-Sofie Back, Damaris, PPQ.

Top Shop also works with recently established designers such as Sophia Kokosalaki, Julie Berube and Emma Cook. Graduate Fashion Week is an established showcase for graduating designers and provides valuable media coverage and visibility within the industry for award winners. It was launched in 1991 as a forum for the very best of graduate fashion design talent in the UK and is a registered charity, which is entirely dependent on the sponsorship it attracts. River Island has taken over the sponsorship for the next two years.

Careers in fashion retailing

The number of jobs and particular responsibilities associated with roles within functions such as buying will often vary among companies. In general, the smaller the company the broader the range of activities and responsibilities is for a position that can be quite 'generalist'. By contrast the larger the company the more specific the roles and responsibilities tend to be. For example in larger fashion multiples the career progression is very clear and individuals have to be 'signed-off' at different levels of a role to demonstrate that they have achieved certain competences. This is not always the case with smaller companies.

Fashion retailers have changed a great deal over the last fifteen years, with most now considered to be (retailer) brands in their own right. As a result there are important distinctions for the roles and responsibilities of some functions between fashion retailers that develop and sell their own brand of products and department stores such as Selfridges which sell only other brands. This is particularly true for buying and design functions which are quite different between department stores that stock brands and fashion retailers that sell their own branded merchandise. Buying offices of fashion retailer brands will be full of rails holding product samples that are in varying stages of development from fit to seal. By contrast, a department store such as Selfridges that sells only other brands will not have such samples.

Key head office fashion functions in retailing

Buyer	Decides on the styles to be bought and stocked, negotiates with suppliers/brands over terms
Merchandiser	Works with buyers on planning stock mix according to trend analysis, manages buying budget, stock control and distribution to stores
Designer	Provides creative direction and produces product designs for buyers to select from
Garment technologist	Provides technical (fabric and construction) advice and controls sample development
Supply chain	Oversees the processes involved in delivering the products from suppliers to the DC, including stages in product development, from sampling to labelling/ticketing
Marketing	Responsible for all brand and product communication; works with fashion journalists, PR agencies, photographers, stylists and production companies

How to access careers in fashion retailing

The most common routes are either through a recruitment agency which specialises in fashion industry careers or directly to a fashion retailer. The larger fashion retailer brands have very specific recruitment processes, which vary among companies and according to whether or not an applicant is a graduate. Graduate training schemes have come and gone over the years within some fashion retailers, depending on the preferences of their senior management teams. However Next and the Arcadia Group are two major fashion retailers that operate a graduate training programme, but they have different approaches to the interview process. Most companies offer specific points in the year when graduates should apply, with some using assessment centres that test applicants' suitability across a couple of days. In general applicants are being assessed on their team-working, communications, numeracy, leadership, organisational and commercial skills. Companies also look for applicants to demonstrate initiative, problem-solving capabilities, creativity and commercial awareness.

Case study | The Arcadia Group

Arcadia is now owned by Philip Green but used to be a public company, which was formed from the former Burton Group. The Burton Group set the standard for buying and merchandising methods and careers throughout the 1980s and 1990s. Still today a career developed within an Arcadia brand such as Top Shop provides and excellent basis for an individual to move on to other companies. The Arcadia Group is Britain's largest multiple fashion retailer, with 7.9 per cent market share in womenswear and 4.7 per cent in menswear by sales expenditure, as opposed to units (*Fashion Trak* 2004). It owns and operates the following retailer brands (although Philip Green has recently bought Etam which includes the niche Tammy brand): Top Shop, Miss Selfridge, Wallis, Dorothy Perkins, Evans, Burton, Top Man, Outfit.

ARCADIA GROUP GRADUATE REQUIREMENTS ACROSS FASHION RETAIL FUNCTIONS

Readers should note that, while common to within the industry, the following relate specifically to the Arcadia Group.

Below are brief descriptions of career paths and specific job requirements for a variety of fashion functions within the Head Office of the Arcadia Group.

What does the Arcadia Group look for in graduates?

Retail management
- A graduate or an HND holder in any subject, and 5 GCSEs including maths and English (Grades A–C)
- Ability to influence, motivate and lead by example
- Flexibility
- Understands the importance of being 'hands on', ensuring the store is at its best for our customers
- An excellent communicator
- Committed to personal and business success
- Able to identify opportunities to move the business forward

Distribution
- A graduate or an HND holder in a numerical, business- or fashion-related subject, and 5 GCSEs including maths and English (Grades A–C)
- Numerate and analytical
- Fashion retail experience/strong interest in fashion retail
- Commercial awareness
- Well organised and able to identify priorities
- Keen to work in a team
- Committed to personal and business success

Merchandising
- A graduateor HND holder in a numerical, business- or maths-related subject, and 5 GCSEs including maths and English (Grades A–C)
- Numerate and analytical
- Fashion retail experience/strong interest in fashion retail
- Commercial awareness

continued

- Well organised and able to identify priorities
- Keen to work in a team
- Committed to personal and business success

Buying
- A graduate or HND holder in a fashion-related subject, and 5 GCSEs including maths and English (Grades A–C)
- Fashion retail experience and a passion for fashion
- Up-to-date knowledge of trends and designers
- Commercial awareness
- Well organised and able to identify priorities
- Keen to work in a team
- Numerate and analytical
- Committed to personal and business success

Human Resources
- Degree in a human resources-related subject
- Confidence
- Communication and relationship management skills
- Team-working commitment
- Commercial awareness
- Problem-solving ability
- Flexibility/adaptability

Finance
- Have an interest in fashion and retail
- A graduate in business studies or finance
- Flexibility
- Commercial awareness
- An excellent communicator
- Able to thrive on variety and challenges
- Able to plan and prioritise
- Looking for the 'big' picture but also has an eye for detail
- Committed to personal and business success

Source: Arcadia Group Recruitment Team (2005).

Arcadia's requirements are typical of the clearly defined and quite specialised roles that exist in the fashion multiples. Each level of a job has clearly defined roles, responsibilities and competences that help individuals progress along their chosen career path.

ARCADIA CAREER PATHS

Figure 10.1 gives examples of possible graduate career paths with the Arcadia Group.

Retail management

Retail management trainee

Store manager (medium store)/deputy manager (large store)/sales manager (outfit) – 12 months

Senior store manager/outfit sales and operations manager – 3 years

Area manager/outfit store manager/mega store manager – 5 years

Distribution

Distributor

Senior distributor – 18 months–2 years

Stock distribution manager – 3–5 years

Entry into merchandising via distribution is also actively encouraged

Merchandising

Merchandise administration assistant

Assistant merchandiser – 18 months–2 years

Junior merchandiser – 3–5 years

Merchandiser – 5 years

Buying

Buyer's administration assistant

Assistant buyer – 18 Months–2 years

Figure 10.1 *continued on p. 194*

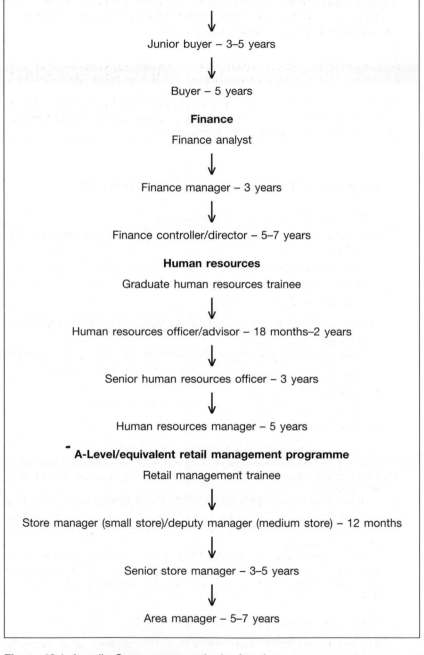

Junior buyer – 3–5 years

↓

Buyer – 5 years

Finance

Finance analyst

↓

Finance manager – 3 years

↓

Finance controller/director – 5–7 years

Human resources

Graduate human resources trainee

↓

Human resources officer/advisor – 18 months–2 years

↓

Senior human resources officer – 3 years

↓

Human resources manager – 5 years

A-Level/equivalent retail management programme

Retail management trainee

↓

Store manager (small store)/deputy manager (medium store) – 12 months

↓

Senior store manager – 3–5 years

↓

Area manager – 5–7 years

Figure 10.1 Arcadia Group career paths by function

Source: Arcadia Group Recruitment Team (2005).

Arcadia states: 'These career paths and timelines are only a guide – speed of progression is very much down to the individual; however all the support networks are in place to make these achievable.'

ARCADIA RECRUITMENT PROCESSES

In common with the larger fashion multiple retailers, Arcadia has a very structured recruitment process for entry to graduate and management training positions. This is outlined in the display below.

Arcadia Group recruitment process

Retail management

Our recruitment and selection process for Retail Management has three stages prior to offer:

- Online application form;
- Assessed group exercise (30 minutes–1 hour);
- Assessment Centre (one day).

The competences that are assessed throughout the above stages are:

- Working with people;
- Putting the customer first;
- Maximising own impact;
- Inspiring performance;
- Driving the business;
- Making the right choices;
- Understanding of the role.

You will be assessed only against the above competences and will not be competing against other candidates attending the assessment events with you.

We will inform you of the outcome of your application within five working days of each stage. Offers are made following the assessment centre.

If you are unsuccessful at any stage, you would be eligible to reapply after three months.

We have one intake into Retail Management each year, starting in early September. We recruit approximately 50 graduates and 50 management trainees into retail, but do not have any specific quota per assessment event.

Finance and Human Resources

Our recruitment and selection process for Finance and Human Resources has two stages prior to offer:

- Online application form;
- Assessment centre (one day).

continued

The competences that are assessed throughout the above stages are:

- Working with people;
- Maximising own impact;
- Driving the business;
- Making the right choices;
- Understanding of the role.

You will be assessed only against the above competences and will not be competing against other candidates attending the assessment events with you.

We will inform you of the outcome of your application within five working days of each stage. Offers are made following the assessment centre.

If you are unsuccessful at any stage, you would be eligible to reapply after three months up to the closing date.

We have one intake into Finance and Human Resources each year, starting in early September. We recruit approximately 4–8 graduates into finance and 2 graduates into human resources.

Buying, merchandising and distribution

Our recruitment and selection process for head office positions (buying, merchandising and distribution) has three stages prior to offer:

- Online application form;
- First interview;
- Second interview OR a half-day assessment centre.

Along with the competences in the 'What we look for in our Graduates' section we look for the following in successful candidates:

- Understanding of the role and enthusiasm;
- Knowledge of our brands;
- Passion for retail and our brands.

If you are unsuccessful at any stage, you would be eligible to reapply after three months.

We recruit all year round for head office positions, therefore you can apply for positions at any time. If you are successful at screening stage, your application will be considered for vacancies close to the 'date available to start work' stated on your application.

We recruit approximately 100–120 buying, merchandising and distribution graduates per annum.

All graduates are recruited to the graduate training scheme through the online application process.

Recruitment agencies

A common way for individuals to begin or advance a career in fashion retailing is to use the experienced services of a recruitment agency which specialises in procuring candidates for jobs on behalf of their fashion retailer clients. Retail Human Resources plc (RHR) is a long-established and leading specialist retail recruitment consultancy for the fashion industry. In addition to having a bank of jobs it provides expert guidance in matching individuals to types of career, assists in preparing candidates for interview and offers detailed information on the roles available in fashion retailing. RHR's fee is paid by the recruiting client retailer and not the applicants themselves! This applies to recruitment agencies in general.

Although some fashion retailers have specific points in the year when they recruit for their graduate training programmes, all fashion retailers recruit to fill head office posts throughout the year. The simple fact is that the fashion industry is relatively young and people progress along career paths quite quickly, creating a high turnover in positions. It is therefore possible to apply speculatively to an agency at any point throughout the calendar year.

Most head office positions within fashion retailers now require applicants to have a first degree, HND or equivalent. It is important that applicants demonstrate enthusiasm and commitment to a fashion career by having gained some work experience prior to seeking employment – indeed, this is a requirement of many fashion retailers, especially for marketing and buying functions, where there is huge competition for jobs. The specific kind of work experience required varies between function. For example, for buying, many retailers require store sales experience (usually through a part-time job) and 3–6 months' work experience in a buying office. Undergraduate programmes that include a placement period are obviously attractive to potential employers in this respect.

RHR graduate process

The agency will ask for a CV and discuss an individual's experience, career aspirations and suitability for particular jobs before putting him or her forward for a specific job opportunity. RHR will also undertake a numeracy test prior to sending an individual's details to a retailer in order to prepare the candidate for the inevitable tests that accompany first interviews for entry-level buying and merchandising jobs. The level of numeracy being tested is not abnormally high and is more concerned with testing specific skills and concepts, including multiplication, division, the use of percentages and ratio, and the ability to spot trends and draw conclusions from data. Most fashion retailers are looking for speed and accuracy from the candidates.

RHR advice on interviews

If a candidate is successful in obtaining an interview, RHR communicates this to the individual and begins his or her preparation for the interview process. This involves giving the candidate advice on how to research a fashion retailer's stores and products; a consultant at the agency will also brief candidates on the type of interview, typical questions and key skills that the retailer will be looking for.

The interview offers an opportunity for an individual to show the prospective employer why he or she should be given a particular job. In most cases the employer has already formed a view about an individual's ability to do the job in question – the employer is not going to waste time on a candidate who lacks the potential to do the job in the first place. However, RHR has observed that too many candidates arrive at an interview with only the vaguest idea of what they are going to say. The agency provides a detailed checklist on preparing for buying and merchandising interviews, which gives useful tips on interview preparation, the asking and answering of questions, and an individual's approach to the event.

Buying, merchandising, design and marketing roles in fashion retailing

Buying and merchandising

The vast majority of fashion retailer (own-brand) buying offices are open plan, with the buying, merchandising, design and garment technology functions all closely located. Most buying and merchandising functions are structured by product departments with a dedicated buying and merchandising team working on specific product areas. For example, jerseywear, lingerie and swimwear, denim and dresses are examples of product areas that are common in multiple fashion retailer businesses. Smaller fashion retailers often structure their operations according to the size of their business and so product areas maybe separated into men's women's and children's departments. The common *competences* that relate to roles in the buying and merchandising functions are listed below. They are sourced from a variety of multiple fashion retailers.

Buying competences

Personal characteristics

- Commercial with creative flair;
- Multi-tasking flexibility;
- Retentive memory;
- Mental agility;
- Energetic;
- Positive approach to problems/criticism;
- Self-motivated consistent temperament;
- People/action oriented;
- Tough but fair;
- Creative.

Awareness

Fashion awareness

- Understands customers' changing fashion requirements;
- Anticipates future looks;
- Interprets relevant future looks in new ranges;
- Can develop coordination opportunities in new ranges;
- Can improve perceived garment quality;
- Anticipates and plans for gaps in ranges;

Commercial awareness

- Can accurately judge cost and selling prices on seeing garments;
- Can predict sales potential of a product;

- Understands the different contributions to sales targets of mark-down and repeat lines;
- Actively seeks and develops new suppliers;
- Coordinates buying with other garment departments where appropriate;
- Understands target customers' buying behaviour;
- Understands and evaluates data in broad market context.

Planning

- Tracks and knows status of all orders for a season through a critical path;
- Understands the need to prioritise the critical path according to stock needs;
- Has contingency plans in place;
- Manages time of self and team through effectively sharing and prioritising work;
- Prepares thoroughly for meetings, negotiations and presentations.

Action

- Accepts responsibility for own and team's decisions and actions;
- Picks up bargain-buying potential for out-of-season products;
- Ensures commercial balance of new fashion and core best-selling lines;
- Reacts to poor sales while minimising price reductions;
- Stays calm and provides direction for others in a crisis.

(Source: Jackson and Shaw, 2001).

Merchandising competences

Personal characteristics

- Logical, rational;
- Multi-tasking flexibility;
- IT-oriented;
- Numerate;
- Analytical;
- Detail conscious – but also aware of 'the bigger picture';
- Assertive;
- Retentive memory.

Awareness

This is separated into two categories.

Data awareness

- Balances interpretation of data with commercial common sense;
- Looks for ways to improve range, collection and use of data;

- Understands the procedures for calculating figures;
- Can spot and interpret trends;
- Can cope with multiple tasks and remain accurate;
- Can produce accurate forecasts based on all available data.

Commercial awareness

- Remembers product sales' histories and can judge optimum selling prices;
- Builds up knowledge of the style, design and colour characteristics of best and worst sellers;
- Makes commercial recommendations to buyer about supplier performance;
- Understands how the garment type's budget and performance affects the company;
- Monitors and influences the progress of products in the garment type's critical path;
- Manages the balance of mark-downs and repeated products (full-price stick) to maximise.

Planning

- Collects all relevant information to contribute to range-planning;
- Develops a commercially balanced range plan with the buyer;
- Monitors sales' performance against stock levels;
- Develops and maintains efficient administrative systems for self and team;
- Manages self and team by prioritising work load effectively.

Action

- Combines analysis of information with experience in the management of risk;
- Adjusts forward stock commitment according to sales' performance;
- Times new deliveries and repeat orders to optimise sales' opportunities and profits;
- Negotiates appropriate discounts (from cost price) in response to late or incorrect deliveries.

(Source: Jackson and Shaw, 2001).

Jobs and their responsibilities

What follows are summaries of the main responsibilities taken from actual job descriptions issued by two leading fashion retailer brands.

Buyer's administrator

Administrator is the entry-level job in fashion buying: no one can enter a buying career above administrator level unless they have proven buying experience at an equivalent level elsewhere. This entry level job is also referred to by other companies as buying admin assistant, buying assistant, buying associate and buyer's clerk.

Job purpose: to maximise profitability through efficient administration to support the buying team.

Principal responsibilities

- Assist the buyers and assistant buyers to prepare products for selection purposes, ensuring that each item is correctly ticketed and presented to required standards.
- Assist in the collation of information from any 'competitor shopping' undertaken by the buying team.
- Assist in the preparation and filing of product specification sheets, ensuring that information is correctly recorded on sheets that are both sent out to and received from suppliers.
- Liaise with the DC on new deliveries, quality control and product/delivery presentation.
- Define and set up new lines in accordance with the new line sheets, ensuring accuracy and that all relevant information is in place.
- Assist in the input and maintenance of all data on the system.
- Develop a thorough knowledge of all relevant systems.
- Liaise with marketing on press sample requirements.
- Actively manage samples.
- Coordinate samples for fitting/product review and assist in the fit sampling process.
- Under the guidance of the buyer and the quality manager, communicate relevant quality information to suppliers.

The job may seem very administrative on a daily basis; nevertheless, it is really the only way to understand the buying function and, more importantly, how all the other functions integrate with it.

The salary scales shown in Table 10.1 are broad. While they are fairly uniformly applied across most fashion retailers at the junior levels, salaries can vary significantly at buyer and merchandiser level and above. Some senior buyer/merchandiser positions have attracted salaries of up to £80,000, although this is rare.

Table 10.1 Salary scales and positions for buying and merchandising

	Buying	Merchandising
Entry level £15–17,000	Buying assistant	Merchandising assistant/allocator
Assistant level £18–26,000	Assistant buyer	Assistant/junior merchandiser
Principal position £30,000+	Buyer	Merchandiser
Senior position £55,000+	Senior buyer	Senior merchandiser

Source: Information supplied by RHR (2005).

Fashion design – the roles explained

The role of design in fashion retailing is extremely important, especially for fashion retailers selling their own branded products. The role of a designer in a fashion retailer brand is quite specific and operates within a number of constraints, including brand and product positioning and competitive retail prices. New design graduates can sometimes be surprised by the lack of autonomy in the role, as the function works closely with the buyer's and suppliers' design teams. Displayed below is a description for a position in an Arcadia brand design team. It is interesting to note the extent to which the job involves working with the buyer and the suppliers.

The design team role

To work closely with the buying, merchandising and technical services teams to develop the most suitable product range for the target customer.

Gathering and using information

Research and gather information from both internal and external sources on trends, colour, fabric and styling and interpret appropriately for the target customer.

Developing product strategy

- Working with buyers and designers to interpret emerging trends.
- Develop seasonal colour palettes, themes and fabric direction appropriate for target customer.
- Work with buyers to translate the department's product strategy into key shapes, fabrics, colours and looks.

Designing the range

- Use information gathered to originate design ideas.
- Design product in accordance with department strategy.
- Work with buyer and supplier to develop a suitable product which has the right level of commerciality exclusivity, excitement and innovation.
- Provide technically accurate working sketches, using technical services where required.

Evolving the range

- Monitor and evaluate success of designs, developing where necessary to ensure range continues to meet the needs of the target customer.
- Visit branches to assess impact of range and research local competition.
- With buyers and merchandisers, draws conclusions from trading results, trials and emerging trends.

Key skills

Ability to sketch designs; meet deadlines and work under pressure; organisational capability; effective communication; creative capacity; good time management.

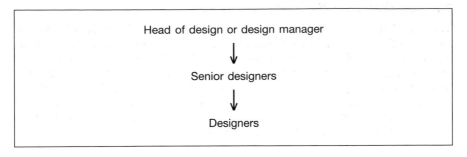

Figure 10.2 Typical departmental structure

Marketing positions

The marketing function within a fashion retailer varies among companies and is commonly a marketing communications role rather than a product one. Specific roles vary although they are all concerned with promoting a retailer's product ranges and communicating brand image to customers. As the marketing and PR roles are relatively narrow, focusing on communications as opposed to products, pricing and other aspects of the marketing mix, so there are relatively few positions within companies. Compared to the product roles of buying and merchandising, for which a fashion retailer might have 30–40 people working in a buying office, the marketing teams will probably only number about 5–10 individuals. Fashion retailers rarely need to use recruitment agencies to find new marketing and PR staff, as agencies tend to attract a large number of speculative approaches in relation to the number of positions available. The marketing department will often include both marketing and PR roles.

Marketing Manager, Marketing Coordinator, Marketing Assistant
Marketing responsibilities:

- advertising;
- national and regional promotions;
- account cards;
- website management (if only a promotional site);
- brand communications;
- customer research;
- charity links/corporate and social responsibility;
- customer relationship marketing;
- in-store graphics.

PR roles
Common PR responsibilities:

- national/regional product placement;
- national/regional press campaigns;

- third party PR;
- brand communications;
- press days;
- celebrity dressing.

Below are two job descriptions that relate to PR jobs at a UK fashion designer label. It is interesting to note that this PR role contains some overlap into what would normally be considered marketing responsibility, for example, the development of an advertising campaign. In fashion, the roles of marketing and PR are often blurred as the marketing function is so specifically linked to communications.

Head of PR
Responsibilities include:

- building and developing brand recognition and awareness of the designer;
- increasing press and editorial coverage of specific product categories and lines in target media;
- maintaining existing good relationships with key editors and developing new ones with a specific focus on the international press;
- planning, implementing and controlling media advertising campaigns;
- planning and coordinating the seasonal RTW fashion shows;
- selecting runway shots for look books and transparencies to be distributed to key fashion press in Europe and the USA;
- coordinating production and distribution of seasonal brochures;
- coordinating in-store events with store managers;
- organising sample sales for press and employees;
- circulating monthly editorial reports to all departments;
- looking after any press or VIP clients who wish to buy from the collection.

Press and PR Assistant
Key roles:

- undertake the distribution (and collection) of all press samples;
- provide details of prices for products when they are requested by the press and keep the editorial file up to date;
- update the press cuttings book regularly and print out editorial reports for all internal departments on a monthly basis;
- assist in the organisation of RTW fashion shows, advertising shoots, brochure production and other projects undertaken by the press office;
- cover the press office when the head of PR is away.

Any marketing or PR role in fashion requires excellent communication skills as the job involves contact with the press and servicing the needs of fashion journalists who often want samples and product information very quickly. Good organisational and planning skills are also important to keep track of the limited sample collections (used for photo shoots and regularly being sent to and returned from the press) and in organising press days. Analytical skills are needed to evaluate media coverage; this varies from weekly to monthly according to the role and company.

Conclusion

It is clear that even within fashion retailing the range of careers is wide. Despite the increasing numbers of graduates applying for careers in fashion retailing, the authors' fashion contacts still complain about the shortage of 'good applicants'. When questioned about what they mean by 'good' in this context, most employers refer to 'likeability', 'motivation' and 'communication skills', things that are not on the curricula of most university degrees.

Applicants for head office jobs in large fashion companies can now expect to undergo some form of assessment, even if they do hold a good degree. Although the tests are objective and aim to gauge relatively basic skills, interviews focus intensively on an individual's personal qualities and are really only about finding out whether or not they would fit in with organisation.

The recently announced Fashion Retail Academy, supported by Philip Green, the owner of Arcadia, will aim to give opportunities in the fashion business to 16-year-olds who do not want to go into standard academic study. Green believes that there are many young people with the potential to do well by following a vocational rather than an academic regime of learning. The Fashion Retail Academy, supported also by the London College of Fashion, is based in London's West End fashion district.

So-called 'front-line' fashion retailing (i.e. sales and management on the shop floor) is generally not perceived as prestigious in the UK. This view is not one that is held in the USA, France and Germany, where *selling* is seen as an important and vital part of the overall business effort. Those who work 'on the shop-floor' are probably the most important part of the overall marketing effort, as they are the link between the business and the customer. Shop-floor selling and customer interaction are more accurately described as marketing at the customer interface. It is these aspects of the service element of the product offer that either make or break a transaction in the fashion industry.

11 The future for fashion

Matthew Jeatt

So, what of the future? How will fashion change and adapt to the emerging world? Can fashion survive the continuing rise of self-expression?

Fashion has shifted enormously in recent years. The rise of individual self-expression has driven the 'democratisation of fashion'. Released from the tyranny of the designers and the power of the couture houses, the consumer has more choice then ever before and is 'listened to' more than ever before. Customers are no longer willing to be 'defined', to have the length of our skirts dictated for us and be told what is and is not 'acceptable'.

At the heart of fashion is a dichotomy: the desire to fit in and the desire to stand out. Perspectives differ between cultures. For example, the powerful shift towards a middle class in China and India is likely to find expression in a desire to fit in at this stage in their development. Because Chinese and Indian consumers perceive the benefit of identifying with wider, more global, values, a 'smart casual' American style is being adopted in the same way that Europe and the UK in particular adopted the 'jeanswear' styles of the US GIs following the Second World War. The adoption of someone else's *style* indicates a desire to adopt the values of that other's culture – a desire to share in its perceived success and power.

Currently embedded in the media of the 'developed' West is the desire to be someone else. Celebrity Wear would appear to be an entirely new category, but is it? Fashion has always been driven by a desire to be modern and fashionable. From the incredible influence of the young Queen Victoria; who almost single handedly forced the adoption of the colour purple, to the lives of the spoilt Hilton sisters, there has always been a desire to emulate the style of others. It is as if, by wearing what they wear, we share their lives and privileges.

So, in developed and emerging cultures, the desire to fit in is tremendously important. Fashion manufacturing is engaged in this process, trying desperately to spot the important details and products in time to maximise the potential profit that they represent.

The other side of the equation is the goal of all creativity, the desire to *stand out*, to be different. The need to be seen as exceptional, and not as a follower of the herd, is the ultimate engine of fashion. This is also the risky side of fashion. For every 'grunge' or 'goth' success there is a 'puff-ball skirt' waiting to bite your ankles. Creativity often recycles in extreme genres, and the designers at the heart of the couture houses are engaged full time in this with the necessity for every new design head to express their own ideas and skills while, at the same time, evoking the style and skills of previous designers. Would Tom Ford's designs have been so desired and praised without the heritage of Gucci? Would Galliano have been seen as so 'radical' without the archive of Dior? Would any of this be possible without the access to money and lack of taste of those very few women who can avail themselves of the imagination and skills of these designers? The couture houses have become ever more 'virtual', the thrust of their businesses being the sale of accessories and coloured and scented water at huge profit. The clothing at this level exists only to drive the perceived value of a brand by providing an endless series of images for consumption by an ever-eager press which, in truth, prefers the ridiculous to the exceptional.

So, couture *stands out,* although not always in the way imagined. There is only so much value that the major fashion manufacturing companies can extract from this feast of self-indulgence. It is no longer simply a matter of copying details from the catwalk to the high-street. The high-street is often further forward than the catwalk. Zara could not exist by copying the couturiers alone. Couturiers, the high-street, fast fashion and manufacturers are all influenced by 'street style'. The ability of the individual consumer to be creative with what is already on offer is the key to this. Major corporations spend fortunes on finding individuals who tie their laces in a different way, who adapt RTW clothing, mixing together garments from different sources or cultures in such a way as to create a unique expression.

This unique expression is both the Holy Grail of fashion and the inevitable poisoned chalice of style. The problem lies in its very *uniqueness.* As soon as a style becomes available to the many it ceases to be of interest to the few. Those very important few, often called 'early adopters', are believed in our culture to be the very barometer of style. Those who are seen to be *different* very rarely are: if their style persists, they must become mainstream. The true exceptions to this are those who are able, either by their own innate sense of style or by the skills of behind-the-scenes stylists, to constantly re-invent themselves and their sense of style and self-expression. Madonna and Kylie Minogue are two obvious examples.

Fashion has for many years tried to 'pigeonhole' people, understanding them and their needs by defining them ever more closely. This process is fundamentally flawed because today's consumer is increasingly complex and more powerful, expressing themselves very differently at different stages of their lives and even at different times of the day. The more they feel they are being targeted the more they will react and resist. This drives the success of mail-order and online retail as the consumer invariably feels more in control of the process; it also drives the search for the different, the stand-out product or brand. To have found 'your own way' to a brand or product is unusual, and calls into question the mass advertising approach. Word of mouth remains one of the most powerful and long-term strategies.

So, given the above, what of *trends*? Trend forecasting has always been open to misinterpretation. The belief in the working of the crystal ball persists to this day. However, the reality is different, with most trend forecasters remembering the words of Nostradamus who once said: 'It is impossible to predict the future; all that I do is project future possibilities out of current events.'

Trends in, and of, themselves, have no value. It is the interpretation and application of trends that releases potential to any given individual or company. Following trends is the easiest thing in the world: all you have to do is identify a trend and watch it evolve. Luxury, well-being, and anti-fashion are there for all to see. The trick is to choose those trends that are relevant to you and your business, and find ways that you can make use of that information to adapt and create new products or communications. Sometimes the most difficult part of the process is to ignore and let go those trends that are not relevant. Just because something is fashionable or trendy does not mean that it is of value to you. Creative people often find it difficult to reject ideas or concepts but this is often the most creative use of their skills. A good idea does not cease to be a good idea just because it is not used immediately. Let the good ideas that are not relevant go; they will still be good ideas when you do find a way or a time to use them.

So, trend-watching is easy; trend-following is sometimes irrelevant; and trends themselves have no value. So why care about trends? Simple. There is only one crime and that is to be unaware of trends. Awareness of trends should be considered a necessary business tool just like having a phone or a computer. Without an awareness of trends you are operating in a void, oblivious to what is happening and why it is happening. This is like selling socks without caring what is available, who your competitors are, and whether or not shoes have a future.

What can we say about the near future?

- Midriffs are out, other exposures will be in.
- Tattoos become unfashionable again.
- 'Dumb' uses for 'smart' materials.
- New comforts will be discovered or developed.
- DVDs will become obsolete.
- Landlines will become uncommon.
- Cars will become more 'dangerous'.
- M&S will be owned by Philip Green.
- A 'new Asian' spirit will invade fashion.
- Good clothes will cost more.
- Poor clothes will cost less.
- Good stores will know your name and your size.
- eBay will call to let you know what will fit you.
- The revolutionary will become mundane.
- The mundane will become art.
- Consumers will continue to buy what they love.

Bibliography

....

Access Asia (2004) International Herald Tribune Conference: *Luxury 2004 – The Lure of Asia*, Grand Hyatt Hotel, Hong Kong

Adanaur, S. (2005) *The Handbook of Weaving*, CRC Press, London

Adburgham, A. (1989) *Shops and Shopping 1800–1914*, Barrie & Jenkins, London

Adburgham, A. (1964, 1981) *Shops and Shopping 1800–1914,* George Allen & Unwin, London

Agins, T. (1987) *The End of Fashion*, William Morrow, London

Alderman, E. (2002) 'Luxury and the downturn: diamonds in the rough', *International Herald Tribune*, 6 December

Allen, M. (2002) *Selling Dreams*, Dent, London

Ander, W. N. and Stern, N. Z. (2004) *Winning at Retail: Developing a sustained model of retail success*, John Wiley, Hoboken, NJ

Angeloni, U. (2001) International Herald Tribune Conference: *Fashion 2001 – The Business and The Brand*, Hotel George V, Paris

Angeloni, U. (2004) International Herald Tribune Conference: *Luxury 2004 – The Lure of Asia*, Grand Hyatt Hotel, Hong Kong

Anon (2002) *Global Offer – Burberry*, Merill Lynch International and Morgan Stanley

Anon (2002) *How To Write Articles for Newspapers and Magazines Arco Step-by-Step Guides* Thomson Arco, London

Anon (2005) *The Marketing Pocket Book 2005*, WARC, Henley on Thames

Anon (2004) *Retail Futures 2009*, Verdict, London

Anon (2005) *The Retail Pocket Book 2005*, WARC, Henley on Thames

Anon (2005) *Summary Data to December 2004,* TNS Fashion Trak, London

Anon (2004) *UK Clothing Survey by Fashion Track*, TNS, London

Anon (2004) *The UK Retail Rankings*, Mintel, London

Anon (2004) *WGSN News Headlines*, May 19 2004

Armani, G. (2005) International Herald Tribune Conference: *Modern Luxury – 2005*, Hyatt Hotel, Dubai Creek

Arnault, B. (2004) International Herald Tribune Conference: *Luxury 2004 – The Lure of Asia*, Grand Hyatt Hotel, Hong Kong

Barclays (2004) *Broker's Report*, December

Barnard, M. (2002) *Fashion as Communication*, Routledge, London

Barr, A. and York, P. (1983) *The Official Sloane Ranger Handbook*, Ebury Press, London

Barthes, R. (1967/1983) *The Fashion System*, trans. M. Ward and R. Howard, Hill and Wang, New York

Beaton, C. (1954, 1989) *The Class of Fashion*, Cassell, London

Benady, D. (2005) 'Arcadia Abandons Plans to use Television Advertising', *Marketing Week*, 31 March 2005

Berger, A. (1998) *Media Analysis Techniques*, Sage, London

Berger, J. (1972) *Way of Seeing*, Penguin, Harmondsworth

Bertelli, P. (2002) International Herald Tribune Conference: *Fashion 2002 – Luxury Unlimited*, Hotel George V, Paris

Birkett, N. (2003) *Shopping for New Markets*, Jones Lang Lasalle, London

Bolton, A. (2004) *The Supermodern Wardrobe*, V&A Publications, London

Bravo, R. (2002) International Herald Tribune Conference: *Fashion 2002 – Luxury Unlimited*, Hotel George V, Paris

Breward, C. (2003) *Fashion*, Oxford University Press

Briscoe, L. (1971) *The Textile and Clothing Industries of the UK*, Manchester University Press

Bull, A., Pitt, M. and Szarka, J. (1993) *Entrepreneurial Textile Communities: A comparative study of small textile and clothing firms*, Chapman and Hall, London

Buxbaum, G. (1999) *Icons of Fashion: The 20th Century*, Prestel Verlag, Munich/London/New York

Carter, E. (1981) *The Magic Names of Fashion*, Weidenfeld & Nicolson, London

Carter, E. (1974) *With Tongue in Chic*, Michael Joseph, London

Cartwright, S. (2004) *International Herald Tribune Conference (Luxury 2004 – The Lure of Asia)*, Grand Hyatt Hotel, Hong Kong

Chapkis, W. (1986) *Beauty Secrets: Women and the politics of appearance*, South End Press, London

Charles-Roux, E. (1981) *Chanel and her World*, Weidenfeld & Nicolson, London/Chittenden

Coleman, E. (1989) *The Opulent Era: Fashions of Worth, Doucet and Pingat*, The Brooklyn Museum

Coleridge, N. (1998) *The Fashion Conspiracy*, Heinemann, London

Coleridge, N. and Quinn, S. (1987) *The Sixties in Queen*, Ebury, London

Coxon, I. (ed.) (2005), *The Sunday Times Rich List 2005*, Times Newspapers, London

Crane, D. (2000) *Fashion and its Social Agendas: Class, gender and identity in clothing*, University of Chicago Press

CSO (2005) *Consumer Trends*, HMSO, London

Cunnington, C. W. (1990) *English Women's Clothing in the Nineteenth Century*, Dover, New York

Davidson, W. E., Bates, A. E. and Bass, S. J. (1976) 'The Retail Lifecycle', *Harvard Business Review 54*, pp. 89–96

De La Torre, J. (1986) *Clothing Industry Adjustments in Developed Countries*, Macmillan, Basingstoke

Deane, P. and Cole, W. A. (1969) *British Economic Growth 1688–1959: Trends and structure*, Cambridge University Press

Deeny, G. (2002) www.hindustandtimes.com, accessed 13 August

Dennis, C., Newman, A. and Marsland, D. (2005), *Objectives of Desire: Consumer behaviour in shopping centre choices*, Palgrave Macmillan, Basingstoke

Deslandres, Y. (1987) *Poiret*, Thames & Hudson, London

De Marly, D. (1980a) *The History of Haute Couture*, Batsford, London

De Marly, D. (1980b) *Worth, Father of Haute Couture*, Elm Tree Books, London

Doherty, A.-M. (2000) 'Factors influencing international fashion retailers' market entry mode strategy: qualitative evidence from the UK fashion sector', *Journal of Marketing Management*, Vol. 16, pp. 223–45

Entwhistle, J. (2000) *The Fashioned Body*, Polity Press, London

Esten, J. (2001) *Why Don't You? Diana Vreeland Bazaar Years*, Universe, New York

Fiorito, S. S., May, E. G. and Straughn, K. (1995) 'Quick response in retailing: components and implementation', *International Journal of Retail & Distribution Management*, 23, (5), 12–21, Bradford, MCB

Fisher, M., Obermeyer, W., Hammond, J. and Raman, A. (1994) 'Accurate response the key to profiting from QR', *Bobbin*, 35, February, 48–62

Flugel, J. C. (1930) *The Psychology of Clothes,* Hogarth Press, London

Ford, T. (2001) *International Herald Tribune Conference (Fashion 2001 – The Business and The Brand)* Hotel George V, Paris

Forty, A. (2000) *Objects of Desire*, Thames & Hudson, London

Frankel, S. (2001) *Visionaries*, V&A Publishing, London

Gobé, M. (2001) *Emotional Branding*, Allworth Press, New York

Goldman Sachs (2004a) *Luxury Goods Europe*, 20 December

Goldman Sachs (2004b) *Luxury Goods Global*, 20 January

Grant, L. (2004) 'She's Gotta Have It', the *Guardian*, 21 September

Grayson, M. (1984) *The Encyclopedia of Textiles, Fibres, Non-Woven Fabrics*, John Wiley & Sons, New York

Gross, M. (1995) *Model: The ugly business of beautiful women*, William Morrow, London

Halter, M. (2000) *Shopping for Identity;The marketing of ethnicity*, Schocken Books, New York

Hankinson, G. and Cowking, P. (1993) *Branding in Action*, McGraw-Hill, Maidenhead

Hasty, R. and Reardon, J. (1997) *Retail Management,* McGraw Hill Irwin, Columbus

HBS (1984) 'Bennetton', *Harvard Business School Case Study 6–985–014*, HBS, Boston, MA

Healy, R. (1996) *Couture to Chaos: Fashion from the 1960s to now*, National Gallery of Victoria, Melbourne

Heller, R. (2000) 'Can this woman do a Gucci on Burberry?' *Forbes Global*, 24 January

Hines, T. (2005) 'Fast Fashion: Myths and realities', *Working Paper*, Manchester Metropolitan University Business School

Hines, T. (2001) 'Globalization: an introduction to fashion marketing and fashion markets', in eds. T. Hines and M. Bruce, *Fashion Marketing: Contemporary issues*, Butterworth Heinemann, Oxford

Hines, T. (2004) *Supply Chain Strategies: Customer driven and customer focused*, Elsevier, Oxford

Hollander, A. (1994) *Sex and Suits*, Alfred A. Knopf, New York

Hollander, S. C. (1960) 'The Wheel of Retailing', *Journal of Marketing*, 24, pp. 37–42

Horner, G. (1981) *The Retail World: The concepts*, Scrimgeour Kemp-Gee, London

Hunter, A. (1990) *Quick Response in Apparel Manufacturing*, Textile Institute, Manchester

Hyde, L. (2003) 'Twenty Trends for 2010: Retailing in an age of uncertainty', *Retail Forward*, Columbus

Jacobi, P. (1991) *The Magazine Article: How to think it, plan it*, Indiana University Press

Jacobs, E. E. (2001) (ed.) *Handbook of U.S. Labor Statistics*, Fifth Edition, Bernan Press, New York

Jackson, T. and Shaw, D. (2001) *Mastering Fashion Buying and Merchandising Management*, Palgrave Macmillan, Basingstoke

Jones, R. M. (2002) *The Apparel Industry*, Blackwell, Oxford

JP Morgan (2004) *European Equity Research – Christian Dior*, 20 December

Kalt, G. (2004), 'He's Got the Luxe, How To Spend It': 10th Anniversary edition, *Financial Times*, Issue 132, November

Keeble, R. (2001) *Ethics for Journalists*, Routledge, London

Kent, C., Macdonald, S., and Deex, M. (2000) 'Luxury Status: Achieving and exploiting it', *November Industry Report*, Morgan Stanley Dean Witter

Khanna, S. R. (1994) 'The New GATT Agreement', *Textile Outlook International*, 52, 10–37

Klein, N. (2000) *No Logo*, Flamingo, London

Ko, E. and Kincade, D. (1997) 'The impact of quick response technologies on retail store attributes', *International Journal of Retail & Distribution Management*, 25, (2), 90–98, Bradford, MCB

Koolhaas, R. (2001) *Projects for Prada Part 1*, Fondazione Prada, Milan

KSA (1997) *Quick Response: Meeting customer needs*, Kurt Salmon Associates, Atlanta GA

Lauren, R. (2002) International Herald Tribune Conference: *Fashion 2002 – Luxury Unlimited*, Hotel George V, Paris

Laver, J. (1937) *Taste and Fashion: From the French Revolution to the present day*, Harrap, London

Lehman Brothers (2004) *Luxury Goods – Tax-free sales development in Europe*, 19 November

Leymarie, J. (1987) *Chanel,* Rizzoli International Publications Inc, New York

Lowson, B., King, R. and Hunter, A. (1999) *Quick Response: Managing the supply chain to meet consumer demand,* Wiley, Chichester

LVMH (2004) 'Passionate About Creativity' *First Half Interim Company Report*, 14 September

Malmsten, E., Portanger, E. and Drazin, C. (2002) *Boo Hoo*, Random House, New York

Mannes, M. (1947) 'The Fine Italian Hand', *US Vogue*, January

Marsh, L. (2003) *The House of Klein: Fashion, controversy and a business obsession*, Wiley, Chichester

Martin, R. (1997) *The St James Fashion Encyclopaedia*, Visible Ink, Detroit and London

Mathias, P. (1969) *The First Industrial Nation*, Methuen, London

McDowell, C. (2003) *Fashion Today*, Phaidon, London

McDowell, C. (1984) *McDowell's Directory of Twentieth Century Fashion*, Frederick Muller, London

McNair, B. (1999) *News and Journalism in the UK*, Routledge, London

McNair, B. (1998) *The Sociology of Journalism*, Arnold, London

McQueen, A. (2002) in 'Paul Smith rips into fashion deserters Maurice Citterden and John Elliott', *Daily Telegraph*

Menkes, S. (2004) International Herald Tribune Conference: *Luxury 2004 – The Lure of Asia*, Grand Hyatt Hotel, Hong Kong

Menkes, S. (2002) 'Is luxury's triangle eternal?', *International Herald Tribune*, 5 December

Merrill Lynch (2002) *Lap of Luxury – Do Giant Stores Mean Giant Killers?*, 20 February

Milbank, C. (1985) *Couture: The great fashion designers*, Thames & Hudson, London

Mintel (2004a) *'Bling Bling' Luxury Goods Retailing – Global*, August

Mintel (2004b) *Clothing Retailing in the United Kingdom*, September

Moore, L. (1999) *Britain's Trade and Economic Structure: The impact of the EU*, Routledge, London

Morgan Stanley Dean Witter (2000) *Industry Report; Luxury Status – Achieving and Exploiting It*, November

Morgan Stanley Dean Witter (2001) *Luxury Goods – Living Legends*, 6 March

Muller, F. (2000) *Art and Fashion*, Thames & Hudson, London

Mulvagh, J. (1988) *History of Twentieth Century Fashion,* Viking, London

Newbery, R. (2004) *Trends in On-line Apparel Retailing – Forecasts to 2010*, www.just-style.com

O'Roarty, B. (2003) *Shopping for New Markets*, Jones Lang LaSalle, London

Okamura, J. (2001) *The Multi-Channel Retail Report*, J. C. Williams, Toronto

Okines, W. and Whitehead, R. (2005) *The UK Clothing Sector – Risk of Excess Capacity in 2005*, Deutsche Bank AG, London

Phoca, S. and Wright, R. (1999) *Introducing Post Feminism*, Totem Books /Icon Books, Cambridge

Polan, B. (1983) *The Fashion Year 1983*, Zomba Books, London

Popcorn, F. and Hanft, A. (2001) *Dictionary of the Future*, Hyperion, New York

Rath, J. (2002) *Unravelling the Rag Trade*, Berg, Oxford

Robinson, J. (1989) *The Art of Fashion*, Bay Books, Kensington NSW

Robinson, J. (1976) *The Golden Age of Style: Art Deco fashion illustration*, Gallery Books, London

Ross, A. (1997) *No Sweat: Fashion, free trade and the rights of garment workers*, Verso, London

Rouse, E. (1987) *Understanding Fashion*, Batsford Books, London

Sanders, K. (2003) *Ethics and Journalism*, Sage, London

Seabrook, J. (2001) *Nobrow: The culture of marketing, the marketing of culture*, Vintage, New York

Seeling, C. (2000) *Fashion: The century of the designer 1900–1999*, Könemann, Cologne

Simmel, G. (1904/1997) 'The Philosophy of Fashion' in D. Frisby and M. Featherstone (eds.) *Simmel on Culture*, Sage, London

Sinha, P. (2001) 'The Mechanics of Fashion' in T. Hines and M. Bruce (eds.) *Fashion Marketing: Contemporary issues*, Butterworth-Heinemann, Oxford

Smith, P. (2002) International Herald Tribune Conference: *Fashion 2002 – Luxury Unlimited*, Hotel George V, Paris

Steele, P. (1988) 'The Caribbean Clothing Industry: The US and Far East connection', *Special report No.1147*, Economist Intelligence Unit, London

Steele, V. (1997) *Fifty Years of Fashion: New Look to Now*, Yale University Press

Stegemeyer, A. (1988) *Who's Who in Fashion*, Fairchild Publications, New York

Steiner, W. (2001) *The Trouble with Beauty*, Heinemann, London

Tyrell, B. and Feenan, R. (2000) *Retail Futures,* Jones Lang LaSalle, London

Tyrell, B. and O'Roarty, B. (2001) *Ten Forces for Retail Change*, Jones Lang LaSalle, London

Underhill, P. (2000) *Why We Buy: The science of shopping*, Texere, London

Varley, R. (2001) *Retail Product Management*, Routledge, London

Veblen, T. (1905/1994) *Theory of the Leisure Class*, Penguin, London

Versace, S. (2004) International_Herald Tribune Conference: *Luxury 2004 – The Lure of Asia*, Grand Hyatt Hotel, Hong Kong

Vreeland, D. (1984) *D.V.*, Knopf, New York

Walkley, C. (1985) *The Way to Wear'em: 150 years of Punch on Fashion*, Peter Owen, London

Webb, W. (2001) 'Retail Brand Marketing in the New Millennium', in T. Hines and Bruce, M. (eds.), *Fashion Marketing: Contemporary issues*, Butterworth-Heinemann, Oxford

Webb, W. (2000) 'Shopping Redefined: Towards a new concept of retailing', *International Journal of Retail & Distribution Management*, Vol. 28, No 12, Manchester, MCB

White, W. and Griffiths, I. (2000) *The Fashion Business: Theory, practice, image*, Berg, Oxford

Wilcox, C. (2001) *Radical Fashion*, V&A Publishing, London

Wilson, E. (1985) *Adorned in Dreams: Fashion and modernity*, Virago, London

Wilson, E. and Ash, J. (1992) *Chic Thrills*, University of California Press

Wolfe, T. (1973) *The New Journalism*, Picador, London

World Bank (2004) *Annual Report*, World Bank, New York

WTO (2004) *International Trade Statistics,* WTO, New York

York, P. and Jennings, C. (1996) *Peter York's Eighties*, BBC, London

Zaoui, M. (2002) International Herald Tribune Conference: *Fashion 2002 – Luxury Unlimited*, Hotel George V, Paris

Zyman, S. (2000) *The End of Marketing as We Know It*, Harper Collins Business, London

Website

www.gerbertechnology.com

Index